MW00782764

# Shakespeare's Other Son?
## William Davenant

# Shakespeare's Other Son?
# William Davenant

## Playwright, Civil War Gun-Runner, and Restoration Theatre Manager

R. E. Pritchard

Pen & Sword
**MILITARY**

First published in Great Britain in 2022 by
Pen & Sword Military
An imprint of
Pen & Sword Books Ltd
Yorkshire – Philadelphia

ISBN 978 1 39909 349 1

A CIP catalogue record for this book is
available from the British Library.

Printed and bound in the UK by CPI Group (UK) Ltd,
Croydon, CR0 4YY.

Pen & Sword Books Limited incorporates the imprints of Atlas,
Archaeology, Aviation, Discovery, Family History, Fiction, History,
Maritime, Military, Military Classics, Politics, Select, Transport,
True Crime, Air World, Frontline Publishing, Leo Cooper, Remember
When, Seaforth Publishing, The Praetorian Press, Wharncliffe
Local History, Wharncliffe Transport, Wharncliffe True Crime
and White Owl.

For a complete list of Pen & Sword titles please contact

PEN & SWORD BOOKS LIMITED
47 Church Street, Barnsley, South Yorkshire, S70 2AS, England
E-mail: enquiries@pen-and-sword.co.uk
Website: www.pen-and-sword.co.uk

Or

PEN AND SWORD BOOKS
1950 Lawrence Rd, Havertown, PA 19083, USA
E-mail: Uspen-and-sword@casematepublishers.com
Website: www.penandswordbooks.com

# Contents

# Preface

Sir William Davenant (1606–68) was in his time widely known as 'Davenant the Poet'. The son of an Oxford vintner (or just possibly the natural son of his godfather, William Shakespeare), he went on to write poems for and about the court of Charles I, and – despite losing his nose to mercury treatment for the clap, which other people thought funny – to replace Ben Jonson and collaborate with Inigo Jones in composing spectacular Court masques, becoming Poet Laureate, as well as writing several successful plays – a few fashionably bloodthirsty, most showing a real comic gift, humanity and sympathy with 'ordinary life'. In the Civil War, he earned a knighthood as an especially successful gun-runner for the Royalists, before escaping to Paris, where he worked on an epic poem. Then sent off by Charles II to colonize Virginia but captured by the Parliamentarians, he escaped execution but was imprisoned in Cowes Castle and the Tower of London for five years. With the Restoration, he practically re-invented English theatre, with the first English opera, women actors, movable scenery and the proscenium arch, as well as reviving interest in Shakespeare with inventive adaptations. Energetic, affable and resilient, he was an appealing and well-liked character.

Despite Davenant's remarkable career, contemporary popularity and importance, and significance in the history of English theatre, what is also remarkable is how his writing and achievements have become relatively little known and appreciated. The development of more recent, though scattered, scholarly discussion has suggested the need for a new, more approachable reconsideration – itself taking such discussion into account – of this important and engaging writer and his work, set in the context of his responses to his changing times. Among features included here, not previously generally discussed, are his varied shorter poems, his ambitious attempt at epic, with its implicit social criticism, his wit and humanity, his increasing scepticism as to Court and aristocratic values, and his developing feminist sympathies. Considered as a whole, this genial figure and entertaining writer – who claimed to write 'in the very spirit of Shakespeare' – should have a wide appeal.

As Davenant's writings, engaging in themselves but also illuminating about the life of their times, are not generally available, on occasion longer excerpts and summaries are included here than would be usual in literary biographies of better-known writers.

# Chapter 1

# Over the Unicorn's Horn (1606–1629)

On 7 April 1668, Samuel Pepys was chatting with Elizabeth Knipp, an actress and bosom friend, backstage at the King's Theatre, in London, when they were told that Sir William Davenant had just dropped dead, probably at his own Duke's Theatre. His Company went on with their advertised performance of his tragedy, *The Unfortunate Lovers* – 'the show must go on' – but everyone turned out for his funeral two days later, when he was buried in Westminster Abbey, under a marble stone inscribed, *O rare Sir Will. Davenant.*

A minor writer of the time, Richard Flecknoe, rose – or sank – to the occasion with his pamphlet, *Sir William Davenant's Voyage to the other world*:

> Now *Davenant*'s dead, the Stage will mourn,
> And all to Barbarism turn:
> Since he it was this later Age,
> Who chiefly civiliz'd the Stage.
>
> Great was his Wit, his Fancy great,
> As e're was any Poets yet:
> And more Advantage none e'er made
> O'th'Wit and Fancy which he had.
>
> Not onely *Dedalus* Arts he knew,
> But even *Prometheus*'s too:
> And living Motions made of Men,
> As well as dead ones, for the Scene.
>
> And if the Stage or Theatre be
> A little World, 'twas chiefly he,
> That *Atlas*-like supported it,
> By force of industry and Wit.

The praise here seems fair enough: through hard work Davenant had been a major force in Restoration London theatre, pushing his own talents to their limit, training his actors and modernizing theatre design and practice with his use of movable scenery and the proscenium arch. However, Flecknoe went on to criticize Davenant's writing; in his satire, he has Davenant being received in the 'Poets' Elysium' in the Underworld. Challenged by the infernal judges to defend his plays, he is made to reply,

> How that of *The Unfortunate Lovers*
> The depth of *Tragedy* discovers;
>
> In's *Love and Honour* you might see
> The height of *Tragicomedy*;
>
> And for his *Wits*, the Comick fire
> In none yet ever flam'd up higher:
>
> But coming to his *Siege of Rhodes*,
> It outwent all the rest by odds;
>
> And somewhat in't that does out-do
> Both th'Ancients and the Moderns too.

He is reproved for this self-praise, but Flecknoe's lines reflect what many theatre-goers of the time, including Samuel Pepys, would have thought justified. Flecknoe goes on to write that Davenant was 'a good companion for /The rich, but ill one for the poor'; there is no evidence for this – perhaps he had not been very helpful to Flecknoe – but certainly he had worked hard for his money, for his large family and his new theatre. As it is, Flecknoe suggests that Davenant had 'left the Muses for Pluto' (the god of the underworld, also Plutus, the god of wealth), in other words, subordinated his poetic gifts to the desire for money.

Certainly, from his earliest days, Davenant had striven to 'get on' in the theatre and at Charles I's Court, and had in his time made good money (much of it spent in his monarch's cause in the Civil War), rising from relatively modest origins. His childhood was spent in Oxford, where his father, John, and mother, Jane, known as Jennet (née

Sheppard), ran a tavern in Cornmarket, near the city centre. The couple began their married life in London, in about 1593; John, like his father, was a successful merchant vintner, active in the busy, important wine-importation business; a contemporary, Anthony Wood, wrote that he was 'a lover of plays and play-makers, especially Shakespeare'. Of Jane's brothers, two were Court glovers and a third was in the Royal Household catering business. London was an unhealthy place at the time, already choked with smoke from coal fires, with open drains and dung carts, and occasional bouts of plague or typhoid. The registers of their church, St James Garlickhithe, south of the river, (convenient for mosquitoes) record the deaths of five Davenant children between Christmas 1593 and Christmas 1597. In desperation, Jane visited the astrologer/doctor, Simon Forman, experienced in not-very-useful advice for would-be mothers. Another hopeful was Marie Mountjoy, of Silver Street, Cripplegate (landlady of a glovemaker's son, William Shakespeare). Jane's sixth child, named John, was born in early 1599, but must have died soon after, as another John was born in 1607.[1]

In about 1600 the Davenants fled London, embarking on a horse-drawn barge up the Thames to Oxford. It is possible that Shakespeare, a near neighbour, who frequently broke his journeys between London and Stratford at a tavern in Oxford, may have suggested the move. The couple now took over the Cross Tavern at No. 3, Cornmarket, near the centre of the town. It was a large, timber-framed building, with a parlour on the street-front, and a good chamber on the first floor with wainscot panels covering the older wall paintings (discovered in 1927), kitchens at the back and extensive cellarage for the Davenants' wine barrels: as a tavern, not an inn, it was rather like a modern wine-bar.

The change proved successful: a daughter, Elizabeth, was born in 1601, a second daughter, Jane, in 1602, a son, Robert in 1603, and in December 1604, a third daughter, Alice. Three more sons followed: William in 1606, John in 1607 and Nicholas in 1611. John Davenant did well in his new tavern; in June 1604, he paid £8 'to have a lycence of this Cytie to sell Wyne & a Bayliffs place', so becoming a freeman of the city.[2] He could afford to send three sons, Robert, John and Nicholas, to his own school, Merchant Taylors School, in London; William did not go. The older children did well: Robert went up to St John's College and then into the church; Elizabeth and Jane married former college Fellows; Jane married the Tavern's apprentice and went on to run it with him. As for young William, Aubrey writes that 'he went to schoole at Oxon to Mr [Edward] Sylvester [at the corner of Turl Street and the High Street], but I feare he was drawne from schoole before he was ripe enough' (no reason given); he was then taught for a while by Daniel Hough, a Fellow of Lincoln College (and so a sort of landlord of the tavern), and may have briefly been on the books there, 'but his geny,' wrote Anthony Wood, 'which was always opposite to it, led him in the pleasant paths of poetry.' The College still acknowledges the connection, and owns a portrait said to be of him as a young man.

In his *Brief Lives*, John Aubrey reports that John Davenant was 'a very grave and discreet Citizen; his mother was a very beautifull woman and of a very good witt, and of conversation extremely agreeable.' He goes on to write that Shakespeare 'did commonly in his journey lye at this house in Oxon, where he was exceedingly respected. (I have heard Parson Robert say that Mr William Shakespeare had given him a hundred kisses.)'

Shakespeare's own son, Hamnet (named after his godfather, Hamnet Sadler) was baptized in February 1585, with his sister, Judith, and died in August 1596, aged eleven and a half. Shakespeare's grief is suggested in a passage in his play of that year, *King John*, where a parent grieves eloquently on the death of a young son:

> Grief fills the room up of my absent child,
> Lies on his bed, walks up and down with me,
> Puts on his pretty looks, repeats his words,
> Remembers me of all his vacant garments with his form;
> Thus have I reason to be fond of grief.

Young William Davenant, named after his godfather, who was in Oxford in 1605, was born in 1606, the year when Shakespeare wrote *Macbeth*, when another charming, doomed little boy dies. The 'hundred kisses' for little William could have been transferred from Hamnet.

Aubrey goes on to say that

Sir William would sometimes, when he was pleasant over a glasse of wine with his most intimate friends, e.g. Sam Butler, author of *Hudibras*, say, that it seemed to him that he writ with the very spirit that did Shakespeare, and seemed contented enough to be thought his Son. He would tell the story, as above, in which way his mother had a very light report, whereby she was called a Whore.

Presumably he would come out with this when in his cups, and apropos his several transformations of Shakespeare into a successful Restoration playwright.

As for the question of a Jennet/Shakespeare affair. In 1610, when William was nearly 5, Shakespeare wrote *The Winter's Tale* (performed in 1611), the story of a destructively jealous husband, Leontes, who believes his beloved little boy ('Most dear'st ! my collop!') is the result of an adulterous affair between his wife and his friend, and cries out,

> Many a man there is, even at this moment,
> Now while I speak this, holds his wife by th'arm,
> That little thinks she has been sluiced in's absence
>     ... by Sir Smile, his neighbour.

The little boy dies, and is replaced by his sister, like Hamnet; the parents are reconciled at the end of the play. Leontes says that the little boy is just like himself ('in the very spirit'), twenty-three years earlier, when very young ('unbreech'd', less than 5 years old). Twenty-three years earlier was 1587, when Hamnet would have been perhaps 3. The play – especially with Leontes' violent pain and jealousy – could have been, apart from its other concerns, an expiation for harm done earlier.

This story, of Shakespeare's paternity, went the rounds over the following years, with some embroidery. In the early eighteenth century, William Oldys had the story, saying that he got it from Alexander Pope, who claimed he heard it from Thomas Betterton, the celebrated actor in Davenant's company. Here, John Davenant was not only grave but 'melancholy', who, with his wife, 'used much to delight in Shakespeare's pleasant company.' He writes that when young William

> was then a little school-boy in the town, of about seven or eight years old, and so fond also of Shakespeare, that whenever he heard of his arrival, he would fly from school to see him. One day an old townsman observing the boy running homeward almost out of

breath, asked him whither he was posting in that heat and hurry. He answered, to see his *god*-father Shakespeare. There's a good boy, said the other, but have a care that you don't take *God*'s name in vain.

It sounds like an old joke taken over for the Davenant story.[3]

Shakespeare probably stayed with his friends at the tavern, when he came up to Oxford in connection with his company's plays (according to the first quarto edition of *Hamlet* in 1603, it had already been performed 'in the two Vniversities of Cambridge and Oxford'), put on in the inn yard at the King's Head inn, also in Cornmarket, just over the way. He could well have been godfather to William (named after his godfather, as was common practice), the baptism taking place at St Mary's, Carfax, just around the corner. It would be interesting to know when Davenant had the story of Shakespeare as father: presumably not just in the 1660s, when he was producing and adapting whole Shakespeare plays, but possibly long before that, when he was cribbing phrases for his own early writing. If the story was current in his boyhood, how might it have affected his relationship with John (and Jennet)? The story is less interesting in what it says about the mother than in what it does not say about the father. By it, John Davenant is simply dispossessed, deleted. It seems a version of the ancient fantasy/myth about the subject's parentage: the putative parents are really inadequate foster parents. The true father is a superior being, more generally honoured (even, in some versions, divine), whose notable qualities have been transmitted, in some degree, to the son. In one play from the 1630s, *The Witts*, there is sibling rivalry and a question as to the source of the younger brother's superior poetic wit. In many of Davenant's plays, throughout his career, two young men, very close friends or even half-brothers (that is, brothers) compete for the same woman (often withheld by her father), easily identified by Freudians as a displacement of the mother. This Oedipal substitution and sibling rivalry seem to underlie many of his plays. Yeats once wrote that he had often had 'the fancy that there is one myth for every man which, if we but knew it, would make us understand all he did and thought'. This may overstate the case for Davenant, but Shakespeare and his writing filled much of his mind, to the very end.

In 1622, both John and Jane died; John, who had only recently been elected Mayor of Oxford, left a careful will, bequeathing £200 to each daughter and £150 to each son, to be paid within a year. He hoped that apprentice Thomas Hallam would marry one of the daughters, and run the tavern (which he did). As for William, John wished that he be 'put to Prentice to some good merchant of London or other tradesman', with an extra £40 for his future master and 'double apparell', this to be done 'for avoiding of Inconvenience in my house for mast[er]shippe when I am gone.' The implications here are not necessarily to William's discredit, but a simple recognition of the need to avoid confusion in the running of the household business. William, however, had other plans. John Davenant had been a successful, respected, middle-class businessman; his guest and friend, Shakespeare, showed that this could be done more interestingly, without going into trade; and this is what young William was to achieve.

William's first concern, or investment, when he got to London was to order some fine clothes (vestments?) from a tailor named John Urswick, with whom he was to be engaged in conflict for several years over unpaid bills. In court in 1632 he acknowledged ordering 'certain stuffe cloth lace and other necessaries' but objected to what he considered 'vnreasonable' bills. He needed such smart clothes for his new employment, having been, as Aubrey put it, 'preferred to the first Dutches of Richmond to wayte on Her as a Page'. Family connexions got him in. His new employer was Lady Frances Howard (1578–1639), referred to at the time as the 'Double Duchess', in that her second husband had been Edward Seymour, first Earl of Hertford (who married her when she was 25 and he was in his eighties) and her third was Ludovic Stuart, Earl of Lennox and, in 1623, created Duke of Richmond, just before his death in 1624.

More relevant to Davenant was her first marriage, aged 19, to Alderman Henry Prannell, whose father had been a very successful vintner and Master of the Vintners Company, who would certainly have known William's grandfather. Also helpful, perhaps, was the fact that, in 1597/8, Lady Frances had, like William's mother and his aunt, Ursula Sheppard, consulted astrologer-physician Simon Forman as to a possible pregnancy, and so could have had some acquaintance with them then. That his uncles Thomas and Richard had served the Jacobean Court as perfumers and glovemakers might have helped. In any event, she took him on.

One writer refers to her as 'an elderly but stately ruin',[4] which is very severe, as, a former Court beauty, she was only 44 when she encountered young William (a portrait in 1624 suggests she had kept her looks). At the time, she was still trying to catch the Earl of Southampton (Shakespeare's patron). In 1630 she was patron of Captain John Smith, the noted Jamestown colonist (forever associated with Pocahontas). She herself was very grand in her manner at Ely House, her mansion in Holborn; a letter from courtier John Chamberlain on 8 January 1625 mentions her:

> We haue much talke of this Diana of the Ephesians, and her magnificence in going to her chappell at ely house on Sunday last to a sermon preached by Dr Belcanquell, where she had her closet of trauerse, her fowre principall officers steward chamberlain Treasurer controller, marching before her in velvet gownes with their white staves, three gentleman ushers, two Ladies that bare vp her traine, the countesses of Bedford and mungummerie following with the other Ladies two and two, with a great deale of other apish imitation ...[5]

and with, presumably, William and the other pages trailing along at the rear, but within call.

Aubrey reports one anecdote William told him about his time with her, suggesting he was well trusted, when 'she sent him to a famous Apothecary [presumably Forman] for some Vnicornes-horne', an expensive powder which was widely trusted as a general panacea, and thought of as a sexual stimulant and cure for sexual diseases and poisons. Young William 'resolved to try with a Spider which he incircled in it'. The thinking was, that if this was real unicorn – unicorns are notoriously difficult to secure – or if it really worked, the spider should shrivel up on contact: 'but without the expected success; the Spider would goe over, and through and through, unconcerned.' One might see this an early instance of Davenant's scepticism regarding received thinking, or merely, to adapt King Lear, as a spider to a wanton boy to kill it for his sport. Such tests were not unknown, especially to anyone keen on drama; in Webster's *The White Devil* (1612), a character remarks how men 'to try the precious unicorns horn, /Make of the powder a preservative circle /And in it put a spider'. (Webster lived in Holborn, near Davenant, and could have had some acquaintance with him.) Presumably William told the Duchess that her money had been wasted. Perhaps he thought too that, like the undaunted spider, he also might break through into Court circles.

In 1623, Urswick had him arrested for his unpaid bill, which would not have pleased the Duchess (though he paid it off next year). At about the same time, aged about 18, William married (or had to marry) a young woman named Mary, for on 27 October 1624 the first of his many sons, also named William, was baptized at St James, Clerkenwell. A daughter, Elizabeth, died in 1631, and another daughter, Mary, was baptized in January 1642.[6] This family life, such as it was – there is never any mention of his family – made demands on the page's purse, which was particularly unfortunate as, following the death of her husband in 1624 – and perhaps William's marriage – the Duchess decided to let him go.

William was always to prove resilient in difficult situations, and it was not long before he had found a new billet in Holborn, in the employ of Fulke Greville, Lord Brooke, statesman, poet and admirer of Protestant hero Sir Philip Sidney. At 70, Greville was spending his last years in revising his own poetry. Aubrey records that Greville 'wrote a Poeme in folio which he printed not till he was old, and then (as Sir W. said) with too much judgement and refining, spoyled it, which was at first a delicate thing'. Aubrey thought that William had been a page also to Greville, but he would have been rather old for that; it seems probable that he was some kind of secretary to Brooke, who recognized him as having some literary ability and ambitions. A little poem, on 'The Countess of Anglesey led Captive by the Rebels'[7] may belong to this time. The Earl had deforested common land, causing hardship and poverty and provoking some sort of disruption. Davenant's poem dismisses the resentful poor as 'this Gothick Rout', a term calculated to be approved by the Court. His wife and child would not have fitted in at Greville's household, and his own promotion required more fancy clothes from Urswick in 1625, who later billed him for £9 for 'meate & drincke & apparell making' for his wife (presumably living with him at the time).

By this time, it appears, Davenant was busily writing flattering poems to and about those at Court who might give him a helping hand. In his own volume, *Madagascar, with other Poems*, published in 1638, he included a poem addressed to Lord Brooke 'in performance of a vow that night to write to him'. Here, he responds,

> My Lord, it hath been ask'd, why 'mongst those few
> Singled out for Fame, I chose not you
> With early speed the first.

The explanation is that he's not ready yet, that his technique is not adequate to express his love and his subject's merits. The metaphor he uses might not have pleased his Calvinistic-minded employer, when he says that 'There are degrees that to the Altar lead, /Where ev'ry rude, dull Sinner must not tread ...' when lengthy prayer cannot 'privilege a zealous Votarie, /To come where the High Priest should only be'. This is the language of what might be called the 'High' church, associated with the Arminian (anti-Calvinist) Bishop William Laud, who scandalized 'zealous' Puritans by moving the communion table to the chancel, as a railed-off altar. He hopes Brooke will excuse him for not trying to do more than he can. Remarkably, he does not actually praise Brooke.[8] This was his last chance to do that, as, in 1628, Brooke was murdered by his long-serving manservant, Ralph Haywood, for not including him in his will (though he left William a year's wages and pension for board and lodging for four months). The scandal of this was overshadowed by the greater, national shock at the assassination, at almost the same time, that autumn, of the great Duke of Buckingham, beloved by both King James and King Charles. At all events, Davenant had received another stop – but it provided another opportunity.

Buckingham, the favourite of kings, had risen rapidly, to become the most powerful man in the country – and also the most hated, widely regarded as responsible for the wasteful expenditure of English lives and money in futile Continental ventures. Whilst out in the country generally his assassin and servant, John Felton, was almost approved as his country's defender, at Court, of course, his death was generally lamented – though perhaps not greatly by the new young French Queen, Henrietta Maria, his rival for the King's affections. Court poets poured out elegies and epitaphs. Davenant made sure to be among them, with two published poems (and another only in manuscript). In the first (placed second in his volume *Madagascar*), 'Elizium',[9] directed to the Duchess, he dreams of Elysium 'where restored forms nere fade', where she and her husband can meet again and restore their youthful joys, 'the scatter'd treasure of the Spring' (as Davenant remembers Shakespeare's Sonnet 63), now 'blown by autumn winds'. A vestal will attend 'the *Shade* of gentle *Buckingham*' (not an epithet everyone would have chosen) while he 'smiles on the Peoples wound ... for though it touch'd his heart [literally], /His Nation feels the rancour, and the smart'. 'Rancour' cannot but evoke the popular and political disturbance that ensued.

Another, more public and concise, has a crisp, formal vigour, on the passing of a Great Man, one uncontroversial, wholly admirable, as a widow might wish him to be remembered:

> For gone is now the Pilot of the State,
> The Courts bright Star, the Clergies Advocate,
> The Poets highest Theame, the Lovers flame,
> And Souldiers Glory, mighty *Buckingham*.[10]

More interesting is an unpublished poem, 'An Elegy on the Duke of Buckingham's Death'[11] that, for all its many echoes of Shakespeare, evokes some genuine feeling. It is perhaps conventional to dismiss others' elegies as insincere, but 'Buckingham, oh my Lord' sounds a personal cry, as he says that, like Cordelia, he lacks a 'smooth and oyly Art', and the ability to catch Claudio's 'viewlesse' winds carrying Buckingham's fame around the world. Now speaking (improbably) as 'a soldyer', he praises Buckingham as a leader, who could coax 'with low phrayse' and, like Cleopatra, 'Perfume the Neyghbour Ayre'. By contrast,

> Luxurious Sleepe, and surfeits that have made
> This Nation tame, and spoyled our glorious Trade,
> Loud Iron war, he did dismiss the Court,
> And taught our churlish youth the noble sport.

Anger leads him, like Romeo, to defy the 'false stars' that permitted Buckingham's death, before turning to the Court's real enemy, the religiously dissenting merchant and farming classes: 'warme Idolators, that onely bowe /To their fraile metall, and th'industrious plough.'

He accuses 'the precize' (puritans or dissenters generally) of relishing 'murther as a Sacrifice'. The next lines recognize potential revolutionary impulses:

> Dull easy faith and Ignorance no more
> Shall flatter crooked Bondage as before,

[the meaning here is by no means clear]

> Predominance shall cease, the sons of men
> Shall now enjoy Equality agen;

(presumably A Bad Thing); without 'Heroicke Princes', what will become of them? What, he asks, has become of all Buckingham's admirers, Othello's 'plumed Troupes', the ambitious flatterers whose 'supple knees adore for secret ends'? The Duchess may weep, but, he goes on, 'my Art / Out climbes that reach; she may advance thy herse, /But fame shall sing thy story in my Verse.'

Davenant's self-praising poetic vainglory has to discontinue, as he returns to his soldier persona: 'Let a dull soldyer greet thee with a groane,' whose rage has led him to clap on his armoured 'Corslett'; but Davenant was no such soldier, and there was no one to fight – yet. Meanwhile, having made his mark, he had to make his own way, somehow.

His godfather's career and success filled his mind, as he watched the fashionable playwrights of the time, at the Blackfriars Theatre, where, as Sir John Suckling would later write in 'A Summons to Town',

> The sweat of learned *Johnsons* brain,
> And gentle *Shakespears* easier strain,
> A hackney-coach conveys you to,
> In spite of all the rain can do:
> And for your eighteen-pence you sit
> The Lord and Judge of all fresh wit.

The Blackfriars Theatre, a superior, indoor theatre, lit by candles, charged a little more than the Globe, over the river – a basic sixpence for admission to the galleries, more for a seat in the pit, and still more for a stool on the stage itself, for the vain and conceited. Payment for authors was not great: in the early part of the century, one might get an initial advance of £6, followed later by perhaps £12. Here, the youthful Davenant would judge – and learn. In fact, while at Lord Brooke's, Davenant had already started on his career as playwright, with two plays, *Albovine, King of the Lombards* and *The Cruel Brother* (both, *Dramatic Works*, Vol. I). He began by attempting to reproduce what had been successful in earlier Jacobean blood-tragedies. These were frequently set in fictional Italian courts, where any depravity, however implausible, might be expected, peopled by corrupt, lecherous rulers, vicious court ladies, conniving, Machiavellian courtiers, a few very innocent and virtuous young ladies, with coarsely comic servants, and where poison and stilettos were the instruments of choice, in plots of bewildering complexity driven by lust, ambition and revenge. In 1594 Thomas Nashe's *The Unfortunate Traveller* had summarized the popular view of what one might find in Italy: 'The art of atheism, the art of epicurizing, the art of whoring, the art of poisoning, the art of sodomitry … it maketh a man an excellent courtier, a fine close lecher, a glorious hypocrite.' Such luridly imagined visions, the equivalents of modern violent, sexist crime-and-spy films, titillated the audience's relish for sado-misogynistic fantasies, whilst providing hyperbolic, satiric images of court corruption.

The dramatists Webster, Tourneur and Ford were to be general models for him, but Shakespeare (whose First Folio had been published in December 1623, though quarto editions of individual plays were available before that) proved a particular source for dramatic effects and eloquent phrases, notably from *Hamlet*, *Othello*, *Macbeth* and *Romeo and Juliet*. If it had worked for them, might it not work for him? In his early efforts, he attempted to surpass his predecessors in tangled, interwoven plotting and extravagant situations and phrasing, to the extent that any attempted moral portrayal of court corruption and moral chaos developed into a world of grotesque fantasy, driving its tragedy to something bordering on black comedy.

There is no record of *Albovine* ever being licensed or performed; it may well have been his first attempt so it seems reasonable to begin with this. Although never performed, it was printed in quarto in 1629, under the name of William D'Avenant, presumably to pretend to foreign aristocratic origins. Predictably, this provoked general derision; to quote one example:

> As several Cities made their claim
> Of *Homers* birth to have the fame;
> So, after ages will not want
> Towns claiming to be *Avenant*:
> Great doubt there is where now it lies,
> Whether in *Lombard* or the *Skies*.

Some say by *Avenant* no place is meant,
And that this *Lombard* is without descent;
And as by *Bilke* men mean there's nothing there,
So come from *Avenant*, means from *No-where*.[12]

The insinuation here is also that Davenant, in being merely middle-class in origin, is a jumped-up nobody, with no background. In a later poem, he knows that 'The cruell and the Envious' will say, 'from knowledge was he born'.[13] He was soon to attract some hostility at Court, as is suggested in a dedicatory poem by a friend, Thomas Ellis, printed with the play: 'Let not Envy's sulph'rous blasts cast forth /Venomous aspersions on thy noble worth' (unfortunately not 'noble birth'). Another friend, Edward Hyde (the future Lord Clarendon), commended his choice of dedicatee for the play: 'Thy Wit hath purchas'd such a Patron's name /To deck thy front, as must derive to Fame /These tragic raptures …' Many might have been surprised at his choice in dedicating the play to Robert Carr, Earl of Somerset, the disgraced former minion of James I, who was only spared from execution for the murder of Sir Thomas Overbury by the personal pardon of the King. It was a curious choice, in that Somerset's career of royal favouritism and homosexual affection, adultery, machination and murder seemed more than a little echoed in Davenant's play. Presumably Davenant was aligning himself with a particular Court faction – for what good it might do him.

The original story dates from the sixth-century court of Alboinus, King of Lombardy. Its sensational material attracted the attention of several writers; Davenant may have known Belleforest's *Histoires tragiques*, translated late in the sixteenth century, or may have been alerted to it by an account in Thomas Coryate's popular travel book, *Coryates Crudities* (1611).

King Albovine has conquered and killed the king of the Girpides, whose daughter, Rhodolinda, he has married, but who is noticeably more attracted to a captive officer, Paradine. Courtiers comment: 'He is our King's minion, sleeps in his bosom … and the royal fool greets him with such ravenous kisses, that you would think he meant /To eat his lips.' Queen Rhodolinda has acquired political power at Court; as they observe: 'as she ascends, her countrymen /Must rise.' (This seems to echo the situation of Charles marrying a foreigner, Henrietta Maria – to whom

Davenant was later to transfer his loyalties.) Among the newcomers is Hermegild, a villainous Machiavel.

Rhodolinda complains to her lady, Valdaura, Paradine's wife, how she grieves for her father's death and her own marriage: 'My cross fate /Like the raven, croaks a funeral note,' echoing Lady Macbeth. Meanwhile, Grimold, a grim old soldier, leers at Valdaura and grumbles about his lack of pay, observing, like Lear, that 'furr'd gowns hold /There is no sin so great as poverty'. His function in the play is ambivalent, as both comic exemplar of, and satiric commentator on, corrupt court values.

Albovine has a taste for drinking deeply, like Claudius, and demands the bowl of victory, the skull of Rhodolinda's father; not surprisingly, she refuses to drink from it and storms out, closely followed by Hermegild, who encourages her to seek revenge. When Paradine urges her to go to her husband's bed, she is outraged, declaring she would 'sooner choose a mansion /In a sepulchre: there commit incest /With the raw remnant of my father's bones', as Davenant remembers Juliet's imaginings. Meanwhile, Hermegild prepares his plot, and Grimold discusses the king with other, rather camp, courtiers:

Courtier:  The King is now in love.
Grimold:   With whom?
Courtier:  With the queen.
Grimold:   In love with his own wife! That's held incest
           In Court: variety is more luscious.

At this time, Charles was apparently fonder of Buckingham than of the Queen. Lacking money, Grimold will even, like other courtiers, prostitute himself to some old lady: 'some old land-carrack [cargo-vessel]; ay, ay, eight hundred crownes a year will do't.' Such relationships were not unknown in Charles's court.

In the main action, Hermegild pretends to help Albovine make up with Rhodolinda by suggesting practising love-making with Valdaura; he even discusses this plan with Rhodolinda. He takes his chance to plan revolt with her, and to seize the throne. She promises him marriage, and they kiss, with unusual physicality for Caroline theatre: ''Twas moist and luscious,' he declares, before suggesting they retire, 'and I'll /Discover how I've practis'd my revenge.' The lip-smacking relish is inescapably risible (at times like this, it is hard to remember that Rhodolinda was being played by a boy or young man). A woman courtier tells Paradine he is to sleep that night at Rhodolinda's, but absolutely silently, without speech. The next morning, he is shocked to discover that he had slept with Rhodolinda, who explains that this merely part of a revenge scheme: if he tells the king, she will accuse him of rape, but if he helps her, she will be his wife and queen; as for Valdaura, she is 'an open whore', and can be got rid of later. Now Hermegild manages to show Valdaura Paradine embracing Rhodolinda; she is grief-stricken, but he tells her to gain revenge by poisoning Paradine (which will take four days to work); she exits, 'I shall die crying.'

We return to the comic characters, Grimold and the courtiers, to show how rotten Court life is. Grimold is diseased, syphilitic: 'This luxurious [lecherous] city /Hath made me so rotten, I dare not walk /I'th'wind, lest I be blown to pieces.' The others mock him: 'I know /His disease, and whence it came; shortly /You'll see him wear a curtain 'fore his nose; / That's the newest fashion that came from Paris ... He must to Rotterdam, to the fat doctor there /And be stew'd in a stove, until he spits his venom out.' Little did facetious Davenant know what was to come his way.

Albovine is in full 'drunken Claudius' mode, hoping to bed Rhodilinda. Hermegild helpfully soliloquizes, worrying that Rhodolinda might want Paradine, whilst acknowledging that he told Valdaura to tell Paradine that Albovine had told her of the adultery, and worrying also that Paradine must kill the king before the poison works on him. Paradine then drinks from Valdaura's bowl, who tells him that it is poisoned. He imagines the effects: will he 'look goggle-ey'd and stretch i'th'cheeks ... will't make my eyes start from my skull, or drop /Like bullets at my feet?' He stabs Valdaura, who then tells him that not merely is she innocent but that he is not poisoned, though she had told him this in order to provoke him to kill her (as she cannot live without his love).

At the beginning of Act V, Rhodolinda wonders why Albovine, who had doted on Paradine, has now turned against him. Paradine explains how Albovine 'hath of late hung thus – /Upon my neck, until his amorous weight /Became my burden, and then lay slobbering o'er /My lips, like some rheumatic babe. This sport /My serious brain abhor'd', which led Albovine to react against him. It sounds like King James at his worst. She urges him on to revenge, and he plans a violent, sadistic attack:

To make him bleed, and leave his arteries
Where the delighted spirits work, shrink up
Until they curl with heat. The wither'd frame
Straight to convert to dust, then th'umerous wind
To fan it o'er the world.

Albovine is woken in his chamber, thinking Paradine must be drunk, but Paradine tells him that he has bedded his queen 'by a dire mistake', tricked by the 'black adulterous queen'. Davenant goes full throttle for Albovine's outburst:

Howl, meagre wolves and empty tigers! Let the hoarse
Thracian bull bellow till he rend his throat,
And the hot mountain lion roar until
Their clamour wake the dead! The resurrection
Is too long delay'd, since we want horror
To celebrate this new …

He then tells Paradine, Othello-style, to 'draw thy bright weapon', who, however, will not fight him and instead falls on his own sword, again echoing Othello: 'Then glorious war, and all proud circumstance /That gives a soldier noise [fame], for evermore, farewell.' He then tells Albovine what had happened, who then goes mad, with traditional delusions, before dying. Paradine hides the body behind the arras, remarking how, like Lear or Gloucester, 'his heart-strings crack'd' (so no one kills a king). Rhodolinda now enters and says that Hermegild must die, as he knows too much, before seizing Paradine in an unusually explicit sex-and-violence clinch:

Rhodolinda: I sure shall ravish thee,
          My appetite is grown so fierce. Let me
          Begin with thy moist lip –
Paradine:   Let's to't like monkeys or the reeking goat.
Rhodolinda: Oh, oh, oh, help, help! [She has bloody lips]
Paradine:   Cease your loud clamour, royal whore!
Rhodolinda: Thou didst eat my lips.

He then stabs her several times, before dragging the body behind the arras.

Enter Hermegild for the concluding dénouement, to inform Paradine that he gave the poison to Valdaura, told the king of his adultery with Rhodolinda, and Valdaura that it was all Paradine's fault. Paradine snatches Hermegild's sword and draws back the arras to display the tableau of the bodies of Albovine, Rhodolinda and Valdaura, before stabbing him to death, and exits. The Governor enters, to order him arrested, and declares that Albovinus's son shall succeed to the throne.

The play's extravagance of plot, situation and language cripple it as an attempt at satiric-moral analysis of Court corruption. As such, it simply will not do, except as a melodramatic, pulp-fiction horror comic. It is no wonder that it was not performed; but Davenant would soon learn to do better.

On 12 January 1627, Sir Henry Herbert, the recently appointed Master of the Revels, licensed *The Cruell Brother. A Tragedy*, dedicated to Richard Weston, the Lord Treasurer. Apparently about aristocratic conceptions of family honour and class distinction, it again seems more concerned with repressed homosexual love. The Duke of Siena loves Count Lucio, his 'creature': his first words to him are, 'My glorious boy!' Lucio's own dear friend and creature, the lower-born Foreste, urges him not to marry his visually identical twin sister, Corsa, ostensibly because she would be too 'base' socially (it might also be like marrying him). Lucio, however, moves away from the Duke and towards Foreste by marrying Corsa; his words, 'Excellent wretch! I am undone with joy,' inauspiciously echo Othello's words for Desdemona.

In Foreste's own declaration of undying love for Luinna, Davenant looked for Shakespearean eloquence; his 'Time lays his hand /On pyramids of brass, and ruins quite' half-remembers 'brass eternal slave to mortal rage. ... That Time will come and take my love away' (Sonnet 64). He covers her face with a white veil; such veiling was common in Venetian ladies, but here seems an ominous shrouding.

The Duke, displeased, resolves to have Lucio's 'other half', his wife, instead. Urging Corsa to be bolder towards him, he says her modesty is unfashionable:

> In neighbour courts [such as?] the ladies so prevail
> With masculine behaviour, they grow
> In factions able to depose their husbands
> From the charter of their sex.

This sounds like an instance of male unease about women's apparently 'prevailing' sexually. In trying at first to seduce her, he gives her a jewel and, in order not to seem too obvious, also gives one to her friend, Foreste's wife, Luinna (which she, being poorer, unwisely keeps). He then suborns the vicious courtier-satirist Castruchio who, jealous and resentful of Foreste, has his own plans, involving the foolish courtier Lothario ('the court baboon') who boasts, 'Know ye not, rogues, that I can muzzle up / The testy unicorn in a spinner's thread'; his greedy ambitions remember Jonson's Sir Epicure Mammon: 'I'll feed upon the tongues of nightingales /For so each fart I let will be a song.' His servant Borachio's comic motif is to speak almost entirely in 'a bundle of proverbs' and clichés, though the effect is undermined by having the main characters also talk largely in moralistic aphorisms and sententiae. Castruchio then persuades his young woman, Duarte, to bring Corsa to the Duke's room. The Duke then rapes her, noisily, off stage.

Foreste, having returned from having been got out of the way, and seeing Luinna with the Duke's jewel, believes that she has been unfaithful and determines to kill her, in a scene of violent jealousy and misogynistic abuse, derived partly from Webster's *The Duchess of Malfi*: 'Thou shalt die /Like an heroic whore … my she-goat … I will procure ye /Some of larger thighs, … Or bring the riotous horse, and the town bull,' before telling two masked men to "Take her aside /And agree who shall begin.' He also tells Lucio that the Duke has raped Corsa.

Lucio in turn goes on to accuse Corsa of having gone along with it:

> If compulsion doth insist until
> Enforcement breed delight, we cannot say
> The female suffers. Acceptance at the last
> Disparageth the not consenting at the first.

This is unlikely to be Davenant's own idea; one wonders at the mindsets in Charles's court. Lucio proposes a slow killing. Like Othello, he will not harm her soul: 'It is a long way to heaven.' He ties her to a chair: 'Thy wrist-veins are cut. Here /In this bason bleed, till dryness makes them curl /Like lute-strings in the fire.' She manages to echo Desdemona's pathetic death: 'Commend me to my dearest lord.'

After a fierce encounter Lucio and Foreste unite against the Duke, but feel that they cannot honourably kill their ruler. The Duke is afraid of Lucio's return; Castruchio advises him to hide in his bedroom where, panicking and dithering as much absurdly as pathetically, he begs Castruchio not to kill his beloved Lucio. Lucio and Foreste arrive and denounce the Duke, who pleads royal immunity (like Claudius). In a scene of absurd confusion, Lothario mistakenly kills the Duke (conveniently saving Lucio's honour). A sword fight ensues, with the friends, both injured, driving off Castruchio and his henchman. Reconciled, they express mutual forgiveness. Foreste explains that, in killing Corsa, he 'gave liberty to her polluted blood'; now sexually experienced, she is even more 'too base for your use' (before, she was socially too base for closer union); 'use' is an interesting word, here. So, 'I killed /A sister to secure a friend'. Some relationships are more important than others.

With the Duke and Lucio dead, the play concludes with the Governor ordering the capture, torture (like that proposed for Iago) and execution of Castruchio. After wallowing in sadism, rape and murder, the play seems more exploratory of misogynistic, homosocial bonding and its corrupting effect. The last words offer an unconvincing moral:

> So intricate is Heavens revenge against lust,
> The righteous suffer here, with the unjust.

Buckingham's death had dominated 1628 for Davenant, who had probably missed out on joining the bungled campaign against the Ile de Rhé in order to be present for the production of his play. He seems, however, to have got carried away with uncharacteristic martial fervour in support of the cause. The Privy Council then received a letter, unsigned and undated but endorsed in pencil, 'abt 1628', offering to blow up 'the Storehowse, or Magazin of Dunkerck, and is to be effected, by a secret illumination of Powder', from 'Mr Dauenant, Lodging in ye middle temple with Mr hide'. Davenant explains that he can do this 'by the easinesse of a friend; who now is official in the Magazin; and his assistance hath given me power to receave imployments there. I have knowledge of a small Engine, that will inforce a usefull fire … I shall performe the service, though with the losse of my life'.[14] Not surprisingly, nothing came of this hare-brained scheme. It appears that Davenant, now out of Brooke Hall, was lodging with Edward Hyde in the Inns of Court; there would still have been nowhere there for Mrs Davenant.

Meanwhile, he returned to his dramatic efforts, and in July 1629, his next attempt, *The Colonel*, was licensed,[15] but then disappeared (perhaps ousted by *The Just Italian*, licensed that October); however, it probably eventually reappeared as *The Siege* in the 1673 folio of his works. As the play is different from what he had tried before, with less repressed homophile feeling, is less bloodthirsty and more attuned to Court sentiment, it belongs with the next chapter's accounts of Davenant's attempts to fit in there. Meanwhile, with his Court poems and his plays, he had achieved his breakthrough – unicorns or no.

# Chapter 2

# Venus and Mercury (1630–1633)

Apart from some characteristic comedy among the lower orders, *The Colonel* (or *The Siege*) (*Dramatic Works*, Vol. IV) is not wholly successful, and it is not surprising that it did not do well; Davenant's nineteenth-century editors even suspected that some of it was by someone else. Nevertheless, it has some good scenes, and demonstrates Davenant's attempt to satisfy courtier interests; there were better things to come.

The story concerns Florello, a celebrated soldier engaged in the siege of Pisa under the Tuscan general Castacagnio, whom he urges not to destroy the city because of all its fine buildings. His real reason for this, however, is love of a Pisan, Bertolina, daughter of the Governor, Foscari. In pursuit of his beloved, Florello deserts and secretly goes over to Pisa, and offers his services to Foscari. Unfortunately for him, Bertolina, despite her love for him, will have nothing to do with him as a result of his dishonourable treachery: 'Thou art now the ruins of /A man, though heretofore the noblest soldier /In the world,' she declares, echoing Cleopatra on Mark Antony. (Or, as Lovelace was to write, 'I could not love thee dear so much, /Loved I not honour more.')

Distraught, he returns to the Tuscans, where, after initial hostility, he is received again. The siege proceeds, when Florello distinguishes himself by his vengeful savagery. When he at last confronts Bertolina, he is shamed by her pride. Then, in a melodramatic scene, he encounters his close friend Soranzo, also in love with her (the first instance of Davenant's recurrent situation), and asks him to kill him, whilst giving him Bertolina. Soranzo will not do this, and Bertolina refuses to be a mere passed-on parcel. Now that Florello is no longer a traitor, she can accept him as a lover, and Soranzo, a true gentleman friend, has to put up with it. Love and honour are reconciled.

There is also a comic sub-plot, intended as a sort of parallel, of two cowardly Tuscan gentleman volunteers, who pay an ensign, Mervole, to look after them under the aegis of Piracco, his captain. One episode clearly derives from Falstaff's celebrated boasting in *Henry IV, Part One*, as they claim to have driven off large numbers of the enemy:

> Ariotti:  Had I not seen thee engag'd against the
> Other five, I had maintain'd the combat still
> With these seven Switzers –pox o'their two-handed
> Scythes! …
> Lizaro:  Right! But 'twas for the safety of my fame
> To see you skirmish with twelve such,
> And not employ my fortitude to weaken
> Their assault …

Captain Piracco, like Florello, had a reputation as a good fighter, but after Mervole accidentally lanced an 'imposthume' (probably a syphilitic ulcer) in his leg, lost all his courage and was demoted and generally derided, rather as Florello was for a while. His story may derive from Fletcher's *The Humorous Lieutenant*, of a soldier (not humorous in the modern sense, but moody and melancholic), at first brave then, after recovery from the pox, no longer brave (but eventually restored). Military minded members of the audience would have been sympathetic. The play considers the unreliability of reputation, but the cavaliers' favourite theme, the contest between love and honour, would figure largely in future plays.

With Lady Frances and Fulke Greville both gone, Davenant needed to re-establish himself at Court as best he could. There are two poems in which he makes up to the King, who had dissolved Parliament in 1629. One, from late that year, attacks, with some vigour, one Alexander Leighton, who, in the previous year, had 'Prophecy'd a Succesles end of the Parliament',[1] and had attacked not only the bishops and Roman Catholicism (i.e. the Queen) and criticized the King. Here Davenant abuses Leighton, 'froward with Age [like] a beggar'd Chymist, or rich Curtizan'. Leighton is a troublemaker: 'He who esteems thy Northern Prophesie /Does but encourage Fools to learn to lie.' Davenant then turns to Parliament – 'great Senate know, I am your Prophet now' – urging them to pay money to the King, as, 'When Thrones are rich, the People richer grow'. He concludes by warning them of 'the Western Eagle', the Habsburg Emperor, who should be resisted.

On 25 March 1630, he wrote a New-Year's Day Ode to the King [2] (the only poem he ever addressed the King directly), who is, in four refrains, 'the example and the Law, /By whom the good are taught, not kept in awe'. Here he hopes for peace, 'not compass'd by Expensive Treaties' (such as those secretly made with France and Spain) but obtained by fame or prayer; then, for a Parliament 'gather'd to consult, not sway; /Who not rebell' (like Thomas Wentworth, who, when Charles had dissolved Parliament in 1626, was eventually bought off with the Earldom of Strafford in 1628); instead, Parliament should proffer 'timely gifts', to enable Charles to assist the Protestant cause in Europe, and no longer make the exploits of the Swedish warrior-king, Gustavus Adolphus II, against the Holy Roman Emperor, Ferdinand II, 'No more our envy, nor our shame.' (Characteristically, Charles dithered.)

Whilst keeping in with the Buckingham group, he also started in on his campaign of flattery of the Queen, as is suggested by a poem 'To the Queen',[3] on her being entertained at night by the Countess of Anglesey, Elizabeth Villiers, sister-in-law of Buckingham (when her husband died in 1630, Charles granted her an annual pension of £1,000 – add a couple of noughts for a modern equivalent). He had already flattered the Countess (Gibbs 125), now the Queen, who has squeezed her moonshine-like radiance into the small lantern of Anglesey. In 1630, his favoured place with the Queen became apparent, in a longer poem, 'Jeffereidos', written to entertain her and the Court.[4]

With the death of Buckingham, the King and Queen were on notably better terms, and in the winter of 1629/30 Henrietta Maria became pregnant. Apparently not trusting English midwifery, she sent to France for a midwife and nurses. On the return journey, the little ship was captured by Dunkirk pirates, who seized jewels worth £2,500, together with other presents for the Queen valued at £5,000 more, as well as midwives, nurses, a dancing master and her pet dwarf, Jeffrey Hudson. The party was eventually released by the Governor of Calais, and returned to England, none the worse for the experience. Davenant celebrated Jeffrey's part in this later that year, in his very early version of mock epic.

Jeffrey Hudson (1619–82) was a tiny but noticeable figure at Court. He was born at Oakham in Rutlandshire (the smallest county, as whimsical versifiers were happy to point out), the son of a butcher in charge of the bulls for bull-baiting for the Duke of Buckingham, who gave him, then perhaps 9 years old and less than two feet high, to the Queen, for a surprise present. At a grand and sumptuous dinner for the young queen, not then on good terms with her new husband, deprived of her French ladies and in need of cheering up, a large pie was brought to table before her. Such dinners were occasions for cooks to demonstrate special skills; Ben Jonson, in *Neptune's Triumph*, describes how such a cook might proceed:

> He designs, he draws,
> He paints, he carves, he builds, he fortifies,
> Makes citadels of curious fowl and fish;
> Some he dry ditches, some he moats round with broths,
> Mounts marrow-bones, and fifty angled custards,
> Rears bulwark pies, and for his outer works,
> He raises ramparts of immortal crust …

From out of such a (cold) pie burst, not four and twenty blackbirds but, little Jeffrey, smartly dressed as a young gentleman, bowing courteously to his delighted new mistress. He was soon her favourite pet, living 'in great plenty, wanting nothing but humility (high mind in a low body) … and would not know his father' (according to Thomas Fuller, in *Worthies of England*, in 1662). Thomas Heywood, in *Times Wonders* (1636) described him as 'one of the prettiest, neatest and well-proportioned small men that ever Nature bred, or was ever seen'. In 1633, the great Court painter, Van Dyck, painted the Queen with her hand on her pet ape, Pug, seated on Jeffrey's shoulder; the painting can be allegorized, as showing chaste Henrietta Maria controlling sensuality, conventionally embodied in ape and dwarf. Jeffrey is dressed in scarlet velvet trimmed with white lace, a gold chain over one shoulder, and spurred boots. In his heels he reaches to the Queen's waist, as she stands on a low step; as she was less than five feet tall, this would make him barely two and a half feet high – though Van Dyck appears, as often, to have somewhat exaggerated the royal inches.

In his poem of 1630, Davenant describes how 'tall Jeffrey' (the standard epithet for epic heroes), presented however as impossibly minute, is hunted down by the pirates in maggot holes and found behind a pewter candlestick; taken at first for 'a walking Thumbe', he is interrogated, in vain, by the Spanish captain. Carried off to Brussels, he is attacked, in a parody of heroic battle, by a turkey-cock, 'with intent to eat /Him up, in stead of a large graine of wheat'. 'Strike up the wrathfull Tabor! And the Gitthern!' cries the poet; Jeffrey cries, 'St George for England,' and with a five-shilling sword knocks off some feathers. The turkey-cock is probably a parody of the eagle of the voracious Habsburg Empire. In the battle, he is overthrown, and the turkey pecks at him, and he begs the midwife, 'Thou that deliver'd hast so many, be /So kinde of nature to deliver me!' With this, the 'Epick Ode' is discontinued, whilst a continuation is promised – though not delivered (it could have celebrated the successful delivery on 29 May of the future Charles II).

In 1637 Jeffrey was at the Siege of Breda, and in 1638 took part in Davenant's masque for the Queen, *Luminalia*, and, in 1640, in the last pre-war Court masque, Davenant's *Salmacida Spolia*, once again as a comic grotesque. In the Civil War, he 'followed the drum', as the saying was, and was given the title of Captain of Horse at Newark, and was then with the Queen at Merton College, in Oxford, when Davenant was also present; later, he was on the Continent again, at Nevers (again with Davenant). In October 1644, Charles Crofts insulted him, and Jeffrey challenged him to a duel; derisively, Crofts squirted water at him. Jeffrey would not be fobbed off, insisted on a duel on horseback, and shot his man dead. This was not acceptable, and he was banished. His career after that is not clear, but with the Restoration he was back in England, was given a pension by the Second Duke of Buckingham and retired to Oakham. Perhaps his association with Henrietta Maria and time on the Continent created suspicion of Catholic sympathies; at any rate, the 'Popish Plot' in 1678 saw him imprisoned for a while – did they think of him as 'a mole'? – before he was released in 1680.

More important to Davenant than 'Jeffereidos' was his next play, *The Just Italian. A Tragi-Comedy* (*Dramatic Works*, Vol. I), performed at the Blackfriars Theatre by the King's Men and dedicated to Sir Edward Sackville, Earl of Dorset (and Lord Chamberlain to the Queen). There seems to have been some hostility to the play, as the dedication observes: 'The uncivill ignorance of the People had depriv'd this humble Worke of Life; but that your Lordship's approbation stept in to succour it. Those many that came with resolution to dispraise, knowing your Lordship's judgment to be powerful above their malice, were either corrected to an understanding, or modesty.' In a later poem to the Earl, possibly written in the 1640s, he writes, 'you adorn'd my Muse and made her known.'[5] That was later; in the meantime, the play appeared not to be in the popular taste. In a dedicatory poem, a friend, Will Hopkins, wrote:

> Hence, giddy fools! Run to the noise they make
> At Paris Garden; or your selves betake      [bear-baiting venue]
> To the new motion – the fine puppet plays,
> And there adore. Commend the learned lays
> That make a din about the streets, or els     [street ballads]
> Extol the Jew's trump, or the morris bells –

before insisting that the wiser few would appreciate it. Likewise, Thomas Carew, shortly to write the Court masque, *Coelum Britannicum*, also criticized the limitations of vulgar taste:

> – thy strong fancies, raptures of the brain,
> Drest in poetic flames, they entertain
> As a bold impious reach …

Quality writers, such as Beaumont and Jonson, have been neglected –

> So was thy Play, whose clear, yet lofty strain,
> Wise men, that govern Fate, shall entertain.

It may have been the poetic flames and raptures that put off some people, as the material – quite apart from the Italianate melodrama – should have been popular enough, with its traditional theme of power struggles between husbands and wives, or the relatively recent theme of proto-feminist complaint set against resentment of uppity women (as in Fletcher's recent *Rule a Wife and Have a Wife*). In the real Court world, courtiers' marriages with wealthier and/or socially superior women produced their own tensions; the young women had to marry but did not always have much choice in the matter. Here, Count Altamont has fallen out with his new wife, Alteza, the daughter of the Duke (and so of superior birth and wealth), who, he says, has 'forgot th'allegiance of a wife'. He hopes that it is 'not from poison'd malice /But from the feminine mistakes of wit; /

For, modern courts now preach, wit doth reside /In ladies' subtle riots, and their pride.' He pleads that it is only love

> That makes th'eternal wisdom thus forbear
> The silly crimes of dull humanity;
> And suffers us, like each delighted fly
> To play the trivial wantons in his eye.

His memories of King Lear not succeeding, he tries to buy her off, absurdly: 'thy maids shall eat young pelicans and squirrels' hearts', and offers ermine furs, Arabian spices, 'marmosets and dwarfs: the male / And female too, to procreate in thy house, /That thy delights may ever be renew'd'. His claim that he will provide all this from 'my large wealth' only infuriates her: she insists that it is not his, but *her* family wealth that *he* owes *her*. Enraged, she swears that she will banish him from her bed, and divide the house into two properties.

Altamont hopes to make her jealous by kissing young Scoperta, whom he says he will make his concubine – but without revealing that she is actually his sister. Whilst this is intended to show him as not guilty sexually, it does introduce a somewhat queasy note. Alteza in turn introduces her gigolo, a handsome Florentine stud, Sciolto; his outrageous swaggering before Altamont has a brutal comedy:

Altamont: Who art thou?
Sciolto:                    A keen guest, invited here.
Altamont: To what?
Sciolto:                    To taste your wife's gammon...
    I am come to get your children for you.
Alteza:    D'ye want a clearer paraphrase? He is
    My servant, sir, my stallion if I please,
    A courtly implement, and much in use
    Among ladies of my growth and title.

When Altamont draws his sword, Sciolto readily draws his, and Alteza, her stiletto, producing an absurd stand-off. Sciolto mocks him further:

> I come t'ease the labour of your body
> And you want courtship to return me thanks ...
> What hereafter I
> Perform, shall be for your good lady's sake,
> And not for yours ...
> I merit better looks, Sir, that must thrash
> All night for ye, and without wages, Sir.

When he and Alteza go off, he explains that he only put on 'terror masculine' to unnerve Altamont for her sake, and that, really, he is gentlemanly. Now that he is ready to get started, he is surprised that she puts him off, as not quite ready yet: he might instead read a book, Rabelais or Aretino (so both wife and husband remain technically innocent).

Meanwhile, in the sub-plot, Altamont's younger and necessarily poorer younger brother, Florello, hearing that Alteza's sister, Charintha, has a prospective Milanese suitor, Dandolo, decides to pretend to be him. He dresses in fine clothes looted in the recent wars with Pisa, spending his limited money on pearls and jewels to scatter among the ladies, to suggest over-abundant wealth. This is the familiar figure of the fortune-hunter, presented with sympathetic comedy. Alteza urges her sister: 'Milk him, my Charintha. Oft have I preach'd /Unto thine ear a sovereignty o'er men.' (So it is feminist principle that motivates her.) Enter Florello as Dandolo, outrageously lofty with Alteza, scattering jewels – 'there's a saphire chain; tie thy monkey in't.' His soldiers appear as his attendants:

> I've instruments distinct, that take a charge
> O'th'several quarters of my frame. My dwarf
> Doth dress me up to my knees, and, when
> His stature leaves his reach, young Virgins then,
> Th'issue of decay'd barons, do begin
> And govern to the navel. Whilst upwards,
> Barbers, painters and parasites are us'd.

Charinthia, while amused, cannot help but be impressed. Alteza and Sciolto encounter Altamont, who draws his sword again; this time, however, his aristocratic weapon is absurdly impotent, as he is outbid by Sciolto's brace of plebeian pistols (the sexual metaphor is evident).

Sciolto will not kill him and risk execution, coolly explaining, 'I have an odd humour not to be kill'd.' In the meantime, the stallion is feeling frustrated: 'In three hours not so much as a dry kiss. /Th'old amorous deacon that embrac'd his cow /Was not so destitute.'

After he demands that Altamont bring him his wife and has sauntered off, Altamont and his friend, Mervolle, swear revenge.

Now the true Dandolo arrives, unimpressive in person and purse ('this hulk is neither rigg'd nor fraught,' says Charinthia's maid, Besognia), and is mockingly outfaced by Florello – 'Unless you are an estridge, Sir, and can /Digest steel, cool your lungs' – who declares that he is a bastard 'got on the tripe-wife of Lucca'. Sciolto and Scoperta meet, fall in love and embrace (observed by Altamont, outraged at his sister's behaviour with this lout: revenge, revenge!). She explains that she is Altamont's chaste sister; they agree to meet in the garden before dawn, and elope. When Alteza, having prepared with perfumes, lute music and Persian quilts, sends for Sciolto, she is amazed that he – now in love – hangs back; instead he gets out of it by insulting her absurdly, while she screeches in fury:

> Why? – ye are not handsome ... Your face
> As carv'd out of a blue cabbage, and 'tis
> Contracted now to one oblique wrinkle ...
> Thy aged skull, instead of hair,
> O'ergrown with moss, and looks as if't had been
> A thousand years entomb'd...
> Thy solitary teeth in distance stand,
> Like the decay'd arches of a bridge ...
>                Wilt not yet go?
> Thy fingers are all crook'd, like the talons
> Of a griffin. Thou walkst on cloven feet ...

After her rage has subsided, her spirit seems crushed: Altamont had never treated her like this, but praised her beauty. She now apologizes, but Altamont, unsurprisingly, takes some convincing, and says that, though he will not kill her, as originally intended, will not see her again. Meanwhile, ominously, he says that Scoperta 'treads the slimy path' for Sciolto's lust.

Act IV returns to the comic sub-plot, as, in front of Charinthia, Florello and his men humiliate Dandolo and his attendants, who pretend that their good manners cover their cowardice. When Florello kicks them, they insist, 'You see we still are calm.' Charinthia urges on Florello: 'Yon marmalet Count deserves as much too.'

> Dandolo:   I do oppugn the motion with my scorn.
> Florello:   D'ye scorn, sir, to be kick'd?
> Dandolo:                                 Pardon me, sir!
>            I say't aloud; the proudest wight on earth
>            Shall not kick me, excepting your dear self.

With Dandolo gone, Niente reveals Florello's true identity. After an initial rejection, Charinthia tells him to return, and gives him the key to her orchard gate.

Back at the garden gate, Scoperta is surprised by Altamont, who in the course of melodramatic ranting, tells her that he has killed Sciolto: 'Stint thy hoarse dirge, pernicious whore!' She insists on her innocence, and Altamont says he will kill her and Sciolto, whom he has captured and had him bound by his servant mutes, who also seize her. Sciolto challenges Altamont to release him for a duel; Sciolto falls, wounded, and Mervolle takes him off to pray before he is strangled. Altamont now realizes that he also is wounded.

Act V begins with two boys singing about Scoperta's forthcoming death, how despite her beauty,

> Death leads Beauty to a shade
> More cold more darke, than Night.

As in other of his writing, Davenant worries about the uncertainty of the afterlife, if any:

> But aske not Bodies (doom'd to dye)
>      To what abode they goe;
> Since *Knowledge* is, but *Sorrowes Spy*,
>      It is not safe to know.

A lyric of his, 'Endimion Porter, and Olivia'[6] belongs to this time, and echoes these verses' tone:

> Before we shall again behold
> In his diurnal race the Worlds great Eye,
>     We may as silent be and cold,
> As are the shades where buried Lovers lie.

The song and episode are quite plangent and affecting, but seem oddly intrusive in the context of the play's action and generally broad comic tone. Indeed, we now switch back to Florello in his original poorer clothing, who has captured Dandolo and his men after they were caught hiding, waiting to assassinate him. After he has failed to commit an honourable suicide, Dandolo is sent off – on bail, as it were – to obtain his ransom money from the Count of Milan. Charinthia and Florello express their love for each other, while Mervole tells them that Altamont is dead – which would make Florello his successor. (The Davenant theme of the cheeky success of the outsider younger brother is notable.)

Next comes the powerful Sciolto/Scoperta scene, where the lovers, bound and with ropes around their necks, await garrotting by Altamont's mutes. Again, there is a lyrical dialogue on death:

> Ere long we must be cold,
>     Cold, cold, my love ...

> But O! How many ages may succeed
>     In heaven's dark calendar, ere we again
> Material be, and meet in our warm flesh?

> Philosophy doth seem to laugh upon
>     Our hopes, and wise divinity belies
> Our knowledge with our faith; jealous nature
>     Hath lock'd her secrets in a cabinet ...

Such lines – however important to Davenant – may be what some considered 'a bold impious reach', or intrusive. Now Altamont casts off his mask as one of the mutes, and acknowledges Scoperta's innocent love; Mervolle urges that he also pardon Sciolto, especially as his uncle has just died and he would be the wealthy, high-caste heir. Everything is now tidied up: Sciolto and Scoperta embrace, Charinthia and Florello are united, and Altamont and submissive Alteza are reconciled. Dandolo is sent off to ride naked on a mule, and the others gather for a celebratory dance.

As tragi-comedy, the play contains episodes of dramatic intensity, with 'raptures of the brain drest in poetic flames', with some melodramatic absurdities; the best thing about the play is its vigorous comedy, an early instance of his real talent.

John Aubrey noted how he had written 'Playes and verses, which he did with so much sweetnesse and grace that by it he got the love and friendship of his two Maecenases, Mr Endymion Porter and Mr Henry Jermyn'. Jermyn (1605–84) had gone to Spain with Buckingham on Charles's unsuccessful courtship trip in 1622, before becoming Henrietta Maria's vice-chamberlain in 1628 and her particularly close friend (and perhaps more, according to Court gossip). A bilingual Francophile – his father was governor of Jersey – he was reputed the 'stallion' of the court. Years later, Andrew Marvell wrote of his 'draymans shoulders, butchers mien /Member'd like Mules, with Elephantine chine'. Porter (1587–1649) had also gone to Spain, and married Olivia Boteler, Buckingham's niece. A patron of art and literature, he had a substantial unearned income as Groom of the Bedchamber, worth £500 a year, and Receiver of fines in Star Chamber (£750), with emoluments for diplomatic service and many properties; it is estimated he had an annual income of £3,000 – as usual, add at least a couple of noughts for a modern equivalent. He was to prove a particularly good friend to Davenant over the next few years.

Davenant's then friend, Edward Hyde, later wrote of this time, that there was

> never an age in which, in so short a time, so many young gentlemen, who had not experience in the world or some good tutelar angel to protect them, were insensibly and suddenly overwhelmed in that sea of wine, and women, and quarrels, and gaming, which almost overpowered the whole kingdom, and the nobility and gentry thereof.[7]

Davenant was one of those so overwhelmed. At some time between 1630 and 1633 Davenant experienced what Aubrey called an 'unlucky mischance', when he 'gott a terrible clap of a Black handsome wench that lay in Axe-yard, Westminster' (behind what is now Downing Street, and where Samuel Pepys came to live in 1658). Aubrey suggested that Davenant had her in mind later, in his incomplete epic, *Gondibert*. There he wrote of 'a black beauty' named Dalga, who 'did her pride display / Through a large window' and 'with black eyes [did] Sinners draw /And with her voice hold fast repenting Men'; her seductive skills (or 'wicked Woman's prosp'rous Art') are supposed to excuse the enthusiastic response of the young man, whether the character, or the author. (Aubrey himself acquired some venereal infection in 1656 – it could happen to anyone.)

He soon found himself repenting, not only as a result of the infection but of the initial attempts at the traditional treatment: mercury, often taken either by swallowing or being daubed on in ointment form. Later in the century, Sir Henry Savile at Charles II's Court complained of the 'mass of mercury that has gone down my mouth in seven months'. The more common method was to absorb mercury vapour in a steam bath (in a 'hot house'); in one poem, John Donne had remarked on an unfaithful mistress's 'quick-silver sweat'. In any event, the effects of the treatment could be horrific, with ulceration of mouth, tongue, gums and throat, with constant spitting. In Davenant's case, faulty treatment caused the septum of his nose to collapse, leaving an unsightly hole, and his life seemed threatened.

He was rescued from this disaster by Endymion Porter, who got the Queen's physician, Thomas Cademan (a Catholic, like Henrietta Maria) to treat him. He later wrote a poem to Cademan,[8] beginning,

> For thy victorious cares, thy ready heart;
> Thy so small tyranny to so much Art;
> For visits made to my disease
> And me (Alas) not to my Fees ...

(These were probably paid by Porter)

> For setting now my condemn'd Body, free
> From that no God, but Devill *Mercurie* ...

Cademan provided him with 'benigne' medicines and rescued him from the fate endured by sailors he had seen lying rotting in seaport hospitals, their 'rheum' (phlegm) dribbling in 'slender Ropes', their 'revolted teeth' threaded like imitation pearl necklaces (he could never resist a grotesque image).

Syphilis was known as 'the French disease' or *morbus gallicus*; his friend Suckling wrote in 'A Session of Poets' (1637) that Davenant had caught the disease travelling in France, probably because that rhymed with 'mischance' and was an easily understood euphemism. As such, it was of course un-English, so that, in the course of his account of his earlier sufferings, his cheeks are described as swollen like a Saracen's head on the signboard of a tavern; his own head was sewn into a hood, rendering him speechless, like a suppressed dissenter preacher or a 'Turk's poison'd Mute', reduced to spitting and foaming at the mouth; when he tried to swallow, he grimaced like an Israelite forced to eat quails (*Exodus* XVI: 13). The horror of his experience is offered to his unsympathetic courtier readers as a kind of comic-grotesque amusement.

Each verse begins with 'For', leading the reader to expect a concluding expression of thanks – which never arrives. As he was not able to pay his tailor, here he could neither pay Cademan's bills nor quite express his gratitude in his verse. Just as he frequently inverted conventional expectations in his commendatory poems, here the joke is not to express thanks directly. Instead, more imaginatively, he concludes by hoping that every spring will bring 'Ripe plenty of Diseases' to the rich, who will pay Cademan well, and 'Health to the Poore', so that Cademan will not have to treat them out of pity – or 'such as pay like mee /A Verse, then thinke they give Eternity': as if a poet could guarantee this.

When a friend of his, one I.C., was robbed of his cloak by his manservant, Davenant wrote to commiserate,[9] regretting his inability to join him in the hunt:

> my sick Joints cannot accompany
> Thy Hue-on-cry; though Midnight parlies be
> Silenc'd long since 'tween Constables and me.

The poem concludes,

> But hark! who knocks? good troth my Muse is staid
> By an Apothecaries Bill unpaid,
> Whose length, not strange-nam'd Drugs, makes me afraid.

Porter would have seen to such bills, even if Davenant liked to think that 'naught justly payes /Physitians love but faith, their art, but prayse'. He seemed to reserve his supreme gratitude to his lifesaver (and substitute god-father) Porter, who would now be his model, whose 'wisedome … hath taught this world an art /How (not enform'd by Cunning) courtship may /Subdue the minde and not the Man betray'.[10] This probably relates mostly to Porter's Court life but could also include his married life (Olivia was excessively jealous), or Davenant's own disastrous infidelity. Nevertheless, he promises,

> If mee (thy Priest) our curled Youth arraigne
> To wash our Fleet-street Altars with new Wine,
> I will (since 'tis to thee a Sacrifice)
> Take care, that Plenty swell not into vice:
> Lest by a fiery Surfet I be led
> Once more to grow devout in a strange bed.

Perhaps he could have made such a promise to his young wife, wherever she was. In the meantime, he would devote himself to his writing, and to Porter. So, in another poem to Porter,[11] written after his recovery and lengthy convalescence, now overconfident in himself, he feels his 'strength so giantly' that the Titans could choose him to throw mountains at Zeus. Now he will try

> if Art, and Nature able be
> From the whole strength and stock of Poesie
> To pay thee my large debts.

Having been away from Court and the theatre (wherever he may have been convalescing) for so long, there were other debts to pay, and he had to get back to work; soon enough, he would find occasion to thank Porter yet again.

# Chapter 3

# Wit, Honour and Love (1634–1635)

Now, after an intermission of perhaps three years, he turned to the theatre again, with a play that might please the King and his advisers. In 1632, Charles had issued a proclamation against the growing numbers of country gentry coming to London, directing them to return to their estates and responsibilities as magistrates and upholders of law and local order, serving the King 'according to their Degrees and Ranks, in aid of the Government'. The King was becoming uneasy about the development of London as a centre of political debate, and possible dissension and even disorder, with the Court having increasingly to take into account the growth of the gentry and merchant classes, with their distinct concerns and values. Davenant's new play, then, was to provide not only entertainment but also some comic discouragement of such out-of-place country gentlemen.

By the end of 1633, *The Witts* (*Dramatic Works*, Vol. II) had been drafted, shown to Endymion Porter and presented to the Master of the Revels, Sir Henry Herbert, to be licensed. Unfortunately, Sir Henry censored it heavily, which led Porter to complain to his friend, the King. Sir Henry's records for 9 January 1634 report:

> This morning ... the kinge was pleased to call mee into his withdrawing chamber to the windowe, wher he went over all that I had croste in Davenant's playbooke, and allowing of *faith* and *slight* to bee asseverations only, and no oaths, markt them to stande, and some other few things, but in the greater part allowed of my reformations. This was done upon a complaint of Mr Endymion Porter in December.
>
> The kinge is pleased to take *faith, death, slight,* for asseverations, and no oaths, to which I humbly submit as my masters judgment; but, under favour, conceive them to be oaths, and enter them here, to declare my opinion and submission.[1]

With Herbert's grudging consent, then, the play was finally licensed on 19 January 1634, and performed by the King's Men at the Blackfriars. Herbert later wrote that it 'had a various fate on the stage, and at court'; in fact, it was very successful at both, despite some possible ill-will from Herbert and his friends. Thomas Carew praised

> this play, where with delight
> I feast my Epicurean appetite
> With relishes so curious, as dispense
> The utmost pleasure to the ravish'd sense ...

In Davenant's prologue, he writes:

> Bless me you kinder Starrs! How are we throng'd?
> Alass! whom hath our harmless Poet wrong'd,
> That he should meet together in one day
> A Session, and a Faction at his Play,
> To judge, and to condemne?

In his dedication of *The Just Italian* he had mentioned the 'many that came with resolution to dispraise'. Later, in 'To Endimion Porter, When my Comedy (call'd *The Wits*) was presented at Black-Fryars',[2] he wrote

> I that am told conspiracies are laid,
> To have my Muse, her Arts, and life betray'd,
> Hope for no easie Judge; though thou wert there,
> T'appease, and make their judgements lesse severe ...

before adding defiantly,

> But I am growne too tame! What need I feare
> Whilst not to passion, but thy reason cleere?

In this play, he turned from his Jacobean-style Italianate grotesque tragedy to contemporary London, in a style of realistic comedy. The play is indeed witty and funny, very Jonsonian in style, tightly plotted, with 'type' comic characters of cunning or folly, concerned with the contrivances of con men out to defraud others, and 'live by their wits'. The main characters are naïve would-be swindlers, Pallatine the Elder and Sir Morglay Thwack, come up to London from the country to cheat ladies of their money. (The choice of the name of Pallatine for the brothers, in view of the well-known troubles on the Continent of the King's needy nephews, Charles and Rupert, known as 'the Pallatine Princes', is intriguing.) Thwack explains their scheme to the younger Pallatine:

> Your brother and myself have seal'd
> To covenants. The female youth o'th'town are his;
> But all from forty to fourscore mine own.
> A widow, you'll say, is a wise, solemn, wary
> Creature. Though she hath liv'd to the cunning
> Of dispatch, clos'd up nine husbands' eyes,
> And have the wealth of all their testaments,
> In one month, sir,
> I will waste her to her first wedding-smock,
> Her single ring, bodkin, and velvet muff ...

Young Pallatine, himself city-smart, warns, 'But sirs, /The city, take't on my experiment, /Will not be gull'd.' In practice, the women are witty, undeceived and more skilful in outmanoeuvring the men. Lady Ample, an 'inheritrix', was herself once poor, living on her wits, as she explains to the romantic young heroine, Lucy:

> My guardian's contribution gave us gowns:
> But cut from th'curtains of a carrier's bed;
> Jewels we wore, but such as potters' wives
> Bake in the furnace for their daughters' wrists;
> My woman's smocks so coarse, as they were spun
> O'th'tackling of a ship ...

Davenant has a good eye for everyday life, but also shows gifts of whimsy, as she continues:

> Our diet scarce so much as is prescrib'd
> To mortify: two eggs of emmets, poach'd,        [ants]
> A single bird, no bigger than a bee,
> Made up a feast.

He also has a delightful gift of comic exaggeration, as when describing an upper room hung with cobwebs,

> and those so large they may
> Catch and ensnare dragons instead of flies,
> Where sit a melancholy race of old
> Norman spiders, that came in with th'Conqueror.

Ordinary life can be evoked simply and memorably, in a few lines, as when Thwack, chivvied to hurry up, contrasts himself with

> the dexterity
> Of a spaniel, that with a yawn, a scratch
> On his left ear, and stretching his hind legs,
> Is ready for all day.

(What other dramatists could do this?)

The play is filled with references to familiar London places, giving a local habitation and a name to the action: the landing-stage at Billingsgate, archery at Finsbury Fields, the regrettable 'decays of Fleet Ditch', Cheapside, the Dutch brewers at Ratcliffe, Covent Garden and many more. There are improbable petty crimes – stealing a font-cover or a vicar's surplice, the hearse cloth and winding sheets 'that have been stol'n about the town this year' (a reference to a recent plague?); a newly impoverished, hungry man will now

> Betroth himself to raddish-women for their roots,
> Pledge children in their sucking-bottle,
> And, in dark winter mornings, rob small school-boys
> Of their honey and their bread.

Appealing to the snobbish prejudices of his courtier and upper-class London audiences, he mocks country-dwelling ladies, in a satiric sequence shared by four speakers, preening themselves on their superiority:

Elder Pallatine:                                    ... poor villagers,
            They churn still, keep their dairies, and lay up
            For embroider'd mantles against the heir's birth.
Lady Ample:      Who is begot i'th'Christmas holidays.
Elder Pallatine: Yes, surely, when the spirit of
            Mince-pie reigns in the blood.
Lady Ample:      What? penny-gleek I hope's   [simple card-game]
            In fashion yet, and the treacherous foot
            Not wanting on the table frame, to jog
            The husband, lest he lose the noble that
            Should pay the grocer's man for spice and fruit ...
Sir Morglay:      Poor country madams, th'are in subjection still;
            The beasts, their husbands, make 'em sit on three
            Legg'd stools, like homely daughters of an hospital,
            To knit socks for their cloven feet.
Elder Pallatine: And when these tyrant husbands, too, grow old,
            As they have still th'impudence to live long,
            Good ladies, they are fain to waste the sweet
            And pleasant seasons of the day in boiling
            Jellies for them, and rolling little pills
            Of cambric lint to stuff their hollow teeth.
Lucy:            And in the evenings, warrant ye, they
            Spend with Mother Spectacle, the curate's wife,
            Who does inveigh 'gainst curling, and dyed cheeks,
            Heaves her devout impatient nose at oil
            Of jessamine, and thinks powder of Paris more
            Prophane than th'ashes of a Romish martyr.

When it came to reflecting and mocking real life, Davenant outfaced his audience with an unblushing, unlovely grin, as he has Lucy reproving Young Pallatine:

            Pall, you are as good-natur'd to me, Pall,
            As the wife of a silenc'd minister      [a suppressed Dissenter]
            Is to a monarchy, or to a lewd gallant
            That have lost a nose.

The Elder Pallatine in his folly is the chief victim of the comedy, shut up in a chest like Falstaff in *Merry Wives*. There are other Shakespearean borrowings: the comic constable, Snore and his wife, echo Dogberry in *Much Ado*; the aptly named clever servant, Engine, necessary for complicated action, half-remembers Hamlet, with 'you may persuade him more like a crab, backward', and Elder Pallatine, lamenting his own downfall, conflates Lear and Macbeth, anticipating when 'the virgins of our land ... will ... throw my dust before the sportive winds, till I am blown /About in parcels ...'

Like Jonson, his chief model here, Davenant can elaborate fantasies, like those of Sir Epicure Mammon, in the imagined delicacies proposed to Elder Pallatine:

> Young Pallatine:   Nothing could please your haughty palate
> But the muskatell, and Frontiniac grape;
> Your Turin and your Tuscan veal, with red
> Legg'd partridges of the Genoa hills...
> ... your angelots of Brie;
> Your Massolini and Parmesan of Lodi,
> Your Malamucka melons and Sicilian dates ...

None of this reaches him, of course. After all the plotting and counter-plotting, he is taken on by Lady Ample, who has coolly outwitted him (and hoodwinked him into giving money to Young Pallatine), as he realizes that his previous 'lazie method, as slow rule of Thrift' is no match for the younger men of the town – and younger brothers, such as Davenant. Thwack, also, resolves to 'write down to the Country, to dehort /The Gentry from coming hither, /Letters of strange dire Newes' with off-putting reports, such as 'That our Theatres are raz'd down; and where /They stood, hoarse Midnight Lectures preach'd by Wives /Of *Comb*-makers, and Mid-wives of *Tower-Wharfe*'. He offers an amusing way to excuse deliberate misinformation – that is, lies. The message is: stay where you are.

Young Pallatine, who has shown responsibility and urban wit, can look forward to a country manor, the unwilling gift of his older brother, and marriage to Lucy. The Pallatines might be versions of the Davenant brothers, as Elder mistakenly reproves Younger (as Robert might have

William): 'the stock my Father left you, if your care /Had purpos'd so discreet a course might well /Have set you up i'th'Trade.' Those keen to see Davenant as Shakespeare's son might be interested, when Elder Pallatine says of his brother,

> This is the wittiest offspring that our name
> Ere had; I love him beyond hope or lust;
> My father was no poet, sure; I wonder
> How he got him.

Meanwhile, Davenant had done his political job; though 'a cruel Faction' was critical, the play proved to be one of his most successful, as Herbert acknowledged: 'before the King and Queene. Well liked.' In the Restoration, he revived it, and Pepys saw it several times, considering it 'a most excellent play'. In the epilogue, Davenant hoped for a generous judgement, when 'our youthful Poet ... Will tread boldly then, /In newer Comick-Socks, this Stage agen'.

However, after this realist London comedy, he switched back to territory familiar to his courtier audiences and their ladies, the unrealistic courts of northern Italy; the new play was originally entitled *The Courage of Love*, and then, when it was licensed on 20 November 1634, he changed it to *Love and Honour*, before asking Sir Henry to alter it to *The Nonpareilles, or The Matchless Maids*. Nevertheless, when it was performed at the Blackfriars in December 1634, it was as *Love and Honour* (*Dramatic Works*, Vol. III).

It must be admitted that, even by his standards, the story is far-fetched, contrasting improbable, high-flown posturing by the aristocrats with coarse comedy by the needy soldiery. As often with Davenant, it opens with a discussion not obviously related to the theme of the play, but on a topic he used more than once, suggestive of his sympathies with the lower orders. There has been a war between Savoy and Millain (Milan), and the soldiers comment on the lack of care by the elegant aristocrats for their soldiers and ruined poor traders:

> Your highway, sir, is now
> Your only walk of state for your maim'd soldier;
> Your hospitals and pensions are reserv'd

> For your maim'd mercers, decay'd sons of the shop,
> That have been often cracked, not in their crowns
> Like us, but in their credit, sir.

Davenant had no time for war; a character observes,

> It is a mystery
> Too sad to be remembered by the wise,
> That half mankind consume their noble blood
> In causes not believ'd, or understood.

In the attack on Milan, the captain, Count Prospero (a name derived, curiously, from the Milanese duke in *The Tempest*), has captured Evandra, the beautiful 'heir of Millaine', and her wounded attendant, Leonell. Remarkably, when he claims that capturing such beauty confers honour on the conqueror, she ripostes scornfully,

> Honour? Is that the word that hath so long
> Bewray'd the emulous world, and fool'd the noblest race
> Of men into a vexed and angry death?
> If 'twere a virtue, 'twould not strive t'inthrall
> And then distress the innocent.

Her speech introduces the concern of the play, which is to devalue the macho culture of aggressive honour, and suggest instead the honour in generous altruism.

When Prospero takes her to Turin, he finds that Alvaro, son of the old Duke of Savoy, is furious that Evandra, whom he loves, has been put in the power of the Duke, who hates all Milanese, whom he holds responsible for the death of his brother; the Duke is determined to execute her, in revenge. After Alvaro has calmed down, Prospero arranges to shelter her in a cave in his garden. While they are there, he tells another courtier, Calladine, that he too has fallen in love with her.

By contrast with the high-flown sentiments directed at the beautiful heiress of Milan, the soldiers discuss the lower-class women they have captured. Tristan, the younger, has acquired Lelia, a maid, dismissed by the older soldier, Vasco, as only 'heir to a brass thimble and /A skene of brown thread. She'll not yield thee in Algiers [slave market] above a ducket, being stript.' He has a widow whom he believes to be wealthy, who is absurdly ancient and decrepit, and tells Lelia to tell her mistress not to catch cold, 'Having a persistent cough, /And so will die before I marry her.' Asked if he intends to court her at her window with 'rare music', he replies, 'No: she's very deaf; so that cost is sav'd ... What other charge? She hath no teeth fit for /A dry banquet, and dancing she is past, unless with crutches in an antimasque.'

Meanwhile, the Duke threatens to execute Prospero instead of Evandra, but when Alvaro pleads for him, he vows to execute Alvaro if she is not found; when they try to dissuade him, he threatens to execute Calladine (he's worse than Alice's Red Queen, for wanting to chop off heads). Vasco and his friends determine to marry the old woman that night; when Vasco kisses her, she observes, 'these comforts come /But seldom after four score.' After a physical-comedy scene, where she totters about when they try to make her dance, she consents to marry, and tells Lelia to 'provide a broom /And sweep away the rheum near the green couch; /And, d'you hear, look for one of my cheek teeth /Which dropt under the wainscot-bed.'

At the entrance to Evandra's cave, Leonell also declares his love for her; Prospero, who has overheard, is enraged and challenges him to a duel. While Leonell is away, Alvaro also declares his love for her, and announces that he is to die for her; characteristically for Davenant, he expresses uncertainty about any afterlife in 'the place of absence, where we meet, by all /The guess of learned thought, we know not whom'. Prospero now offers to die instead of Alvaro, to which Alvaro objects. She persuades Alvaro to enter the cave, and she locks him in. Prospero says he will now go to the Duke, to provoke him to have him killed, in hope that the Duke will then release her; she persuades him to take some food and drink into the cave for Alvaro, and promptly locks him in as well. After instructing Leonell to look after them, she and her friend, the Lady Melora, decide to go to the Duke themselves, as sacrifices to save the men: 'An act,' they are sure, 'as will outlive all history.' As they go, Leonell declares,

> This sure is such
> A great example of a female fortitude
> As must undo all men, and blushing make
> Us tear off our saucy beards before
> The scatt'ring winds that give us the pre-eminence
> Of sex; when this is known let women sway
> Counsels, and war, whilst feeble men obey.

The speech would have gone down particularly well with the Queen. When Melora goes to Calladine in disguise, pretending to be Evandra and so be executed instead, he is immediately smitten with her beauty and resolves to save her, and find Evandra, who he believes is Melora, to send in her place.

Meanwhile, Vasco and his friends celebrate the wedding with a grossly comic song, including the verse,

> Let not her Husband e'er vex heaven
> And for a plenteous off-spring begge,
> Since all the Issue can be given,
> Is that which runneth in her legge.
> Chorus: So old, so wondrous old, i'th'nonage of Time,
> Ere Adam wore a Beard, she was in her Prime.

Tristan remarks, 'I've seen a corse look better in a shroud.' The old woman asks, 'Look I so ill, Lelia?' and is reassured: 'As you were wont, forsooth: most strange and ugly.' When Vasco complains of having sex with her, 'coffin'd up /With clouts and a skeleton', he is reminded, 'Those that seek gold must dig for it in mines.'

Now Evandra and Melora present themselves before the Duke, arguing which of them shall die; despite having received pleading letters from Milan, he insists they must both die and Alvaro and Prospero are to be released and watch the execution (which Vasco hopes to block). Prospero accuses Leonell of keeping them imprisoned so as to improve his own courtship chances, which infuriates Leonell and they duel until Alvaro stops them, and all three are reconciled. Two bearded ambassadors from Milan now arrive, to plead in vain to a self-declared 'Prince that rather loves /To be cruel than to break his vow'. Leonell offers himself as a substitute, and reveals himself to be the Duke of Parma's son and heir. Evandra, disappointedly, cries out, 'O Melora! Thy brother will reveal /Himself and quite undo our glorious strife.' The Duke commands that they be unbound and Leonell prepared for death. At this, the first ambassador removes his false (saucy?) beard, to reveal himself as the Duke of Millain; the Duke commands that Leonell be released and Millain executed. Melora in turn laments, 'Our hope of endless glory now is lost,' as their vainglorious posturing is frustrated. The second ambassador now takes off his own false beard, to reveal himself as the Duke of Savoy's brother, long presumed dead but having lived quietly in Milan for ten years. The old Duke's malevolent 'honour' vow has been based on an ignorant mistake, and inflexible intransigence is exposed.

Executions are stopped, dukes and brothers reconciled, aristocratic young couples paired off; Prospero, left over, goes off to war, and Vasco is granted a divorce – 'She writes a hundred and ten, sir, next grass' – and promised to receive what he would have got as the widow's dowry.

It is hard to understand now that this preposterous stuff could have been taken at all seriously, but it went well – a lot of it is very funny – and Henrietta Maria, no doubt in response to its feminist element, had it revived at Hampton Court in March 1637, during the temporary closure of the theatres caused by plague. Davenant himself revived it successfully in 1661, when Pepys saw it three times, when the theatre's bookkeeper, John Downes, recorded, 'The Play having a great run, produc'd to the Company great Gain and estimation from the Town.'

Meanwhile, the Queen had plans for him; his campaign of flattery and reputation as a competent writer had paid off when he was commissioned to write for her his first Court masque, *The Temple of Love* (*Dramatic Works*, Vol. I), in collaboration with the celebrated Inigo Jones, who was to be responsible for scenery, costumes and special effects. Davenant was replacing Jones's previous collaborator, Ben Jonson, who had flounced out in disgust at what he saw as the dumbing-down of the intellectual element of masques in favour of spectacle. As he wrote, in his 'Expostulation with Inigo Jones':

> O Shows! Shows! Mighty Shows!
> The eloquence of masques! What need of prose
> Or verse or sense t'express immortal you?
> You are the spectacles of state! 'Tis true
> Court hieroglyphics! …

This was to overstate the case somewhat. The masques went on with less erudite classical references – which largely went over the heads of most spectators – but still with a considerable amount of intellectual – especially political – content, usually implicit.

As it was put on at the Queen's command, Davenant had a pretty good idea of what she wanted the masque to mean, or at least suggest, when it was put on, on Shrove Tuesday, 10 February and then on the 11th and 12th, 1635. It has been pointed out that 'masque splendour depended on resources being seen to be squandered in a single act of stupendous prodigality. That a masque be danced only once, then thrown away, was a testimony to princely magnificence, whereas to repeat it could suggest that its sponsors had an eye on economy'[3] – or were concerned that its message should reach as wide an audience as possible.

In theory, the Court masque was a private entertainment of dancing, music and spectacle, intended for the King and Queen and the royal family, but a considerable number of other people could also attend. Members of the nobility, courtiers and those associated with the court, officials and attendants, honoured guests, moneyed senior citizens and merchants, and politically significant gentry might all combine to swell the audience numbers, to several hundred on occasion. There could be so many that, in 1634, the King had introduced a system of ticket entry for *The Triumph of Peace*, even with 'a turning Chair', a temporary turnstile.[4] In a poem 'To Sir Robert Wroth', Jonson complained of the people crowding in

> When masquing is, to have a sight
> Of the short bravery of the night,
> To view the jewels, stuffs, the pains, the wit
> There wasted, some not paid for yet.

Masques were not just social occasions for an élite, but political events, intended to intervene in an uneasy social and political context. As the Renaissance scholar, Roy Strong, wrote:

A study in depth of any of the Caroline masques reveals that no other form gives such a penetrating glimpse into the mind of Charles I. The seriousness and the passionate belief in their [politically] remedial efficacy [are] reflected above all in the closing masques of the reign. They offer overt evidence of the confidence the King and Inigo Jones placed on the effect of these spectacles in staving off the oncoming tide of disaster. In 1635 the famous Rubens canvases were inserted into the ceiling of the Whitehall Banqueting House … [providing] in permanent form a pattern of Neo-Platonic ideas hovering above the heads of the Court below, just as the masques did in a more ephemeral way.[5]

Henrietta Maria had recently been engaged unsuccessfully in a minor power struggle against the Lord High Treasurer, Richard Weston, a crypto-Catholic, pro-Spanish sympathizer who favoured Charles's peace policy, as against her wishes at the time. Now she was pushing her own 'feminist' policy.[6] *The Temple of Love* was part of the Queen's campaign of social control, directed initially against sexual looseness in the Court, proposing the royal marriage as the model, but aimed also beyond, at a disturbed society. The theory behind this was Platonic Love; this cult was mentioned in the *Familiar Letters* of the courtier James Howell, in 1634, writing of 'a love call'd *Platonick Love*, which much sways there of late; it is a Love abstracted from all corporeal gross Impressions and sensual Appetite, but consists in Contemplation and Ideas of the Mind, not in any Carnal Fruition.'[7] This derived partly from the youthful Henrietta Maria's experience in the French Court, via her mother, Marie de' Medici, and was concerned less with high-minded celibacy than with a more refined social harmony governed by religion, with women controlling manners (and, in the case of the Queen, influencing policies); in her case in particular, it was associated with a moderate form of Catholicism and devotion to the Virgin Mary. Thomas Carew's 'To the Queen'[8] summed it up satisfactorily:

> Thy sacred Love shows us the path
> Of modestie, and constant faith,
> Which makes the rude Male satisfi'd
> With one fair Female by his side.

(It is not easy to see little Charles as a 'rude Male'.)

As Davenant was to admit in the following year, in his play, *The Platonic Lovers*, this was not an idea that appealed to him, any more than to many Cavalier courtiers. John Cleveland's poem, 'The Anti-Platonick',[9] expressed most male courtiers' attitudes:

> For shame, thou everlasting wooer,
> Still saying grace, and ne'er fall to her!
> Love that's in contemplation placed,
> Is Venus drawn but to the waist ...

Nevertheless, Davenant did his best. The piece works as a promotion of the Catholic Queen, whose Temple of Love could be seen as the locus of true spiritual authority, together with a celebration of royal superiority over a restless people. In the early 1630s, Henrietta Maria had been having some success in obtaining a degree of acceptance of Catholicism at Court, with some notable converts. She was having a personal chapel prepared for her in Somerset House (opened in 1636), which was seen by some as the return of the true faith; the masque's establishment of the Temple of True Love could be linked with that.[10]

The masque, set on a raised stage, was initially framed by, on one side, the figure of an Indian linked with the sun, seated on an elephant, and, on the other, an 'Asiatique' with a half-moon, seated on a camel. The masque's orientalism may be associated with early Eastern commercial developments (the East India Company had grown considerably since its foundation in 1600). Now, rosy-coloured clouds open to enable the descent of a beautiful woman dressed in sky-coloured clothes set with stars of gold: Divine Poesy. She has come to the 'Indian' kingdom of Narsinga, to persuade Indamora, the Queen, to re-establish in 'the dull Northerne Ile, they call Britaine', the Temple of Chaste Love, at present hidden by clouds to thwart the magicians who are its enemies. She declares:

> As cheerful as the Mornings light,
>     Comes *Indamora* from above,
> To guide those Lovers that want sight
>     To see and know what they should love.

The famed brilliance of Indamora's eyes seems to have a worrying searchlight power of surveillance:

> Her beames into each breast will steale,
>     And search what ev'ry Heart doth meane …[11]

At Court, at least, there will be no hiding for the disaffected.

The Temple's fame has induced a company of noble Persian youths (probably representing French exiles) to seek it out. Together, Divine Poesy and the Queen will disperse the mists of error, as her superior royal power can magically transcend all dissension, and the young Persians are duly inspired by 'chaste flames' for Indamora and Platonic Love. The deities Orpheus and Arion are sent in 'an antique barque' to calm the (political) seas (that had troubled Charles), so that a 'maritime Chariot' can carry the Persians to the Temple. (Charles was already contemplating reinforcing his own maritime chariots with Ship Money charges, introduced later, in 1637.) Now it is the turn of the Brachmani (Indian Brahmins, perhaps equivalents of Henrietta Maria's Capuchin priests) to celebrate Orpheus's beneficent powers:

> Hearke! *Orpheus* is a Sea-man growne,
> No winds of late have rudely blowne,
>     Nor waves their troubled heads advance![12]

The song registers, indirectly, the advance of troubled heads out in the real world. The entry of the Queen is welcomed again – 'So fit and ready to subdue.' Another song brings in marine imagery:

> More welcome than the wandring Sea-mans starre,
> When in the Night the winds make causelesse warre,
>     Until his Barque so long is tost,
> That's sayles to rages are blowne, the Maine-yard beares
> Not sheet enough to wipe and dry those teares
>     He shed to see his Rudder lost.[13]

Are the 'wars' really causeless? Storm imagery and a damaged ship with a rudder (directing power, or king) lost, sit oddly in an entertainment ostensibly concerned with chaste love: the political situation overshadows the nymphs, naiads and idealizing visions.

Indamora /Henrietta Maria now enters enthroned on scallop shells, so combining Venus and the Virgin Mary. After a dance, Sunesis (Understanding – a male dancer, of course) and Thelema (Will, female) express their true union, the Temple appears and 'Chaste Love' descends, to invite Indamora's royal lover to witness the consecration of the Temple (the union of the Crown and the Faith). Divine Poesy reproves the assembled company of poets for their previous celebrations of sensual love, but the magicians criticize the beauties of Indamora's train – the Court ladies – 'who sure /Though they discover summer in their looks, / Still carry Winter in their blood', with their 'strange doctrines' and new sects of love, 'which must not court the person, but /The mind.' A second verse has some disabling wit:

> Believe me, my magical friends,
> They must bring bodies with 'em that worship
> In our pleasant Temple: I have an odd
> Fantastic faith persuades me there will be
> Little pastime upon earth without bodies:
> Your spirit's a cold companion at midnight.

An antimasque of elemental spirits follows, with amorous men and women, alchemists, drunken Dutch skippers, witches and usurers – all the usual suspects – together with notably different and clearly politico-religious enemies: Puritans –

> a sect of modern devils,
> Fine precise fiends, that hear the devout close
> At every virtue but their own, that claim
> Chambers and tenements in heaven, as they
> Had purchas'd there, and all the angels were
> Their harbingers …

Davenant went on to describe in his notes to the published text 'a modern devil, a sworn enemy of poetry, music and all ingenious arts, but a great friend of murmuring, libeling and all seeds of discord, attended by his factious followers: all of which was express'd by their habits and dance'.

Some of the context of this was a resentment of the royalist-Anglican religious pressure at the time (use of altars rather than of a communion table, the imposition of the Prayer Book), not confined to Puritans. In particular, there was William Prynne's *Histriomastix, or a Scourge for Stage Playes* of 1633, a thousand-page-long abusive attack on the corruptive effect of the theatre and all associated with it, whether naïve, innocent or sinfully inclined: 'will not then the premeditated voluntary delightfull beholding of an unchaste adulterous Play, much more contaminate a voluptuous, carnall, graceless Play-haunter, who lies rotting in the stink of his most beastly lusts?' Not much might have come of this, had he not gone on to attack royalty. 'It hath always been a most infamous thing for Kings and Emperours to act Playes or Masques either in private or publike, or to sing, or dance upon a stage or theatre, or to delight in Playes and Actors.' He particularly attacked 'women actors notorious whores', so especially angering Henriette Maria and her fellow lady performers in masques. The Star Chamber condemned him to the pillory, the cropping of both ears, imprisonment in Guernsey and a heavy fine of £5,000; John Aubrey says that Archbishop Laud was a spectator of this, having been his judge. The sentence was repeated in 1637 (this time sent to Caernarvon Castle), when he was also branded on both cheeks with S.L., for Seditious Libeller. He proved irrepressible: Aubrey describes him, continually writing, a peaked quilted cap over his eyes shading him from the candlelight in his cell, a servant bringing him a bread roll and ale every few hours, to keep him going. Parliament released him in 1641, when he became am MP, trailing his old long rusty sword. Until then, England was in a more troubled condition than this masque could acknowledge.

Extremes of puritanism and anti-courtly resentment were to be countered with less extreme versions of Court discipline and Platonism. Here, a perky page jestingly discounts any cult of soul-love that undervalues the demands of the body. Henrietta Maria's Platonism was not celibate: the proper end of virtuous love was union of the mind and then marriage, relationships that 'keep love warm, yet not inflame'. Now Indamora sits beside her royal lover, the King, complementing each other like Sunesis and Thelema, transcendent figures of control. The final chorus proclaims the royal union as the pattern of both sexual relationships and political governance, concluding:

> To CHARLES the mightiest and the best,
> And to the Darling of his breast,
>    (Who rule b'example as by power)
> May youthfull blessings still increase,
> And in their Off-spring never cease ...

(The Queen was pregnant at the time.) Platonic Love, rather than a sterile fancy, was intended as a reining-in of Court behaviour in the face of a growing swell of discontent; but 'rule by power' was still an available option.

Meanwhile, the after-show dances and revels went on for a large part of the night; Davenant's concluding notes boasted that 'for the newness of the invention, variety of scenes, apparitions and richness of habits, [the masque] was generally approved to be one of the most magnificent [and, presumably, expensive] that hath been done in England'.

# Chapter 4

# For Queen and Country (1635–1637)

From these courtly caperings, Davenant returned to the world outside, the London of ordinary people, that his comic gifts could well represent: his next play, *News from Plimouth*, and his engaging comic poem, 'The Long Vacation in London, in Verse Burlesque, or Mock-Verse'. Whatever private circulation the poem may have had in manuscript, it was not printed until 1656, in a collection entitled, *Wit and Drollery, Jovial Poems*, before appearing in amended form in his posthumous collection, *Poems on Several Occasions*, dated 1672. Both the play and the poem (itself not really a burlesque, rather a series of humorous character sketches of London types) are filled with well-observed detail and local colour, and simple fun.

With the London law courts closed for the summer vacation and the Court and courtiers away, life went quiet and poor, as Davenant, still only on the fringe of Court circles, may well have known. In the poem,[1] a 'Town Wit' summons his 'witty friend' (almost certainly Davenant, named as 'Will' later in the poem) to go off into the country, to profit there as best they can. Likewise, early in the morning, a poor gambler sneaks out of his lodging to evade his landlady, keeping his last crown to pay for a room in some country inn that night, where he will not be able to pay for a meal. A merchant's wife and daughter from Cheapside hire a six-shilling coach for Islington, a village outside London, for a picnic of chicken and rabbit pie followed by cream; her husband, son and apprentice follow, intent on duck hunting with their dog, Ruffe. Left in town, the fat, hungry bawds in Turnbull Street send their 'roaring swash' pimp to sell their spare clothes for food. A poor poet hides from his moneylender, lamenting his inability to write successfully – 'Quoth he, do noble Numbers chuse /To walke on feet that have no shoose?' –and the failure of his readers to pay him. The original version read, 'Kings pay no scores but when they list, /And treasurer still hath cramp in fist' (it sounds as though Davenant knew what he was talking about); the later version tactfully amended this to 'Courts pay no Scores ...' Out steals the poet to the Globe Theatre (where *Plimouth* was performed), swearing that four acts of his promised play are complete, and telling every actor that his is the best part, all in hope of a modest advance. As for the actors from the more popular, downmarket Red Bull Theatre, one tries his luck as a ferryman, in vain, and fishes for eels, while another, perched on a dung lighter, fishes with worms as bait.

Up the social scale, the Mayor, looking big, rides into Bartholomew Fair, with an eye on the pig-meat stall (central to Ben Jonson's play on the Fair). Aldermen play at quoits, and, together with a lean, mean attorney who never 'verses took for fees' (as Davenant had hoped Dr Cademan might) and an old proctor, who now has no whores to disperse from the nave of St Paul's, they go off to Finsbury Fields for a day's archery – perhaps the contemporary equivalent of businessmen's golf. The exodus continues: time-served apprentices 'spynie [skinny] *Ralph* and *Gregorie* small, /And short hayr'd *Stephen*, Whay-fac'd *Paul*' (they sound under-fed) hire 'meagre' horses to visit their families, away in the Peak District, who give them money to help them set up for themselves, 'That babes may live, serve God and cheat.' Popular entertainers, such as the 'Vaulter good, and dancing Lass /On Rope', the tumbler, the puppeteer with 'old Queen Bess' and models of Sodom and Gomorrah, the chained monkey and Marocco the famous performing horse (mentioned in *Love's Labours Lost*) now all 'trudge from Town, /To cheat poor Turnep-eating' countrymen. There's no money left in town, for the debt collector or to lend a friend.

> But stay, my frighted Pen is fled;
> My self through fear creep under Bed;
> For just as Muse would scribble more,
> Fierce City *Dunne* did rap at Door.

The poem is not ambitious – with no narrative and only a series of sketches – but it has a humour, humanity and sense of real life that might have been beneficial in his Court writings.

Such qualities were present in his city comedy, *News from Plimouth* (*Dramatic Works*, Vol. IV), that was licensed on 1 August, and intended for the more popular, commercial theatre, The Globe.

Like the Vacation poem, it was not very ambitious: the prologue admits, 'this house, and season, does more promise shows, /Dancing, and buckler fights, than art or wit', but hopes that it will 'please those who do not expect too much'. For all that, it is lively, with broad comedy and sense of everyday life – and political reference. In it, three sea captains – Seawit, Cable and Topsail – find themselves 'wind-bound' (trapped by an unfavourable wind) and with little money in a dull seaport (there is a possibility it was originally to have been Portsmouth). Cable complains:

> This town is dearer than Jerusalem
> After a year's siege; they would make us pay
> For day-light, if they knew how to measure
> The sun-beams by the yard. Nay, sell the very
> Air too if they could serve it out in fine
> China-bottles. If you walk but three turns
> In the High Street, they will ask you money
> For wearing out the pebbles.

The port is also 'vilely destitute of women' (unusually for a seaport), but they set out to catch some, the wealthy Widow Carrack (the word for a large cargo ship), Lady Loveright and Mistress Joynture (a wife's marriage portion), without having to marry them. Loveright is known to be rich; the gossip is, that 'the very housewives of /Her dairy play at cent [a card game rather like piquet] and her plough-boys /Double their wages at cribbage and picket'. (Interestingly, Aubrey wrote that Davenant's friend, the poet and gambler, Sir John Suckling, 'invented the game of Cribbidge'; the *OED*'s earliest citation is 1630, when Suckling would have been 22: it's not impossible.) Also present is Sir Studious Warwell, a long-term if unexciting suitor to Lady Loveright; Mrs Joynture thinks that Loveright is looking for a rougher lover, and tells her that people say that

> you hold a courtier
> Too soft, a country gentleman too dull,
> To make a husband, and that your main end is
> To be kiss'd to the purpose in the gun-room,
> Upon a cannon by a rough commander,
> Then brought to bed in his cabin of two boys.

The speech, entertaining as it is, is misleading for the audience: it is not really what Loveright has in mind, though Topsail woos her with a charming aubade:

> O Thou that sleep'st like *Pigg* in Straw,
>     Thou *Lady* dear, arise:
> Open (to keep the *Sun* in awe)
>     Thy pretty pinking eyes:        [blinking, half-open]
> And, having stretcht each Leg and Arme,
>     Put on your cleane white Smock,
> And then I pray, to keep you warme,
>     A *Petticote* on *Dock*.            [tail]
> Arise, Arise! Why should you sleep,
>     When you have slept enough? ...

Loveright plays along with her suitors, rather like Lady Ample in her cool clarity and demand for submission from her future husband. She is determined not to marry, or be married, for money, but to have control: 'my ambition is /To make a man, not take addition from him. /I would have him poor, and if unlearn'd the better.' Davenant had seen too many Court marriages made for money. The subject of the dominant wife he had treated elsewhere, and was a frequent comic topic by others.

She also has a comic uncle, Sir Solemn Trifle, a long-winded provider of fake news (perhaps partly derived from Jonson's *The Staple of News*), of a kind now familiar. The play's title derives from this; Davenant had in mind the various irregular pamphlets and popular newssheets produced at the time; in their commentaries on current affairs, they would not always have been welcomed by the authorities. This part of the comedy exists partly to discredit such unapproved publications. Sir Solemn says his gullible readers

>             come for news; man's nature's greedy of it.
> We wise men forge it; and the credulous vulgar,
> Our instruments, dispose it. I have it for 'em:
> News of all sorts and sizes ...

He gives examples of the current stories:

Though I grieve to report it, Rome is taken
By the ships of Amsterdam, and the Pope himself,
To save his life, turn'd Brownist. Here's a letter  [extreme dissenter]
From the matron of the courtesans confirms it...
                                    From Florence:
All the silkworms are dead, and an edict made
Unbenefic'd ministers must give o'er their satin ...

His stories are true, he insists; and even if not, the popular reaction to
them will inform the government of public opinion. Later, Topsail is able
to expose and denounce him: his servant, Prattle, has gone too far, and

> hath tasted of the rack for venting of
> Your trumperies, and the rack will make him yield
> A reason why he holds intelligences
> Without commission, and with foreign Princes ...

It does seem familiar; having been exposed, Trifle must flee the town
(though that will not be the end of fake news).

Among other Jonsonian-humour characters are Sir Furious Inland,
a ridiculously combative youth from the country (related to Kastrill,
the quarrelling boy in Jonson's *The Alchemist*) and a Dutch sea captain
(foreign accents always being good for a laugh). Their bickering friendship
and counter-challenges, that reflect unease about Dutch commercial
competition, fill up much of the middle of the play. The amorous comedy,
the best part of the play, is led perhaps by the Widow Carrack and Cable.
She admits her wish to remarry, missing her husband's sexual energy
('rest his soul in Neptune's bosom, /For his body hath fed haddocks'):

> He was a woman's man, captain,
> A good one, too; he lay not idle, he,
> I speak it in my tears ...
>      ... you are so like my husband,
> And just, as they say, such a rough hewn man
> Was he: so troublesome to maids and women
> Of meek behaviour, that they would all cry
> Out on him, yet they loved him too. Truly, he was
> Scarce to be trusted in the dark ...

Sexual harassment was not a concept available at the time. Their badinage is light-hearted, with cheery innuendo about his pinnace being well rigged. There are good simple jokes:

Cable:     Your breath is /As sweet as my mother's red cow's.
Carrack:  Which you have kiss'd, sir!
Cable:     Every one as he likes. You know the proverb.

They have a good comic scene, when she dresses as a whore in order to lead him on, but she is quite clear that only marriage will do, and has a warning speech with extra significance for the author:

> If you do desire to be still a rambler
> Till you are so pepper'd, that you hate the sight of't,
> And then become a prey to your apothecary,
> And defy your chirurgeon, or perhaps
> Be practis'd on in the spittle, who can help it?
> Be honest, and you may be rich, and happy;
> Continue a whoremonger, and you know what follows.

Meanwhile, the men's financial situation does not improve. Cable gets creditors' demands from London, that is normally

> the Sphaere of light and harmony,
> Where still your Taverne bush is green, and flourishing,
> Your Puncke dancing in Purple,
> With Musicke that would make a Hermit frisk,
> Like a young Dancer on a Rope.

(It all sounds good fun; no wonder Prynne disapproved.) Now, however, London has become

> that unlucky town; where now, in dead
> Vacation too, a time of great calamity
> With younger brothers, men o'th'camp, and the
> Distress'd daughters of old Eve, that lie windbound
> About Fleet-Ditch ...

He reads a letter from a tailor, begging for overdue payment:

> Hum! forborne you above seven years – hum! promis'd
> With oaths to pay me last Cales [Cadiz] voyage – hum!
> Never drunk for my worship – hum! Three of my children
> Lie sick of the measles – hum! – but one bunch of turnips
> Among twelve of us these four days – hum! – commit
> Myself to your conscience – hum! – your friend as you
> Use him, Gregory Thimble.

Tailor Urswick might not have been greatly amused.

Now, as the wind changes, the story is wound up: Loveright at last takes Warwell, who has given up absolutely everything for her. Jointure snaps up Seacourt. Royalist Davenant makes a subdued Cable throw in a crack against Puritanism: "I'll cut off my main mast, and for /No other reason, but because me thinks /It looks like a may-pole' (future sexual sobriety is also hinted); he is told to go back to sea and then to return, rich or poor:

> Come home ne'er so poor, forswear you whoring,
> And I am your wife; and to encourage you to it,
> Give a particular of your debts, I'll pay 'em.

What more could be hoped for? As usual, marriage and money make a happy ending. A revival could do well today, as an example of popular period comedy.

Now it was time to re-engage with the Court, and about this time he wrote a curious poem, intriguing both in the light it sheds on his connexion with the complex inter-relationships of great families there, and on what it suggests about his views on the positions of the King and Queen with regard to the current difficult political situation. The full title is, 'To the Queene, /presented with a suit, in /the behalf of F.S. directed, /From Orpheus Prince of Poets, /To the Queene of light; in favour of a /young listener to his Harpe.'[2] Here the writer refers to himself as 'your poet', and Davenant had just used the title 'her Majesties Servant' in *The Temple of Love*. His modern editor seems to interpret the title to mean that Davenant is presenting a suit directed to the Queen on behalf of a young poet, F.S., whom he cannot identify. An alternative interpretation is that it is F.S. who has directed Davenant to present a suit to the Queen on behalf of a 'young listner' to the harp – a listener, therefore not a poet himself.

A sequence of Davenant poems may be helpful. In 1632 he had written a poem[3] to Richard Weston, Earl of Portland (to whom he had dedicated *The Cruell Brother*), on the marriage of his son Jerome to Frances Stuart, daughter of the Third Duke of Lennox and sister of James Lennox, who took part in two of Davenant's Court masques. Later, in 1637, he wrote a poem[4] celebrating the marriage of James (himself the nephew of yet another, older Frances Stuart, whom Davenant had served as a page in the 1620s), to Mary Villiers Herbert, daughter of the Duke of Buckingham and widow, at the age of 14, of Charles Herbert, son of Philip Herbert, Fourth Earl of Pembroke (to whom, with his brother, William, the Shakespeare First Folio was dedicated). Then, in 1639, Davenant wrote to James, Duke of Lennox and Richmond[5] in relation to his help with Davenant's plans for a theatre. Given Davenant's continued connexions to these families, it seems very probable that F.S. is Frances Stuart, wife of James, asking 'the family poet' to help some other 'listner'.

The poem itself has its oddities. It is written in the person of Orpheus, singing in the Underworld, though he blurs into Davenant in referring to his poetic silence since 'my *Euridices* sad day'. (One would expect this to refer to the death of his wife, Mary, at some time after 1632, the time of the last previous poem – unless this has to do with the sad death of a daughter in 1631.) Orpheus spends some time preparing the Underworld garden for the eventual arrival of the Queen. Remarkably, the attendants he proposes for her are Tamiris, the Scythian warrior queen who slew Cyrus the Great, Penelope, chaste wife of Ulysses, and Artemisia, another warrior queen, who built a monument for her dead husband and brother, Mausolus, at Helicarnassus (the site of the spring in Davenant's later masque, *Salmacis Spoliae*); she is referred to as 'a living Tomb unto her Lord', in that she drank his ashes, so absorbing his spirit. The Queen is thus associated with faithful warrior women (as Henrietta Maria became less patient with Parliamentarian opposition). By contrast, when the King is to die, he will not be associated with warriors – 'testy Pyrrhus, or malicious Hannibal', or Alexander the Great; when he is linked with 'mighty Julius', Caesar is thought of as a philosopher, 'who had thoughts so high /They humble seem'd when th'aimed at victorie'. Charles is 'In anger valiant, gently calme in love'. Conventional gender roles have been reversed. Having now anticipated the eventual deaths of the Queen and the 'God-like Monarch' of her breast, Orpheus can now retire in favour of 'her Poet' – Davenant – crowned with everlasting wreaths and established as his 'Deputy' throughout Britain. Nothing is known of the suit tacked on to the poem by means of the title.

In November, he followed his masque on platonic love with a comedy, *The Platonic Lovers* (*Dramatic Works*, Vol. II). Perhaps significantly, when it was printed in 1636, it was dedicated to his patron, Henry Jermyn, the Queen's very close favourite and possibly the least platonically minded man at Court. In the prologue, Davenant expresses bafflement at the new term and concept, not expecting it to be well received by the general public.

In the opening scene, we are told of the Sicilian Court's riches: 'the garden gallery /Adorn'd with Titians pictures and those frames of Tintoret.' (Charles was an avid and extravagant purchaser of such art; in 1631 he had acquired from the Mantuan collection stocks of statues and paintings – 'the prized Titians, Raphaels, Corregios and Giulio Romanos were hung in Charles's privy lodgings in the heart of the palace.').[6] Here, the tables are 'spread with napery /Finer than Poppea's smock' while 'cupboards crack' with stacked plates and 'crystal vials', together with 'cellars so fill'd that they would make /A Danish army drunk'. An audience might see regrettable similarities between the luxurious – if imagined – Sicilian Court and the real English one. Cynical elderly courtiers discuss the noblemen's wars, their attitudes and the consequences, the

> triumphs of a war. But yet
> If midnight howlings heard in cities sack'd
> And fir'd, the groans of widow'd wives,
> And slaughter'd children's shrieks can pierce the ears
> Of Heaven, the learned think their glorious ghosts
> Will have a dismal welcome after death.
> However, in this world, 'tis good to follow 'em.

The condemnation, perhaps reflecting reports of the continental Thirty Years' War, could hardly be more emphatic. Neither of these passages has anything to do with the action of the play; a Court poet, Davenant was rarely at ease with Court practices and courtier values.

Courtiers now introduce the main characters and situation. Duke Theander and Eurithea, sister of his friend, Duke Phylomont, are 'lovers of a pure Coelestial kind, such as some style Platonical; /A new court epithet scarce understood'. In contrast are Duke Phylomont and Theander's sister Ariola, who 'still affect /For natural ends ... such a way as libertines call lust, /But peaceful politicks and cold divines / Name matrimony'. In the comic sub-plot, old Lord Sciolto tells his man, Fredeline, that he has brought up his son, a young soldier, Gridonell, in complete ignorance of women. They fear that Theander is wasting his youth and inheritance, and plan to slip him an aphrodisiac powder, made by chemist Buonateste.

In Act II, Gridonell meets Amadine, sister of courtier Castragno – 'she's old and poor. He may safely confer with her' – and is immediately enchanted, and thinks her an angel. 'Those I think are petticoats! I've heard /Of such a word. Sure it hath wings, and they are made, I think, / Of cambric and bone lace.' She responds, 'I'm mortal, sir, no spirit, but a maid. Pray feel me, I am warm,' but he is too naïve. Meanwhile, Ariola complains to her maid that she may not marry without Phylomont's permission, and Theander and Eurithea have a chaste meeting in her bedroom, about how he can go off to war while she has to stay at home. Dawn breaks off their conversation, as in *Romeo and Juliet*: 'To bed! to bed! methinks I hear the lark, /The morning's merry officer', in words that paraphrase one of Davenant's best-known and frequently anthologized lyrics, 'The Lark now leaves his watry Nest'[7] (itself echoing the song in *Cymbeline*, 'Hark, hark the lark at heaven's gate sings').

Buonateste gives Fredeline the aphrodisiac for Theander's wine, when Sciolto asks for some for Gridonell, who is, he fears 'very much Platonically given', which arouses Buonateste's indignation:

> My Lord, I still beseech you not to wrong
> My good old friend Plato, with this Court calumny;
> They father on him a fantastic love
> He never knew, poor gentleman. Upon
> My knowledge, sir, about two thousand years
> Ago, in the high street yonder
> At Athens, just by the corner as you pass
> To Diana's conduit, – a haberdasher's house
> It was, I think, – he kept a wench!'

Fredeline then tells Castragnio he loves Eurithea, but without hope of marrying her, and Phylomont asks Theander for permission to marry his sister.

Theander:   How! marry her! your souls are wedded, Sir.
            I'm sure you would not marry bodies too;
            That were a needless charge. Come, you shall save
            Your bridal feasts, and gloves …
            To what purpose would you marry her?
Phylomont:  Why, sir, to lye with her, and get children.
Theander:   Lye with my sister, Phylomont? How vile
            And horridly that sounds …

He has to admit, with brutal, aristocratic condescension towards the lower orders, that

>                   if such deeds
> Be requisite, to fill up armies, villages,
> And city shops; that killing, labour, and
> That cozening still may last, know, Phylomont,
> I'd rather nature should expect such coarse
> And homely drudgeries from others …

He goes on to tell Phylomont that, in wanting to marry, he is 'too masculine!' (The implication here is that the new Court fashion is effeminate.) He then says that he will lock Ariola away, provoking Phylomont to give him three days before he attacks his palace.

Castragnio now urges that Gridonell should marry Amadine ('she's old, and tough') for money; Fredeline promises him a captain's commission, and asks Amadine to praise him to Eurithea, as a way of getting to her:

> That's the platonic way; for so
> The balls, the banquets, chariot, canopy,
> And quilted couch, which are the places where
> This new wise sect do meditate, are kept,
> Not at the lovers' but the husband's charge,

so that, besides her husband, the wife may have 'A sad platonical servant to help her meditate. /Were Eurithea married, I would teach /Her the true art: she is unskilful yet'.

He points out, 'All the modern best authors do allow it.' Davenant regards the cult with profound scepticism, as hypocritical.

At last, the aphrodisiacs work, as Theander tries to control his desires, and is ready to marry. Fredeline asks Buonateste for a potion to make the beloved reciprocate, and explains that, after Eurithea has married, she'll want to try other men, and also that he wants to make Theander jealous, which will provoke her to give him cause. Meanwhile, Theander warns her of what might be involved in marriage: 'new /And undiscover'd trials … Dark deeds, and practis'd in the night.' Gridonell is wishing he could exchange places with the Great Turk and his seraglio –

> Yet 'tis a chargeable place.
> He can't spend less than a Colonel's pay
> In pins among these damsels, besides ruffs,
> And fine white gloves…
> Fetch me your sister straight … I've occasion to use her.
> Something I must do, I know not what 'tis
> But I begin to feel she will be very
> Convenient for me at this time.

Sciolto now takes him away, for his own sake.

Perversely, it seems, now that Phylomont and Ariola are together, she seems cooler, and wonders whether they need marry. Eurithea and Theander wonder what they are to do when they get married: Amadine explains. The next day, Theander is with Fredeline when they hear Castragnio and Amadine talking about their own night-time activities, and Fredeline tells him they have committed incest in Eurithea's bed – perhaps with her. Fredeline develops his plot, offering Castragnio promotion if he and Amadine sign to say that they lay together, and with Eurithea; after he has forced them to do this, he locks them away.

Now the action moves to its complicated climax: Phylomont is 'weary of this cold Platonic life' and demands that he and Ariola marry (Buonateste will persuade her). The Fredeline/Castragnio plot collapses, with Buonateste's assistance, and they are exiled. The four main lovers are now reconciled and reunited, proceeding towards marriage. In the epilogue, the speaker tells the audience that 'not these two long hours amongst you all /[Could he] find one will prove Platonicall'. So much for platonic love.

Despite this send-up of her latest fad, the Queen had more work for Davenant. In January 1636, the dispossessed princes of the Palatine, Charles and Rupert, had come to England to stir up support for their efforts to reclaim the Palatinate from Maximilian of Bavaria, if only with courageous individual volunteers. In 'An Epistle to a Friend, To Persuade Him to the Wars', Ben Jonson urged:

> Wake, friend, from forth thy lethargy; the drum
> Beats brave, and loud in Europe, and bids come
> All that dare rouse: or are not loth to quit
> Their vicious ease, and be o'erwhelmed with it.

The Queen and the English Protestant 'war party' were keen on opposing the enemy of the French, the Habsburgs, though the moderate Anglicans, more pragmatic, favoured simply getting on with Spain and the Habsburgs and dealing with problems provoked by the rise of the Dutch. In the circumstances, the King welcomed the princes for their mother's sake, but did not provide any notable entertainment. The Queen, however, was active in welcoming and encouraging them, especially the more dashing, militaristic Prince Rupert, with frequent meetings with French ambassadors. One courtier reported: 'Comedies, festivities and balls are the order of the day here, and are indulged in every day at Court for the prince's sake, while all the greatest lords vie with each other in entertaining him at noble and sumptuous banquets.'[8] Young gentlemen postured as soldiers and enjoyed their opportunities, as Jonson also observed:

> How much did Stallion spend
> To have his court-bred filly there commend
> His lace and starch? And fall upon her back
> In admiration of his rich suit and title, lord?
> Aye, that's a charm and half!

Now Davenant had to set up a masque for them, to be performed by the young lawyers of the Middle Temple, entitled 'The Triumphs of the Prince d'Amour' (*Dramatic Works*, Vol. I). This was usually an annual celebration, in which one of them was declared the 'Prince d'Amour', with a parody court, which debated issues drawn from law and current affairs, received petitions, dubbed 'knights' and generally had a good time, culminating in a feast. In the event, Davenant had to set it up in short order – he complained that it had to be 'devis'd and written in three days' – though at least the music was by Henry and William Lawes; that his friend Bulstrode Whitelocke had been Master of the Revels at the Middle Temple may have helped. That it was a semi-official occasion is indicated by the Queen and her ladies, the Marchioness of Hamilton and the Countesses of Denbigh and Holland, attending dressed only as citizens, together with her favourite, Henry Jermyn, and other lords, 'somewhat disguised also'. The young Princes were there as guests of honour.

It began with an antimasque of swaggering, debauched soldiers, 'such as are said to roar, not fight' in an alehouse, with black kitchen boys smoking pipes, together with two Dutch sea officers, an 'old overgrown Cavalier', a begging soldier and a sutler's wife (poor seller of soldiers' provisions) – not a glamorous portrayal of military life. The first scene, however, framed with Doric pillars, showed a camp of tents: the Temple of Mars. The priests of Mars now entered, singing a song of war, accompanied by drums and trumpets. Five verses presented the progress of a battle, from the initial charge to the final defeat of the enemy, the survivors allowed to live. A chorus followed each verse:

> Heark! heark! some groane, and curse uncertaine Fate,
> Which us for blood and ruine, doth create.

If this was meant to celebrate any forthcoming military campaign, it was half-hearted; Davenant was no enthusiast for war. The episode concluded with eleven men dancing in Roman dress, imitating the Knights Templar (supposed originators of the Middle Temple).

Then came another antimasque, in a scene supposed to show an Italian piazza, occupied by a sequence of incompetent, absurd amorists – Spanish, Italian, French and Dutch, followed by 'a furious debauch'd English lover' angry with a Frenchman. After their dance, the scene changed to a grove of cypress, framed by Corinthian pillars: the Temple of Venus. Her priests call upon them to

> Unarme, unarme! no more your fights
> Must cause the virgins teares …

They are told,

> Such diff'rence as when Doves do bill,
> Must now be all your strife:
> For all the blood that you shall spill,
> Will usher in a life.

The bloodshed is not from war but either from the taking of virginities or from 'the common Renaissance notion that sperm is a product of the blood'.[9] They are reassured that the ladies would 'faine enjoy what they pretend to feare'.

Next, the Temple of Apollo is framed by pillars of the Composite order – the most sophisticated; his priests declare how 'with the powers of War and Love, /Hee shall unite his wiser Deity … T'inspire and breath himself in every Knight'. 'Behold, how this conjunction thrives!' they sing, before summoning 'industrious slaves of plenty' to 'bring All that is hop'd for in an Eastern Spring, /Or all that Autumne yields', suggesting the usual colonial exploitation of non-Europeans. Twelve half-naked 'wild men', dressed in leaves, emerge from trees, bearing baskets of food for a banquet for the guests.

Now a priest of Mars sings how 'The furious Steed, the Phyph and Drum /Invite you still to Triumphs of the War'; two priests of Venus urge them to love; three priests of Apollo hope that their 'Language will be of force … full of wonder their discourse'. All the priests combine to hope that their souls will be raised and sense rarefied.

It was a simple entertainment, knocked up quickly, intended merely to amuse, but without encouraging any hopes of military assistance that the princes might have had. After this, the Queen took them to the Blackfriars Theatre to see *Alphonsus, Emperor of Germany*, an Elizabethan patriotic melodrama, depicting the sufferings of Germany under Spanish tyranny, opposed by valiant English noblemen. Her political message could hardly be clearer – and hardly more obviously not attuned to the King's policy. Davenant's final note was not altogether happy: 'Thus, as all pleasures and triumphs are full of haste, the envy of such as were absent do not rebuke the courteous memory of those who vouchsafed to enjoy it.'

At some time during the year, he appears to have been unwell again – perhaps the aftermath of his previous serious illness – indicated by a poem, 'To the Lady Bridget Kingsmill; sent with Mellons after a report of my Death'.[10] Here he refers to his 'new Play' and the proclamations closing the theatres in 1636, which points to his *Platonic Lovers*, recently acted and published. Late in the year he fitted in a contribution[11] at the end of a volume entitled, *Annalia Dubrensis. Upon the yeerely celebration of Mr Robert Dovers Olimpick Games upon Cotswold-Hills*, adding to the preceding thirty poems, including verses by Jonson and Michael Drayton. The games were a celebration of traditional rural sports and activities – archery, bowling, racing, wrestling, dancing, hare-coursing – of the kind encouraged by King James in his *Book of Sports* in 1617, and had been revived by 'Captain' Robert Dover, a retired lawyer and country gentleman. These Whitsun pastorals were not wholly innocent politically, but held in opposition to puritan criticism – Charles had reissued King James's *Book of Sports*, approving vaulting, bowling, Morris dances and maypoles, as recently as 1633 –and were by no means artless, with 'the Captain' riding about wearing a large hat, ruff and other items of the King's old wardrobe donated by Endymion Porter, 'purposely to grace him and consequently the solemnity'. Participants might be rustics, taking part in traditional rural sports. The popular versifier, Samuel Rowlands, described such games:

> Man, I dare challenge thee to throw the sledge,　　　　[hammer]
> To jump or leap over a ditch or hedge,
> To wrestle, play at stoolball, or to run,　　　　[like rounders]
> To pitch the bar, or to shoot off a gun,
> To play at loggets [throw sticks at a staff], nineholes or tenpins …
> At leaping o'er a Midsummer bonfire,
> Or at the drawing Dunne [a log] out of the mire:
> At any of these, or all these presently,
> Wag but your finger, I am for you, I …

There might also be hunting and coursing with hounds, and mock sieges, with guns firing blanks. The visitors and spectators, however, were often gentry and upper class, come to demonstrate their resistance to merchant-class priggishness and moralism. Here, Davenant, in reaction to his legal arguments with his tailor, Urswick, approves Dover's turn from law to the country, and attacks the greedy London lawyers, 'gown'd Lackeys … Whose hollow Teeth are stuff'd with others Bread':

> Ere you a Yeare are dead, your Sonnes shall watch
> And rore all Night with Ale, in house of Thatch …

As for Dover,

> His Girles shall dow'rlesse wed with Heires of birth;
> His Boyes plough London Widows up like earth,
> Whilst Cotswald Bards caroll their Nuptiall Mirth!

Davenant himself had done his share of night-time roaring, and, as *The Witts* had shown, had little time for country life, but aligning himself with the royalist Countryside Alliance could only do him good.

Throughout the summer of 1637, when the ceiling of Banqueting House in Whitehall was being 'richly adorned with pieces of painting of great value, figuring the acts of King James of happy memory' (the great paintings by Rubens, as Davenant described them in his introduction to 'Britannia Triumphans'), no masques were performed at Court. During this enforced 'intermission', as he called it, he and his friends Sir John Suckling and Jack Young, a minor poet from Oxfordshire, took a leisurely outing to Bath, later described by John Aubrey. (In August that year, Ben Jonson died, and was buried in Westminster Abbey; legend has it that it was Jack Young who paid the masons there to inscribe the words *O rare Ben Jonson* on his stone.)

Aubrey's account of this trip fills a large part of his *Brief Life* of Suckling, and clearly derives from Davenant's report of his friend. While the friends rode slowly down the Bath road, such as it was, Suckling 'came like a young Prince for all manner of Equipage and convenience' and had a cart-load of books carried down for him (as the equipment for his little book on Socinianism – *An Account of Religion by Reason* – that he wrote en route). Aubrey reports, presumably echoing nostalgic Davenant, ''Twas as pleasant a journey as ever men had, in the height of a long peace and luxury, and in the Venison season.' The chief anecdote from the trip derives from their second night, when

> at Marlborough, and walking on the delicate fine downes at the Backside of the Towne, whilest supper was making ready, the maydes were drying of cloathes on the bushes [clothes lines were not thought of for many years yet]. Jack Young had espied a very pretty young girl, and had got her consent for an assignation, which was about midnight.

The others overheard this and decided to trick him. That night they all played cards, until Young, feigning tiredness, insisted on going to bed early. They then warned their landlady: 'Observe this poor Gentleman, how he yawnes, now is his mad fit comeing upon him. We beseech you that you make fast his doors, and get somebody to watch and looke to him, for about midnight he will fall to be most outrageous. Gett the Hostler, or some strong fellow, to stay-up, and we will well content him.'

At midnight, Young tried to get out, but found his door locked; shouting and swearing were in vain. 'Sir John and W. Davenant were expectant all this time, and ready to dye with laughter.' At last, somehow, he got the door open, but, coming downstairs,

> the Hostler, a huge lusty fellow, fell upon him, and held him, and cryed, Good Sir, take God in your mind, you shall not goe out to destroy yourself. J. Young struggled and strived, inasmuch that at last he was quite spent and dispirited, and was faine to goe to bed to rest himself.

In the morning, the hostess kindly brought him a warm gruel to comfort him after his 'heavy fitt'; he, however, 'thought the woman had been mad', and furiously threw the bowl in her face. 'The next day his Camerades told him all the plot, how they crosse-bit him.' It is to be hoped that they were generous to the kind, well-meaning ostler and hostess (Davenant's 'turnip-eaters') whom, as much as Young, they had abused for their amusement.

The next night they went on to Bronham House ('then a noble Seate, since burnt in the Civill Warres'), before going on to West Kington, to stay with parson Robert Davenant, William's elder brother, 'where they stayed a weeke – mirth, witt, and good cheer flowing', where Suckling wrote his book before they went on to Bath.

# Chapter 5

# The Arts of Government (1638)

After some seven years of ruling without Parliament, the King was having difficulty in raising money, even by ingenious methods and outdated laws. For instance, any landowner whose property was worth more than £40 a year and had not been knighted, had to pay a fee; landowners whose land had encroached on former royal woodland were fined. Whether the money this brought in was worth the consequent resentment, was another matter. In 1637 he imposed a new levy of Ship Money (ostensibly for shipbuilding and maintenance), a tax hitherto imposed only on coastal counties, to pay for their own defence, but now throughout the country. This provoked widespread resistance, as is usually the case with new taxes, notably from a Buckinghamshire gentleman, John Hampden, who refused to pay what he saw as a constitutional abuse. His representative in court, Oliver St John, argued that if the King could raise taxes as he wished, without consulting Parliament, then he had rights over all his subjects' assets. Ship Money was supposed to protect the state, but the country was at peace, not in danger. Questions of the king's prerogative and the liberties and duties of the subject arose. The case went to the Exchequer Court that winter; when the judges' verdict, delivered in February 1638, went in the Crown's favour by seven votes to five, it was widely believed that the judges had yielded to Crown pressure. In the short term, Charles got his money, apparently to protect English shipping in the Channel and against Moroccan pirates (but also, quietly, to keep his side of secret treaties made with the Spanish against the Dutch); in the longer term, he lost much political credit in the country at large. There were demands that he should summon another Parliament, and the so-called 'Long Parliament' (including John Hampden) eventually met on 5 November 1639.

In this fraught atmosphere, it was decided to have an effort at public relations, in the form of another masque, to reassure the Court and bring over waverers among the political elite: Davenant got the commission.

There had been no Court masques since his *The Temple of Love* in 1635, while the great Banqueting Hall was being expensively redecorated. In the interim, a temporary wooden Masquing Room, with rough brick outer walls and a roof of pantiles, was built next to it; at 112 feet long, 57 feet wide and 59 feet high, it was slightly larger than Inigo Jones's original hall. Now, in January 1638, it seemed the right time for another expensive Court spectacular.

Despite – or perhaps because of – it being such an obviously political event, Davenant's introduction to his masque for the King, *Britannia Triumphans* (*Dramatic Works*, Vol. II), could not have been blander:

> Princes of sweet and humane natures have ever, both amongst the ancients and moderns in the best times, presented spectacles and personal representations, to recreate their spirits wasted in grave affairs of State, and for the entertainment of their nobility, ladies and court.

The contentious subject of Ship Money and ships could hardly be avoided entirely. His introductory 'Subject' declared:

> Britanocles [the King] the glory of the western world, hath by his wisdom, valour, and piety, not only vindicated his own, but far distant seas, infested with pirates, and reduc'd the land, by his example, to a real knowledge of all good arts and sciences.
>
> These eminent acts, Bellerophon, in a wise pity, willingly would preserve from devouring Time, and therefore to make them last to our posterity, gives a command to Fame, who hath already spread them abroad that she should now at home, if there can be any maliciously insensible, awake them from their pretended sleep, that even they with the large yet still increasing number of the good and loyal may mutually admire and rejoice in our happiness.

In fact, the Ship Money ships had forced some Dutchmen to purchase licences to fish in English waters, and pushed back the Dunkirk pirates, which excused the masque's references to victories at sea, and also possibly a representation of the royal flagship, the splendid *Sovereign of the Seas*, launched in October 1637. The traditional image of 'the Ship of State' also enabled suggestions of good government.

With the Queen seated under the State canopy, and 'the room filled with spectators of quality', the show began. The first image was of bound captives; on the right side of the proscenium arch was a woman in pale blue and silver (rather like the Virgin Mary) with a victory garland, holding a ship's rudder, and a little winged figure with a palm branch, all indicating Naval Victory. Opposite was a man with a sceptre and palm, a book, a garland of unfading amaranth and a cuirass of gold, treading on a serpent, presenting Right (strong) Government. Above, was a frieze of naked children riding seahorses and fishes, with tritons blowing trumpets.

The first scene now depicts English houses, the City of London and the Thames, 'which, being a principal part, might be taken for all Great Britain'. After the initial chorus, there is an extended debate on a subject dear to Davenant, the rôle of the arts in society. The first participant is Action, a young man in a purple garment inscribed 'Medio Tutissima', the other is Imposture in an extravagant costume. Action is all for art as moral engagement, with the function of the arts being to educate the people in self-discipline and virtue (that is, obedience). Imposture is a very modern sceptic out of twentieth-century philosophy, insisting that everything is presentation, illusion and deception. He observes that, then as now, imposture (spin, PR and establishment ideology) is useful in 'the manage and support of human works', and that

> Wisely the jealous sceptics did suspect
> Reality in every thing, for everything but seems
> And borrows the existence it appears
> To have – imposture governs all ...

Davenant tends to put this rather well; experience had led him to some scepticism of Court ways, that could be expressed safely through a 'bad' character. Most spectators would dismiss this as anarchic, populist rejection of established values, while Action is a spokesman for the courtly elite, 'a few whose wisdoms merit greater sway' than others, 'some few 'mongst men /That as our making is erect, look up /To face the stars'.

After Action has criticized extremists, the high-principled austerity of Platonists and 'some sullen clerks' – Puritans – Imposture goes on to summon the magician Merlin, 'most ancient prophet of this Isle'. He sets up an antimasque of 'the great seducers of this Isle', linking popular music (low musicians with knackers, bells and tongs, balladeers with kitchen maids), charlatans (sellers of mousetraps, entertainers with baboons and apes), mountebanks selling fake medicines, parasitical courtiers and radical social critics such as John Cade, Jack Kett and Jack Straw. Now Bellerophon, mounted on Pegasus, the winged horse, intervenes to reinforce Action and denounce the ostentatiously principled, who

> of late
> Have got a fine feminine trick to rail
> At all they will dislike, refer to what is
> Not easily understood onto a kind
> Obedient faith, and then call reason but
> A new and fancy heretic

Now Merlin presents a 'Mock Romanza', in a burlesque of old-fashioned popular chivalric romance, with its simplistic morality, intended to contrast with Charles's more sober, up-to-date policy. The action is lively, with simple action and comic-pantomime rhyming (it must have been fun). In a forest, a dwarf and damsel are fleeing a giant in archaic armour and with a Saracen face, but are defended by a knight in old-fashioned armour. The dwarf warns of the approaching battle with the giant:

> They come! In's rage he spurns up huge tree roots,
> Now stick to lady, knight, and up with boots.

She excuses their presence in the giant's forest, as only a fruit-picking trip:

> I'fecks, if you'll believe it, nought was meant sure
> By this our jaunt, which errants call aventure.

The giant says she will have to slave in his kitchens, and the knight protests:

> O monster vile! Thou mighty ill-bred lubber!
> Art thou not mov'd to see her whine and blubber?

The knight and giant engage in a comical fight, as the giant threatens:

> I'll strike thee till thou sink where the abode is
> Of wights that sneak below, call'd Antipodes.

Merlin transforms the fight into a dance, before they all depart.

Now it is definitely time for royal glory. A richly adorned golden palace with silver pilasters and doors with bas-reliefs in gold, with a frieze of jewels, appears. Fame, in gold-trimmed carnation (flesh-pink) coloured robes, with a gold trumpet and olive garland, enters, to celebrate both arms and mercy, and sings to Charles as a sun-god:

> Break forth thou Treasure of our sight
> That art the hopefull morne of every day ...

and continues:

> What to thy Power is hard or strange?
> Since not alone confined unto the land;
>    Thy Scepter to a trident change,
> And strait unruly Seas thou canst command!

The Channel engagements are wildly exaggerated. It is time for Charles himself to enter. The chorus sings:

> Britanocles, the great and good appears.

With implicit recognition of the presence of some Parliamentary sympathizers at Court, his nobles and courtiers (some fourteen were taking part) are instructed to be more active in support of the sun-god king:

> Why move these Princes of his traine so slow ...
>
> Move then in such a noble order here,
> As if you each his governed Planet were,
> And he mov'd first, to move you in each sphere ...
>
> Each breast like his still free from every crime,
> Whose pensive weight might hinder you to clime!

Otherwise, their court careers might be at risk. Fancy metaphors could carry serious messages.

The debate on the rôle of the arts culminates with the masquers' address to the Queen, conventionally the possessor of bright eyes, and a chorus of poets accompanied by Fame. Her radiance has made the poets blind, like Homer, but it will inspire 'Raptures', with reformed poetry, 'High numbers, though with loss of eyes'.

We return to the main theme of maritime success, with the sea nymph Galatea riding on a dolphin:

> So well Britanocles o're seas doth Raigne,
>     Reducing what was wild before,
> That fairest sea-Nymphs leave the troubled maine,
>     And haste to visit him on shore.

The nymphs and chorus do now surround Charles, inviting him to lead them in their dance. Images show large ships, with a great fleet coming safely into harbour (England into security). The King and Queen are finally serenaded by the whole company, while the coming of night encourages amorous thoughts:

> May ev'ry whisper that is made be chast,
> Each Lady slowly yeeld, yet yeeld at last.

Everyone will be inspired by the royal pair, to a surprising degree:

To Bed, to Bed, may ev'ry Lady dreame
From that chiefe beauty shee hath stolen a Beame
    Which will amaze her Lovers curious Eyes!
Each lawfull Lover to advance his youth,
Dreame he hath stolne his Vigor, Love, and Truth;
    Then all will haste to Bed, but none to rise!

The King and Queen may have gone to bed in good spirits, but the absurd fictions of naval might and resentment about Ship Money tax (some of which, it was suspected, might have been diverted here), together with criticism, not only from Puritans, of the masque being staged on a Sunday – the Sunday after Twelfth Night – might have reduced the emollient effect hoped for.

Almost as soon as Davenant had finished this masque, he was summoned by the Queen to write one for her as a response to the King's *Britannia Triumphans*: this was *Luminalia* (Orgel and Strong, Vol. I), presented in the great Masquing Room on Shrove Tuesday, 1638 (again causing a minor degree of scandal), starring the Queen and her ladies. Inigo Jones was directed to provide 'variety of Scenes, strange apparitions, Songs, Musick and dancing of various kinds'. '*Luminalia* must have been a lovely show,' remarked Allardyce Nicoll, wistfully, in his book on Stuart masques; it cost a good £1,400 (one might add two, or even three, zeroes for a modern equivalent). As it is, it is hard to imagine the overall impression produced by these great masques – the beautiful scenery and elaborate special effects, the varied lighting, the hired speakers, the different kinds of dancing (mostly by the ladies), the musicians, the expensive costumes – so much more than the printed words. Even at the time, their ephemerality, performed as they were, usually only once, was a cause of regret, not least to their creators. Jonson, commenting on his own *Hymenaei* (1606), wrote that it lacked nothing 'either in richness, or strangeness of the habits, delicacy of dances, magnificence of the scene, or divine rapture of music. Only the envy was that it lasted not still, nor … cannot by imagination, much less description, be recovered to a part of that spirit it had in the gliding by'.

The theme on this occasion was to be the defeat of darkness (the political situation), culminating in the light embodied in the Queen. The proscenium frame depicted satyrs 'bigger than the life' carrying baskets of fruit, with young satyrs disporting themselves. *Luminalia* itself began in a scene of darkness, with dark woods, a moonlit river and owls. To solemn music, a 'dusky cloud' rose up, with an elaborate chariot drawn by two great owls, carrying a woman in a purple robe with stars of gold and a golden sceptre, her dark hair flowing loosely: Night. She began impressively:

> In wet and cloudy mists I sloowly rise,
> As with mine owne dull weight opprest,
> To close with sleep the jealous lovers eyes,
> And give forsaken Virgins rest.[1]

The original spelling, 'sloowly', seems to suggest her ascent. The mists billowing around must have been effective. As they cleared, from the wings appeared her attendants: Oblivion, a naked young man in a green mantle, on his head a cuckoo; Silence, an old man in a close skin coat with a tawny mantle and a peach-tree garland (the allegories are not all obvious); and the four Vigil Hours of the Night. The first was in blue, with a bat, the second with an owl, the third in purple and black with a dormouse on her head (presumably 'bigger than the life'), the fourth in watchet blue and carnation (perhaps suggesting pre-dawn light), with a swan. Their song celebrates the rest that Night can provide, before the entry of the antimasque's 'fantasticke creatures of the night'.

These present scenes of social disorder: first, thieves sharing their booty with corrupt watchmen; watermen (noted for their coarse behaviour) and lackeys; five 'fairies', including little Jeffrey Hudson, cavorting as usual; and some coiners at work. After these, 'a new and strange Prospect of Chimeras appear'd', with strangely shaped trees, mountains of gold, collapsing towers and windmills, and, in the background, the 'Great City of Sleep', on top of a rainbow. Sleep was embodied in a fat man in black, with a white mantle, a garland of grapes, and another dormouse, together with his three sons, who bring different kinds of dreams: Morpheus in cloth of gold with poppies presents 'humane shapes'; Icelos, with batwings, brings 'fearfull visions'; and Phantastes in a white robe, produces extraordinary sights. Their song celebrates the power of the unconscious imagination:

> How we shall fill each mortall with delight,
> To shew the soules fond business ev'ry night,
> When she doth inwardly contract her beames,
> To figure out her influence in dreames!
> How they will smile, that mans immortall part
> Works things lesse perfect than if rul'd by Art![2]

More comic antimasques follow: four clowns stumbling in sleep-walking; four witches, with a devil and a goat; the traditional folk-night mischief maker, Robin Goodfellow, with dairy and kitchen maids; five 'feathered men' (perhaps like Green Men); some sailors with a ship floating above (another of Jones's ingenious effects); guardians of the gates of sleep; and a 'cavalier' absurdly wooing a young woman who turns into a frightening fury (perhaps something that some over-enthusiastic young courtiers had experienced).

Dawn is now approaching, as a 'delicious prospect' of a sunlit landscape appears, as Hesperus, the morning star (another naked young man) complains that 'the bright perpetuall Traveller', the sun, is delaying. Aurora in her golden chariot explains that he is giving way to 'a terrestrial beautie here'; together they summon Apollo's priests (poets) to attend on her in the gardens of the 'Britanides' (the equivalent of the Garden of the Hesperides). They all now descend, to sing to the King, urging him to accept their praise (as if there were any doubt):

> Yet mightie spirits raise
>    Their actions up to Fame,
> When lifted high with praise:
>    Then who will blame
> Great virtue for ambition when it strives
> To feed on praise (the food by which it thrives)?
> Who earn'st, yet hat'st, himself of truth deprives.[3]

Now the Queen and the lady masquers appear radiantly from on high, a bright sky with 'a glory' shining around her, her ladies in 'close bodies open before the breasts, of Aurora colour embroidered with silver' and with 'well-proportioned ruffs'. Their accompanying song dismisses the poets' efforts to express 'A beauty that can rule severest eyes', whilst

'Those beauties neare her are made up of beames / They gather'd from her uselesse scatter'd light'. After another saraband and song, they conclude with a song to the King and Queen seated together under a heaven of various deities and muses:

> You that are chiefe in soules, as in your blood ...
>   Ev'n in your passions as in reason good,
>   To whom vast power can adde no ornament.[4]

(They were to find their power less vast than they had thought.) They have superior virtue, 'because 'tis conjugall' (marriage was one of Henrietta Maria and Davenant's preferred themes). They are urged not to die until everyone has appreciated what they have to offer. Now a heaven opens, with bright clouds, gentle zephyrs and dancers with light garments and garlands. Lively dances conclude the evening.

Everybody must have had a lovely time, with the Queen and King particularly happy; what effect a diet of this sort of thing had on them is uncertain. For all its celebration of light in the person of Henrietta Maria, a darker world constituted a surprisingly large amount of time in the antimasques, with scenes of social disorder and admission of psychological disturbances normally suppressed. After the pretty pictures and 'sprightly' trippings were done, the shadowy images of other realities, that Davenant had evoked, might have lingered in the observers' minds.

After the 1636/7 closing of the theatres, Davenant had to wait until April 1638 for the licensing of his next play, *The Unfortunate Lovers* (*Dramatic Works*, Vol. III), which was then performed at three theatres, the Blackfriars, before the King and Queen, the Cockpit and at Hampton Court, so it must have been a success; it was published in 1643. The intriguing prologue[5] was reprinted in the 1673 folio; there, the audience is reproved by 'the melancholly Tragick Monsieur', the author, for having grown 'excessive proud' and more demanding than in the past:

> Since ten times more of Wit then was allowed
> Your silly Ancestors in twenty year,
> You think in two short hours to swallow here.
> For they to Theaters were pleas'd to come,

> E're they had din'd, to take up the best Room;
> There sit on Benches not adorn'd with Mats,
> And graciously did vail their high-crown'd Hats
> To every halfe-dress'd Player, as he still
> Through Hangings peep'd to see the Gall'ries fill ...

The play was first performed by The King's Men (Shakespeare's former company) on 23 April, Shakespeare's anniversary. When it was printed in 1643, the dedication, made in the author's absence on Civil War business, was to a Parliamentarian sympathizer, Philip Herbert, Fourth Earl of Pembroke, to whom, with his brother, William, the Shakespeare First Folio had been dedicated. The signature of the dedicator was, simply, W.H. (the initials, famously, of the 'onlie begetter' of Shakespeare's *Sonnets*). Whilst this was probably a friend of his, William Habington, these coincidences have provoked some speculation.

Once again there is another absurd, convoluted Italian-court-set plot, with a corrupt, conniving courtier, and close friends in love with the same woman. Galeotto, the wicked favourite of Ascoli, Prince of Verona, wants his daughter, Amaranta, to marry Duke Altophil, who is himself in love with the beautiful Arthiope, whose reputation for chastity Galeotto therefore wishes to destroy. Nevertheless, Altophil insists on marrying her, but Prince Ascoli, who has himself fallen for her, forbids this, which provokes some questioning of royal authority.

Through Galeotto's treachery, the city has been captured by Heildebrand, King of the Lombards, and Altophil's men disarmed. Now, as Heildebrand's deputy, Galeotto tells Altophil and Arthiope they may marry, so, he hopes, freeing Ascoli for the virtuous but less beautiful Amaranta. He has promised Heildebrand he can have Arthiope while Altophil has been tied up. When Amaranta learns of this, she is shocked, releases Altophil and takes the lovers into hiding. When Heildebrand and Galeotto expect to meet Arthiope in the bedroom, they encounter only Amaranta, who Heildebrand says will do nearly as well. Later, Galeotto finds Arthiope and brings her to Heildebrand, who carries her off. After this, Amaranta releases Altophil (who keeps getting tied up) and gives him what turns out to be her father's sword; he fights and kills Galeotto, and Amaranta, overcome with grief at her father's death, falls on his sword.

Now Ascoli changes his mind, and he and friend Altophil are united in the cause of virtue; when Arthiope, 'her hair hanging loose about her', tells them of her rape, they go off after Heildebrand, while she hints that she cannot last much longer:

> the clean nice ermine not
> Endures to live when once the hunter doth
> Her whiteness soil, though with a little stain.

Ascoli's faithful captain, now in charge of the citadel, tells Heildebrand that Arthiope is now willing, and that he should go to her room. While he waits for her, there is an extraordinary song, 'Ye Fiends and Furies come along',[6] about hell-fire punishment for rape, before Altophil confronts him and shows him the bodies of Galeotto and Amaranta. They fight, as Arthiope, 'her hair dishevelled as before', looks on. Altophil kills Heildebrand, himself fatally wounded near the heart ('the region of thy love,' she points out), and she also dies, from 'no other wound but grief'. The abuse of power by the monarch (surely a sensitive subject), together with the conflict between Love and Power constitute the theme of the play.

Some comic relief is provided by the attempts of 'an ambitious tailor', Friskin (or Frisklin, in 1673) – memories of Davenant's old nemesis, Urswick – to get payment from a 'young gallant Soldier, much indebted and vexed by Creditors', keen on fashion ('I wear my clothes as well as any man'), who wants the latest Paris styles.

The play was revived after the Restoration, but Pepys, despite seeing it four times, was not impressed: 'no extraordinary play.'

Davenant's next theatrical effort, *The Fair Favourite* (*Dramatic Works*, Vol. IV), was licensed on 17 November 1638 – he seems to have been a virtual play-writing machine at the time – and was printed only in the 1673 folio; there is no record of an actual production (it circled dangerously close to ineffable undercurrents at Court). The story of a king led into a political marriage who persists in affection towards a (female) favourite might not have found favour, even with its celebration of female virtue. Here, the King, told that his beloved, Eumena, is dead (when, really, she has been hidden away) is tricked into a political marriage to a woman he

does not love. He complains: 'He that made such haste to join /Our hands
… was more a statesman than /A priest, and married provinces, not us.'
Having discovered that Eumena is alive, he rejects the Queen, who loves
him, and relentlessly pursues the virtuous Eumena, who will not become
his mistress, and, by making her his influential Court favourite, arouses
resentment and wrecks her reputation for chastity, her honour.

The play sets up a tension between the personal and public responsibility.
The King describes himself as 'a monster … that still between two bodies
groans, /The natural and the politic, /By force compounded of most
diff'rent things'. Meanwhile, Eumena's brother, Oramont, returned from
recent wars, needs money to pay off the ransom owed his captors, but will
not accept it from her, whom he now considers dishonourable, nor from
the King, who has dishonoured her and his family. He goes so far as to
question

> what strange divinity is that which guards
> These kings – the lawful terrors of mankind –
> Keeps them as safe from punishment, when they
> Oppress the tame and good, as it secures
> Them from the treachery of the fierce and bad.

His honour prevents him from moving against the King; but such
questioning, reminiscent of *Hamlet*, would not have been welcome.
Fortunately, the ransom demand is cancelled by the Tuscan king, whose
son, Amadore, pledges eternal friendship with Oramont, who himself is
determined on an 'honour killing' of his sister: 'Fair Favourite; my sister in
thy name, /Not blood, take heed!' Tense verbal battles ensue between the
King and Eumena, as he demands his way (adapting Falstaff: 'Honour's
a word, the issue of the voice') and Oramont denounces her, while the
Queen is loyally submissive.

Amadore goes to test Eumena and is convinced of her virtue, and of
course falls for her, which infuriates Oramont, and they go off to duel;
Oramont then shows her a bloody sword, causing her to weep, as he
assumes that this is the consequence of 'a sorrow that proceeds from sin'.
The King insists on enforcing the law that condemns the survivor of a
duel; both the Queen and Eumena plead for Oramont, and he eventually
relents, whilst demanding Eumena's love as payment. His advisers tell

him that he cannot get her love until the Queen consents to a divorce; she, however, has made Eumena's confessor break the vow of secrecy of the confessional, to reveal her unwavering chastity, so that Oramont must now believe in her honour.

Plot reversals now proceed apace, as Amadore is revealed to be alive; nonetheless, he insists that, by losing the duel, he has lost his own honour, and demands that Oramont duel with him again. Refused this, he contemplates suicide, but Eumena goes off to dissuade him and woo him for herself. Now enters the King, who has suddenly, off-stage and without any preparation, fallen in love with the Queen: 'Proclaim a lasting joy to all that love ...' and explains to the delighted Queen that her 'constant virtue' has vanquished his 'Rash rebellious flames'. He summons the entire Court, 'that they may /Celebrate the miracle of love'. The King and Queen are now united, and he blesses Amadore and Eumena, whilst Oramont goes off to war, to expiate his 'sins of jealousy'.

Oramont's function in the play is to demonstrate the destructive effects of aristocratic conceptions of honour; the King shows the pernicious consequences of obsessive self-will. One might see Eumena as the heroine of the play, in her passive resistance of oppression, as she and the Queen uphold the principles of fidelity and true honour. There is implicit criticism of a king whose personal wishes conflict with his responsibilities as ruler and upholder of law (a subject of some political importance at the time). He observes that it is

> Our worst mistake, to think the arts of government
> So hard; since a perfection in the skill
> To rule is less requir'd than perfect will.

# Chapter 6

# As If (1638–1639)

1638 had been a good year for Davenant, with successful performances of his plays and masques. Perhaps particularly significant for someone seeking recognition as a Court poet was his volume, *Madagascar, with other Poems*, licensed in November 1637 and published late in 1638. It constituted a remarkably varied and ambitious collection of 42 poems, with lyrics, elegies, satires and flattering panegyrics, some written as early as 1628 and others squeezed in very late indeed, marked by wit, inventiveness and some fancy phrasing. Later, in his Preface to *Gondibert*, he wrote that 'Young men … imagine [that wit] consists in the music of words, and believe they are made wise by refining their speech above the vulgar dialects', and he was noted for his style. (Harbage quotes a ballad: 'His art was high although his nose was low.')[1] His primary concern was to establish himself, not as a particular sort of poet, in literary terms, but as a poet for the Court. A friendly biographer acknowledges that he began his career by 'addressing himself to a phenomenally large proportion of the great, the near-great, the once-great, and the to-be-great, never desisting in his tireless siege of their interest and good will'.[2] Indeed, nearly half the poems here were dedicated to Endymion Porter, Jermyn and the Queen; dedicated to his patron and life-saver, Porter, and his other 'Maecenas', Jermyn, the volume had five commendatory poems, one by Porter himself, and others by his poet friends Sir John Suckling, Thomas Carew and William Habington.

The title poem, one of his best, relates to a curious, abortive enterprise originally mooted in Court circles in 1636, to find something to do for the younger of the so-called 'Palatine Princes', Prince Rupert, a soldier and athlete, a more impatient character than his brother, Charles Louis. The suggestion was that Rupert should lead an expedition to Madagascar, conquer it and establish a profitable colony there, to exploit the island's native population and natural resources, and its position for intercepting trade routes from India and the Far East (i.e. piracy), as well as providing

*Masquer*, c. 1638 (pen & ink on paper), by Inigo Jones (1573–1652). Design for *Luminalia* (1638) by William Davenant and Nicholas Lanier. (*The Devonshire Collections, Chatsworth. Reproduced by permission of Chatsworth Settlement Trustees / Bridgeman Images*)

Portrait of Queen Henrietta, attributed to Anthony van Dyck. (*Wikimedia Commons*)

Charles I and his wife Henrietta Maria with their eldest children: Charles, Prince of Wales (Charles II) next to his father and Mary, the Princess Royal, in the arms of her mother. By Anthony van Dyck. (*Wikimedia Commons*)

Queen Henrietta Maria (1609–1669) and her 'Dwarf', Jeffrey Hudson (1619–1682) (after Van Dyck), by Charles Jervas. (*Wikimedia Commons*)

Portrait of George Villiers, 1st Duke of Buckingham (1592–1628), by Peter Paul Rubens. (*Wikimedia Commons*)

*The Suburbs of a Great City*, c. 1639 (pen & ink on paper), by Inigo Jones. Set design for scene IV of 'Salmacida Spolia' (1639) by William Davenant; this was last court masque performed before the Civil War. (*The Devonshire Collections, Chatsworth. Reproduced by permission of Chatsworth Settlement Trustees / Bridgeman Images*)

Inigo Jones by William Dobson.
(*Wikimedia Commons*)

Prince Rupert, 1619–1982, 1st Duke of Cumberland and Count Palatine of the Rhine, by Peter Lely. (*Wikimedia Commons*)

Portrait of Henry Jermyn by Anthony van Dyck. (*Wikimedia Commons*)

Endymion Porter by William Dobson. (*Wikimedia Commons*)

Inigo Jones by William Hogarth. (*Wikimedia Commons*)

Prince Rupert of the Rhine, Count Palatine,
Duke of Cumberland by Anthony van Dyck.
(*Wikimedia Commons*)

Samuel Pepys, attributed to John
Riley. (*Wikimedia Commons*)

Thomas Betterton by Godfrey Kneller. (*Wikimedia Commons*)

John Aubrey by
William Faithorne.
(*Ashmolean Library*)

Thomas Killigrew by William Sheppard. (*National Library of Wales*)

Thomas Killigrew, after Anthony van Dyck. (*Wikimedia Commons*)

Sir Endymion Porter and Van Dyck by Anthony van Dyck. (*Wikimedia Commons*)

Edward Knyaston, 17th-century actor.
From an engraving by R. B. Parkes and artist
R. Cooper. (*Wikimedia Commons*)

William Shakespeare, the Chandos portrait, by John Taylor. (*Wikimedia Commons*)

Mr Cave Underhill y Famous Comedian
in y Habit of Obadiah y Fanatick Elder
R Bing pinx.                    J. Faber Junior fecit 1712

Portrait of Cave Underhill, English actor. Here, he is in character as Obadiah in *The Committee* (1665), by Robert Howard. (*Wikimedia Commons*)

Portrait of George Villiers, 1st Duke of Buckingham by Peter Paul Rubens. (*Wikimedia Commons*)

Sir Fulke Greville, 1st Baron Brooke (1554–1628), English poet and courtier. (*Wikimedia Commons*)

Sir John Suckling, painted by Anthony van Dyck.

Sir William Davenant. Published by W. Walker, 1 March 1822. English School (17th century). (*Look and Learn / Elgar Collection / Bridgeman Images*)

a stepping stone for further conquests. (The island's strategic importance was recognized in the Second World War by both the Allies and Japan.) Naturally his mother was against this, seeing it as an evasion of his true responsibility, writing in a letter to ambassador Sir Thomas Roe, of the 'Romance some would put into Rupert's head of Conquering Madagascar where Porter they say is to be his squire when he shall Don Quixote-like conquer that famous island, but in earnest seek to put such windmills out of his head..[3] At first, Rupert was willing to go, and information was obtained from the East India Company, which had sent a flotilla there in 1628, when the merchant traveller Peter Mundy recorded bartering with the natives. Mundy was there again in June 1636 as part of another fleet sent by the trader Sir William Courten, in which Endymion Porter had himself invested.[4] Somehow it all fizzled out in May 1637, and Rupert went back to The Hague. As it happened, in 1639, the Earl of Arundel, originally a backer of Rupert's enterprise, got Van Dyck to paint him and his wife seated by a globe prominently displaying the island; in the event, he did not go there, either. Instead, Davenant, at some time in 1637, imagined, over 446 lines, what might have happened.[5]

After some lines alluding to two recent bouts of illness, probably the aftermath of his venereal disease and its treatment and mocked by the 'cruell wits' of the Court, he recounts a dream. Perched on a 'crystal rock' – that it is of crystal marks the beginning of his fantasy wonderland – he sees Rupert's royally reinforced fleet (thanks to Ship Money) approaching the island; when they land, the innocent natives – early versions of the European invention, 'Noble Savages' – happily welcome them (unlike the real tribesmen, who had forcibly repelled other would-be European colonists).

Suddenly there is the sound of drums, marking the approach of a heavily armed force (which had arrived before), either Portuguese, who claimed the eastern hemisphere, or Spanish (Portugal was part of the Spanish empire until 1640). Each army sends forward two champions to fight for the island – ostensibly to spare their followers, who 'in their Princes' kinde indifferent eie /Are dutious fooles, that either kill, or die'. Davenant did not expect any 'we band of brothers' sentimentality from the aristocracy, and always had sympathy for poor soldiers. At some time in the 1630s he wrote a 'Song. The Souldier going to the Field', where the soldier regrets having to 'go where lazy Peace /Will hide her drouzy head;

/And for the sport of Kings, increase /The number of the Dead'.[6] For the English, Rupert selects Endymion and 'Arigo' (Jermyn's nickname, acquired in Spain in 1622), compared at length with Sir Philip Sidney, the hero of Davenant's former patron, Fulke Greville (and the anti-Spanish faction's model of Protestant activism). After their inevitable heroic victory (though in a poem 'To Henry Jarmin', he questioned the values of 'the Gallant Warrior ... Why would he kill? Or why for Princes fight? /They quarrel more for glory than for right')[7], the enemy army treacherously attacks. In the middle of the battle, Davenant worries about the futility of such fighting, especially for the losers, since

> That Land, achiev'd with patient toyle, and might
> Of emulous encounter in the fight,
> They must not only yeeld when they must dy,
> But dead, it for the Victors fructifie.

There is, however, no expectation of patient, productive toil on the land so 'fructified', but only military conquest for these raiders.

Davenant now feels the need to divert from the action, where the enemy have been easily slaughtered, to attempt justifications for such colonization. (His former employer, Fulke Greville, in his *Treaty of Warres*, had questioned whether colonial wars were justified.)[8] In Adam's time, the earth was spacious enough, but now, with population expansion, there is not enough room for everyone,

> Which is the cause wee busie ev'ry winde ...
> For Lands unknowne.

First-comers resist new immigrants:

> Not that Man's nature is averse from peace;
> But all are wisely jealous of increase:
> For Eaters grow so fast, that wee must drive
> Our friends away to keep our selves alive:
> And Warr would be lesse needful, if to die
> Had bin as pleasant as to multiplie.

This, of course, was not the case in relatively sparsely populated Europe, where the competition between jostling states was chiefly for empire and exploitation of subject populations. Here, the masters of this 'Golden Isle' (of Golden-Age innocence and golden profit) are not interested in agriculture or the hungry (here or in England) but in piratical interception of others' trade, to 'tribute take, of what the East /Shall ever send in Traffique to the West'. Wonders of submissive tribute from other empires are imagined.

In particular, the English are keen to loot the island: 'Now Wealth (the cause, and the reward of War)' –so much for claims of economic necessity – 'Is greedily explor'd: some busie are [natives, now working for their new rulers] /In virgin Mines [they had not gone there before]; where shining gold they spie.' He rises to lyrical effects:

> Some neer the deepest shore are sent to dive;
> Whilst with their long retentive breath they strive
> To root up Corall trees, where *Mermaids* lie,
> Sighing beneath those Precious boughs, and die
> For absence of their scaly Lovers lost
> In midnight stormes, about the Indian coast.

Further luxury goods are sought:

> Pearles, whose pond'rous size
> Sinks weaker Divers when they strive to rise:
> So big on Carkanets were never seene,          [necklaces]
> But where some well truss'd Giantesse is Queene.

They find sapphires, rubies, a diamond fit for a Sultan's bride, and ambergris. Then in a grove,

> They strait those silken little Weavers spie,
> That worke so fast on leaves of Mulberie:
> The Persian worme (whose weary summer toyles
> So long hath beene the rusling Courtiers spoyles)
> Compar'd to these, lives ever lazily,
> And for neat spinning, is a bungling Flie!

This is the climax of the dream of riches, of wealth of use not for the needy or the nation generally, but for the already wealthy. English appetite for luxury, especially silk, had been growing throughout the century.[9] King James had planted 10,000 mulberry trees for silkworms, and Robert Cecil 500 at Hatfield House; despite many efforts, mulberries would not grow in commercial quantities in England, but demand at the upper levels of society was insatiable; raw silk was a major import, second only to wine.

Davenant's silkworms work for the wealthy. It is interesting to set against these lines, lines from another text, written in 1634 and published in 1637, Milton's masque, *Comus*. There, the villain speaks of the sheer abundance of Nature, that needs to be exploited fully. Why else, he asks, did 'Nature pour her bounties forth', and – in words calculated to appeal to an upper-class audience –

> set to work millions of spinning Worms,
> That in their green shops weave the smooth-hair'd silk
> To deck her sons ... ?

Comus and Davenant knew that conspicuous consumption would be welcome to those that could afford it. In *Comus*, the Lady puts forward a counter-argument, how

> If every just man that now pines with want
> Had but a moderate and beseeming share
> Of that which lewdly-pamper'd luxurie
> Now heaps upon som few with vast excess,
> Nature's full blessings would be well dispensed
> In unsuperfluous even proportion.

Not a thought familiar to the Court, for whom any downward redistribution of wealth was unthinkable; it was not something for Davenant even to hint here.

Now he concludes his vision of an Eldorado, a Xanadu pleasure garden of impossible wealth beyond the scope of his readers' imaginations. Even in dream he cannot presume to such wealth as his aristocratic heroes, and descends with a self-deprecatory grin to a humorous view of the moderate, quotidian corruption and profiteering available to those like himself of modest background and limited ambition, when he imagines how he

> might twirle a Chaine
> On a judiciall Bench; learne to demurre,
> And sleepe out trialls in a Gowne of Furre;
> Then reconcile the rich, for Gold-fring'd gloves,
> The poore, for God-sake, or for Sugar-loaves!

But when he perceives that 'cares on wealth rely,

> That I was destin'd for authoritie,
> And early Gowts,

he wakes to his 'halfe dead Body', to hope instead that as a flattering Court poet he might 'deserve a little sprig of Bay', the poet's laurel, and further recognition. His Court readers could respond to his glamorous fantasy and humour, but might not notice the scattered implicit social questioning.

Carew's commendatory poem remarked on his mixture of real people and fiction, but hoped that this 'adult'rate mixture' would be more inspiring, in providing

> More pregnant Patterns of transcendent Worth
> Than barren and insipid Truth brings forth –

noting that nothing much had actually happened, and hoping for a more active foreign policy. He suggestively contrasts Virgil's Aeneas, only briefly distracted by dalliance with Dido from establishing his true empire, with Davenant's hero, who did nothing. The English remained teetering on the brink of commitment to action in Europe. Suckling observed ironically,

> What mighty Princes Poets are! those things
> The great ones stick at, and our very Kings
> Lay downe, they venter on …

Meanwhile, he noted, '*Dav'nant*'s come /From *Madagascar*, Fraught with Laurell home', and concluded by urging Davenant, 'In thy next Voyage, bring the Gold too with thee.' As it happened, there was soon evidence of the risks of foreign adventures such as Davenant had fantasized. Later that year, Rupert and Charles Louis landed a small force near Bremen, but were soon caught by Imperial forces; Charles Louis got away, but Rupert was captured and imprisoned, far away, at Linz on the Danube.

'Laurel' might be merely complimentary, or a reference to Davenant having been made Poet Laureate, in succession to Ben Jonson, who had died on 6 August 1637; whether he got the pension with it is uncertain. In a poem to Endymion's wife,[10] he urges Tartars, Indians and Negroes to give her ermines, diamonds and pearls, but in vain, and concludes,

> Thus Poets like to Kings (by trust deceiv'd)
> Give oftner what is heard of, than receiv'd.

The third poem in the volume, after that addressed to Buckingham's widow, appears to be on the wedding of her daughter to the Duke of Lennox, where, as one of the sons of Orpheus, he harps on his hoped-for title, for 'small Trees of *Bay* [laurel]' (to hang a broken harp on, echoing Psalm 137's harps 'hanged' upon the willow, remembering Zion, as he and she remember Buckingham).[11]

More engaging is the next poem, an account of 'A Journey into Worcestershire',[12] probably undertaken in 1636, with Endymion Porter and two unnamed gentlemen (one probably his friend William Habington, and the other, 'the Captaine'), leaving behind 'Town, ill Playes, sowre Wine … and the plague [of 1636]', as well as, in his case, a troublesome tailor (probably Urswick). They may well have intended going to Captain Dover's 'Olympick' games, held annually on the borders of Worcestershire and Gloucestershire. On the way, there is torrential rain, drenching their spirits and silencing them 'like to silent Traytors in a Vault', a simile suggesting that they might have been intending to call in on the way at Hindlip Hall, home of William Habington, where the Gunpowder Plotters, originally caught in a vault, had then been captured in 1606. They get as far as Childswickham, near the Worcestershire border, by night; and there they, like the poem, give up.

A couple more poems included in the *Madagascar* volume provoke questions. One is his 'Ode, in remembrance of Master William Shakespeare'.[13] A not very successful exercise, it is sometimes thought to be an early effort, perhaps partly provoked by Milton's verse contribution to the Shakespeare Second Folio of 1632. Here, using the scenery of Stratford, he warns off other poets from letting their 'num'rous Feet' tread 'the Banks of Avon', that is, to copy or seek to overgo Shakespeare. Their poetic flowers will droop and 'hang the pensive head'. Larger efforts will be overshadowed, and the source ('River') of Shakespeare's poetic power cannot be found in any 'Map' – any text, in the Folio or quartos – and will dwindle away.

Intriguingly, the image of the flower hanging the pensive head is found also in 'The Queene, returning to London after a long absence'.[14] There, the Queen's return (perhaps from a gracious royal progress) is like the return of the sun at dawn or in spring, when 'Each Violet lifts up the pensive Head'; the phrase clearly echoes the lines in Milton's *Lycidas*: 'The glowing violet … with cowslips wan that hang the pensive head.' Milton's poem was not published until 'late 1638'.[15] He was composing it in Cambridge in 1637, and, in November of that year, in London, when, in a letter, he suggested he was considering moving into an Inn of Court –where Davenant had friends and was possibly still lodging with Edward Hyde. It would seem that either Davenant had seen Milton's manuscript in 1637, or his Shakespeare Ode and poem on the Queen's return were written and included *very* late in his collection in 1638.

The 'London' poem itself complains of the city's lack of enthusiasm for the Queen. The mean-minded citizens– 'false Sonnes of thrift' – choke in 'Mists of Sea-coale-smoake' – a metaphor for the anti-royalist merchant classes. His friend, Sir John Denham, used it in his politico-landscape poem, 'Cooper's Hill' (1642), describing the City as 'like a mist … Whose state and wealth the business and the crowd /Seem but a darker cloud …' Here, in the citizens' 'narrow gardens' (contrasted with the flowers opening to the Queen's eyes), potted plants and caged larks (repressed poets) are metaphors for narrow minds. They are 'distrustfull Bargainers', but welcoming bells and bonfires (despite the smoke) would gain the Queen's approval, and so help them to 'couzen it [swagger or cheat] out in Silks, next publique Show'. The poem seems calculated to appease her wounded vanity.

Two other poems in the volume are worth separate mention. In 'Madagascar' he had sent Porter and Jermyn on an imaginary voyage; a few months earlier he had sent them off to sea, attempting to sail to Elysium, to find the spirit of George Goring, thought – erroneously – to have been killed at the siege of Breda in October 1637. After comparing him to various heroes, they leave it to Davenant whose 'Verse may [better] make those Sorrowes last'.[16] ('Leave the elegies to me.') The volume's concluding poem, 'To Doctor Duppa'[17] ought to have been an elegy; it is written to pay a debt of gratitude to the Dean of Christchurch for organizing a collection of poems, *Jonsonus Virbius*, published in March 1638, in honour of Ben Jonson, who had died the previous August. He briefly praises Jonson's 'conqu'ring Wit' and 'Judgment's force' – the five lines are his only mention or praise of his great predecessor – but is more concerned to thank Duppa. He did not contribute to the volume (whether or not he was invited); now he pays Duppa a 'hereditary Debt', having earned his 'Bayes', as Jonson's successor since 25 March. In the poem he indicates that he had to stay up late, to get the poem written 'before Day' – presumably a last-gasp inclusion. It was probably after this that he commissioned his portrait by John Greenhill, shown wearing his Laureate garland.

As the political storm clouds darkened, the image of the Ship of State was again in his mind, notably in his powerful, prophetic 'Song. The Winter Storms',[18] unusually written independent of any other work or address to any individual. Here, he remembers the stormy opening scene of *The Tempest*, that begins its examination of the uses and abuses of authority with a ship foundering, its crew and passengers all in conflict. He begins with the storm:

> Blow! blow! The Winds are so hoarse they cannot blow ...
>     The Waves are all up, they swell as they run! ...
>                 ... to wash the face of the Sun.

The political allegory seems obvious.

> Port, Port! The Pilot is blinde! Port at the Helm!
> Yare, yare! For one foot of shore take a whole Realm,
>     Alee, or we sink! Does no man know how to wind her ...

Davenant remembers *The Tempest*'s boatswain and pilot, and Gonzalo's wish to exchange 'a thousand furlongs of sea for an acre of dry ground' – but here the whole realm is at risk, for want of a little certitude. Having called 'alee', to sail to the leeward, the next call is, 'Aloof, Aloof!', to sail to windward: contradiction and confusion. Should one also attempt to keep aloof, at a safe distance (as Jonson advised, in his 'Ode to himself', to sing 'aloofe')? The 'Carracks and Ships [that] fall foul' suggest wrecking in politics. No one knows which way to turn, the Pilot is blind and the weak, fearful boatswain cannot direct with his whistle. It seems apt that the poem is written in a dramatic present tense: the danger is now; and few can hear the warning whistle of Davenant's desperate poem.

In the circumstances, he was not inclined, as Jonson advised, to keep away from 'that strumpet the Stage', and, temporarily diverting 'aloofe' from the Court but with business in mind, made a petition, on 26 March 1639, to put up a 'Theatre or Playhouse, with necessary tireing and retiring Rooms and other Places convenient' behind the Three Kings in Fleet Street, and there 'gather together, entertain, govern, privilege and keep, such and so many Players and Persons, to exercise Action, musical Presentments, scenes, Dancing and the like, for the honest recreation of such as shall desire to see the same'.[19]

No sooner had this been approved than he was swept up in the first Bishops' War. Attempts to impose bishops and the English Prayer Book upon the Calvinistic Scots provoked vigorous resistance: when the Dean of Edinburgh read from a Laudian *Book of Common Prayer* in St Giles's Cathedral on Sunday, 23 July 1637, a market trader, Jenny Geddes, threw a stool at him, and riots ensued. The Scots Church General Assembly declared episcopacy abolished and Presbyterianism restored. The Scots prepared for war: troops were ordered, recalled from the Dutch and Swedish regiments where they had engaged in the Calvinist cause, beacons were prepared around Edinburgh to warn of any assault. In response, the King called for volunteers – Davenant and his friend Suckling went as a matter of course, as courtiers – and on 27 March, the day after the granting of his theatre petition, the Royalist forces began their march north, to Berwick-upon-Tweed. Davenant was under the command of the Master General of the Ordnance, the Earl of Newport. Suckling made a showy figure with his own troop of horse, as Aubrey (probably informed by Davenant) relates: '100 very handsome young proper men, whom he had clad in white doublets and scarlett breeches, and scarlett Coates, hats, and feathers, well horsed and armed. They say 'twas one of the finest sights in those days.' Their performance was not so distinguished, notably at a somewhat shambolic encounter at Kelso, near Berwick, where they retreated before a superior Scottish force; the so-called Pacification of Berwick followed on 18 June.

Shortly before this, Suckling had complained of delays in communications, so that 'unless I had one of Mr Davenant's Barbary pigeons (and he now employs them all, he says, himself for the queens use), I durst not venture to send them, sir ...' This enterprising side interest of Davenant's – here presumably helping the Queen to keep in touch – comes as a surprise, but he had previously mentioned the use of carrier pigeons four years earlier, in *The Platonic Lovers*, referring to the sending of messages 'in a little letter tied to /A Tartarian arrow ... /Or 'bout the neck of a Barbary pigeon'.

Davenant's own participation once again involved difficulties with a tailor. This man, James Fawcett, complained that in that May, about 400 horses needed for hauling the cannon had been put on his land at Goswick, at Davenant's command. He had been promised twelve pence for each horse, but had received only three pence each, 'and half of that unpaid' (it sounds like Davenant's way with tailors), and that Davenant had accused him of injuring some of the horses. In the event, Fawcett was summoned to the bar at the House of Lords, where he was convicted of lack of respect for the Earl of Newport and made to pay the Earl £500. It is not hard to guess where Fawcett's future political sympathies might lie.

Soon enough, the royalists were back in London, trying to reorganize for the next round of the conflict. Among them was Endymion Porter, who in April took a moment to write to one of his employees to get assistance from James Stuart, Duke of Lennox (and later of Richmond), to help with Davenant's continuing efforts to get his theatre. Matters had not been going smoothly, and Davenant wrote to the Duke 'In the Year 1639',[20] using a marine analogy, how 'The Court does seem a Ship'; his analogy broke down, however, as 'Courts breed stormes, and stormes are lasting there'. He is being thwarted, partly because of his modest social origins:

> Where he that feeds a wild ambitious spirit,
> And nourishes desires above his merit,
> Is lost when he imagines to prevail,
> Because his little ship beares too much sayl ...

One has to proceed indirectly to obtain help from Power:

> And, as in Ships, so in a Palace, all
> Proceed by Aids that are collateral.
> The way to highest Pow'r is still oblique ...
> Whilest Money, like the Boatsens whistle, calls
> Reach helper till through haste most hazard falls.

He had seemed to be making progress, until he found obscure enemies wrecking his ship – 'Sure some perverse and undiscover'd hand, /Pulls an odd Rope that by oblique Command' stops him. (This could have been his old, undeclared opponent, Sir Henry Herbert.) He concludes by asking the Duke to be his 'princely Pilot', and hints that it might prove profitable: 'My Bark may Multiply, and grow a Fleet, /And I lay yearly Customs at your Feet.' It was in vain, and on 2 October he had formally to renounce his claim for his own theatre.

Meanwhile, on the great stage of the national drama, events proceeded towards war. Strongman Thomas Wentworth returned from Ireland, was raised to an earldom, taking 'Strafford' as his title, and aroused new fears and hostility. Without sufficient money to fund a campaign against the Scots, Charles had to try to persuade Parliament, but was determined, with Wentworth's assistance, to get his way. Matters rose to crisis point, and, on 5 May, he dissolved the Parliament.

For Davenant, another chance seemed to beckon in May 1640, when William Beeston's company put on at the Cockpit Theatre in Drury Lane, without Herbert's licence, Richard Brome's *The Court Beggar*, taken as a criticism of the Scottish War and the Court, and was put down. On 27 June, the Lord Chamberlain's office recorded that 'William Davenant, Gent., one of Her Majesty's Servants' should take over the theatre. However, there was no time to do anything about this, as the second Bishops' War broke out.

Once again, they trooped north, and, once again, Davenant in the ordnance department had to organize supplies of horses. Suckling's old commander, Lord Conway, had been named General of Horse, and was struggling with insufficient money. A letter of 17 July 1640 complains that 'There are 400 draught horses comme hither [Newcastle], 800 more will be here within fowre days, there is noe order taken for theire payment or any man that knows what to doe with them, there is only one sent downe, a deputy to Mr Davenant, if another man should doe soe he would put it in a play ...'[21]

The fault was not necessarily Davenant's: the royalist party generally was poorly organized and under-funded, led largely by the inexperienced. There is a notably tart letter from him to Conway on 24 August:

> May it please your Lordship I find a command sent hither to despatch from hence [Newcastle] three hundred and 50 horse for draught of the artillery towards Hull, and with all possible hast; but unlesse your Lo[rdshi]p send money (according to your own computation) for their charges thither, and mony for more iron to shoe them and a warrant for theire weekly pay who attend them, it is impossible to sett them forward ... Your Lo[rdshi]p is to consider how many days be allowed them for their journey to Hull; how much shall be allowd each horse when they travaile. And wt to draw after their journey; 350 being the number, besides their carters and conductors, and mony for their shoeing.[22]

His Lordship could consider himself told.

The last play that Davenant could manage to write before the war took over all his attention was *The Spanish Lovers*, which was licensed on 30 November 1639, just before Parliament closed the theatres. There is no record of its performance, but it was printed, however, in 1673, as *The Distresses* (*Dramatic Works*, Vol. IV). For once, a Court play, a sort of serious comedy, is not set in Machiavellian Italy but in Spain (Cordova), possibly reflecting a sense of Spanish obsession with family honour, particularly as embodied in young women. The obsession is personified in the aristocrat, Leontes, described in the cast list as 'hot-spirited', who seems a less obviously absurd version of *Plimouth*'s Inland Furious, in his aggression, violence and compulsion for duelling at any perceived slight, however imaginary. His sister, Claramonte, warns an admirer about his 'jealous honour' and his 'contempt of civil laws' against duelling. As is often the case, the foreign setting provides an exaggerated version of the Court culture its author observed and its intended audience experienced; as such, it is almost feminist in its depiction of compulsive male sexual aggression and victimization of women. Androlio, the witty, spoilt son of the Governor, remarks,

> My dear Don! how go
> Affairs? This is a mad town! The very race
> Of mankind in't are all horrid cats! Such climbing
> Into windows, clambering over house-tiles,
> And scratching for females, was ne'er heard of
> Since first the hot Moors did overcome Spain,
> And met with our grandmothers in the dark.

(As Moors, they were sexually 'hot' – a charge levied against Othello.) A decent young man, Orgemon, while providing a traditional excuse for sexual harassment and misbehaviour, says of Leonte, 'I knew he had some goust of levity /And youth, which unjust custom doth excuse,' and admits, to Claramonte,

> It is the lasting vice
> Of our ill-fashion'd sex, to think those injuries
> We do to yours but pretty triumphs,
> As if it were a dignity in youth to have
> The pow'r and judgement to betray ...

(It is hard to think of any of Davenant's contemporaries writing such lines.) As one young woman, Amiana, says bitterly to a lightweight courtier, Orco, 'Not one of all your promising, pretending sex /Is virtuously inclined.'

The action of the play concentrates on the pursuit – or 'sad distresses' – of two young women, particularly Claramonte, beloved of the apparently socially modestly born Orgemon and then also of Dorando, apparently of equally modest origins, who, in the last act are revealed as brothers, unknown to each other, kept in relative social obscurity by their nobleman father until they have demonstrated their true worth (two favourite Davenant schemes combined). Perhaps the implication is that such upbringing – not unlike Davenant's – makes for more decent behaviour than that of arrogant aristocrats. Honourably, notwithstanding Dorando's later heroics on their behalf, Orgemon and Claramonte remain true to each other, and Dorando makes way for his brother.

Claramonte's main distress, apart from her bullying brother, is her cynical pursuit by Androlio, who has been involved with Amiana but regards marriage merely as a trap:

> A trick your old law-makers first found out
> To keep us tame. And then they fob us off
> With stale deceptions of prerogative,
> That every husband is a monarch in
> His family. Of what, I pray? Of small
> Milk-eaters, that complain of breeding teeth,
> And we of breeding them.

His 'merry gentleman' friend, Orco, agrees, saying

> Marriage is a kind of foolish penance we
> Are often put to, for wasting thus
> Our precious time in making silly love.

Androlio prefers 'the large pleasure of doing little mischiefs', seducing on a whim, merely out of

> a kind of wicked wantonness,
> A sort of doing mischief a
> Fine new way; th'old way of sinning is tedious.

He seduces middle-class wives of 'poor /Shop-traffickers, that spend their precious hours /in narrow lanes –' as Orco confirms –

> Who are a kind of pious eunuchs, and their wives
> Your concubines, whom they keep for your use
> At their own charge.

Androlio's immediate perverse amusement is to use his superior social status to try to spoil Orgemon's wooing of Claramonte, for

> how much it doth concern
> The honour of a cavalier, to be
> Outwitted where a mistress is the prize.

At one point, having made Claramonte weep, he briefly finds himself, to his surprise, affected by her distress –

> I must
> Weep too! But say I prove so curs'd
> A villain now, as to have a mind to her
> In my tears?          [A faint echo of Richard III, here]

He turns to the audience, with a derisive, knowing leer:

> huge double drops, I swear!

(It would have been a good part for the actor: a witty villain playing to the audience.) He even goes on to suggest to Orco that they should share mistresses, whether Claramonte or the hypothetical daughter of an attorney.

This malevolent promiscuity – a typical 'Court project, which no man gets [profits] by /But the inventor' as Orco (or Davenant) has observed, is characteristic of the Court attitudes to women: either to be locked up indoors, or, mere prey, fruit to be picked, as Orco says of his rather young woman: 'She's newly blown, and I am going now /To make her ripe.' In this world, even professions of love are not taken seriously, as in the play's one song, that begins, unromantically,

> None but my self my heart did keep,
> When I on Cowslip-Bed did sleep,
>     Neer to a pleasant Bog ... [23]

The conventional lover's heart is here grotesquely physical, originally 'thick, and fat, and plump before, /Weighing a full pound weight and more', but now 'wasted to the Skin, /And grown no bigger than the Head of Pin'. Each verse ends with a curse:

> A thousand Fiends as black as Soot,
> With all their dirty Dams to boot,
> Take thee, O take thee every day,
> For tempting my poor Heart away.

Davenant stresses that the relationship of the sexes is one of power, as when Claramonte points out to Orgemon that, despite their mutual love, when they marry,

> Then I shall lose
> My freedom, whilst by force of formal law,
> And a devout necessity, I must
> Become the subject of your power, who was
> The mistress of your love. A dreadful change ...

By Act V, Androlio has run out of mischief and reconciled himself to marrying Amiana, when they make a curious, almost Restoration-comedy-teasing bargain of marital contest:

Androlio:   ... being married, I
            Shall prove a very rogue...
            I shall often put you, Amiana, to
            Your morning's draught of tears ...
Amiana:   I shall take order then, that you shall sigh
            For company.

In Androlio, the dominant character in the play, there is an unsettling, almost Wildean character of mocking exposure and inversion of social norms, who serves to express Cavalier values of selfishness:

> Friendship is folly when we suffer it
> To hinder us of what we dearly love
> When young. W'are wise when we our pleasure gain,
> All other documents are grave, but vain.

He seems a precursor of the Restoration libertine wit.

The play is densely plotted, with much complication of action: disguises, cross-dressing, a comic bawdy-house madam, quarrels, duels on and off stage, recognition scenes; the resolution is comic, with money and marriages; nevertheless, it is also thoughtful and serious, as feminist as the social and theatrical conventions of its time would permit. A few, non-aristocratic characters stand up for truth and morality, and the immoral are brought round in the end, but it is a callous, amoral and hypocritical society that is shown, where Claramonte can reasonably observe,

> Virtue and truth are only names on earth:
> And their realities are fled to heaven.

It is remarkable that a Court writer should produce such a critical presentation of aristocratic, Court culture at such a politically tense time. For all its skill and vivacity, had the theatres been available, the play is unlikely to have found favour then.

As the political situation deteriorated, preparations were made for what was to prove the last, but most splendid, of the Stuart Court masques. Without sufficient money to fund a campaign in Scotland, Charles would at last have to summon Parliament, hoping to conciliate but determined, with Wentworth's support, to impose obedience. As part of the political campaign, it was time to put on a spectacular show, not just for some self-pleasing Court entertainment but to reach out to the political and governing classes, not only to royalist supporters but also to those with some sympathy with Parliament's complaints, both outside and within Court circles themselves. 'Almost two-thirds of the male masquers were either moderate critics or future opponents of the King.' [24] Inigo Jones and Davenant were to put on a grand performance, celebrating the King's power to produce harmony and avoid the gathering storm.

The title was to be *Salmacida Spolia* (*Dramatic Works*, Vol. II), its meaning not self-evident even to those who knew its classical referent. The Latin text was provided with a translation: 'Salmacian spoils gained without bloodshed and without sweat, rather than a Cadmian victory when destruction falls upon the victors themselves.' In the original legend, the Salmacian spring was where Hermaphroditus changed sex after refusing the love of the nymph Salmacis, whose spring had the power of making men effeminate. The point was, the calming effect of drinking the waters on the barbarian tribes, bringing them without bloodshed or sweat to peacefulness, law and civilization. The second part of the text referred to the Pyrrhic victory of Thebes (here called Cadmus) over the Argives, which left very few Thebans alive. In the printed introduction, the 'Subject' is explained: 'The allusion is, That his Majesty, out of his mercy and clemency approving the first Proverbe, seekes by all meanes to reduce tempestuous and turbulent natures into a sweet calme of Civill Concord.'

Notwithstanding the critical situation, both the King and Queen took part, busily involved in preparations and rehearsals. The Earl of Northumberland wrote to his sister: 'I assure you their Majesties are not less busy now than formerly you have seen them at the like exercise,' and the King was reported to be busy practising his dance steps, 'dayly so imployed about the Maske, as till that be over, we shall think of little else'. Their presence together made a symbol of unity, and 'a gesture of royal willingness to build bridges to moderate opinion'.[25]

This was a major enterprise, 'the most splendid of all [the masques],'[26] stretching Inigo Jones's imagination and technical powers to their limit, with elaborate backcloths, four flats running in on grooves from each side, large wooden engines to lower performers from the heavens or raise them from below, chariots, thrones, clouds, stages for choric performers to stand on, backstage teams with windlasses and ladders, to say nothing of all the special costumes, props and musicians. The cost was estimated at £1,400 (one might add two or even three zeroes for a modern equivalent); Davenant was paid £40 (again, perhaps two more zeroes).

So, on Tuesday, 21 January 1640, *Salmacida Spolia* was performed in the Masquing House in Whitehall. The proscenium arch contributed to the meaning of the whole, not only with the displayed Latin phrasing. It is to be hoped that the spectators generally appreciated the allegorical significance of its painted and carved figures. On the right, a woman in a sky-blue dress with a golden crown, bridle in hand, embodied Reason; with her, a winged figure in shot silk indicated Intellectual Appetite. Above them, putti, one taming a furious lion, one with an antique banner, one with a palm branch, showed Victory Over Perturbation. On the left-hand column, a grave old man in purple, with a golden heart on a chain embodied Counsel, and a woman in cloth of gold, holding a sword with an entwined serpent, was Resolution. Above them was an altar with Pallas Athene's owl, for Prudence, and three winged children, one with a book, one with a lighted torch and one in adoration, figured Intellectual Light accompanied by Doctrine and Discipline. Above all these was a painted frieze; on top, Fame with wings and a gold trumpet; a figure with an anchor was for Safety; another with a cornucopia demonstrated Riches. Forgetfulness of Injuries (something the King was supposed to be offering) was shown by a figure extinguishing a flaming torch on armour; Commerce, by a figure holding ears of corn; Fertility, with a basket of lilies; a grasshopper, Affection to the Country; Prosperous Success was displayed by a figure holding a ship's rudder, and Innocence by one with a branch of ferns.

The performance began with the antimasque: a storm scene, showing rain, lightning and trees lashed by wind. A great globe of the Earth descended and split open to reveal a Fury, grimacing, her hair wreathed with serpents, who, echoing his poem 'Winter Storms', urges, 'Blow winds! Until you raise the seas so high …' She continues, 'How am I griev'd, the world should everywhere /Be vex'd into a storm, save only here!' (The continental Thirty Years' War had been going on for twenty years.) She invokes an unlovely team of evil spirits directed to stir up trouble, with Davenant very clearly exposing the familiar tensions and stresses in society:

> The great, make only wiser to suspect
> Whom they have wrong'd by falsehood or neglect.
> The rich, make full of avarice as pride,
> Like graves or swallowing seas unsatisfied,
> Busy to help the State, when needy grown,
> From poor men's fortunes, never from their own.
> The poor, ambitious make, apt to obey
> The false, in hope to rule whom they betray;
> And make religion to become their vice,
> Nam'd to disguise ambitious avarice.

The spirits are replaced by a new, painted picture of calm weather, rich cornfields and vines. Into this plenty descends a silver chariot, containing a woman in 'watchet' (sky blue), figuring Concord, and a young man in 'carnation' (flesh pink), with an ancient sword, embodying the Genius of Great Britain. In their duet, he urges her not to leave, 'if but to please / The great and wise Philogenes' (lover of the people, a newly invented title for the King). She regrets that

> though the best
> Of kingly science harbours in his breast,
> Yet 'tis his fate to rule in adverse times,
> When wisdom must awhile give place to crimes.

Their duet concludes:

> O who but he could thus endure
>    To live and govern in a sullen age,
> When it is harder far to cure
>    The People's folly than resist their rage?

The People's folly is the subject of the next lengthy sequence of antimasques, beginning with a Dutch magician, Wolfgangus Vandergoose, suggesting foreign importation of absurdity and misbehaviour, perhaps echoing the disorders of the Thirty Years' War. Among the twenty episodes enacting national ills are young soldiers overdressed in courtly fashions; a rich old man; old-fashioned Irishmen, Scotsmen and an English couple; various grotesques including Doctor Tartaglia, an Italian mathematician (a suspect foreign expert); an 'Invisible Lady' (a jibe at Rosicrucians); an absurdly amorous courtier; two 'roaring boys'; a comically adulterous scene of a jealous Dutchman, his wife and her Italian lover; and a scene of three Swiss, one of them a small figure 'who played the wag with them as they slept': Jeffrey Hudson in his last performance for Davenant. Concord and Good Genius then suggest that such follies are easily controlled, if people are encouraged to 'honest pleasures and recreation'– as in King James's *Book of Sports*.

Then follows a picture of rocks and craggy mountains, indicating the difficult way to the Throne of Honour, which is yet to be achieved. The second song, sung by a 'Chorus of the beloved people ... led by Concord and the good Genius of Great Britain' was addressed to the Queen's mother, Marie de' Medici, widow of Henri IV of France, exiled from

France since 1638, chiefly for her involvement in the Catholic cause in the war. Despite this, she was sometimes seen as an influence for peace, partly for her skill in linking kingdoms through her children's royal marriages. Nevertheless, her presence and presumed Catholic and foreign influence were a cause of some unease, while her closeness to the Queen could be seen as undermining the King's authority. Here she is celebrated as the source of the Queen, the 'Streame from whence our blessings flow', who had encouraged her husband with her 'Tuscan wisdom' (but hinting at Italianate – Machiavellian – cunning).

The printed text included a passage tactfully omitted from performance, asking why the King's ascent to the Throne of Honour had been delayed, perhaps held back by 'o'erweening priests' (whether Calvinist or Laudian) resisting any compromise; but, inviting his entry, concluded, 'You are heere.'

The King now descends in a magnificent golden Throne of Honour, surrounded by ostensibly loyal, adoring courtiers, in white silk costumes embroidered with silver, long white stockings and silver caps with plumes of white feathers. The overall effect of his appearance was itself somewhat ambivalent, as below him were figures of bound captives and trophies of armour and weapons. Whilst this vision might display Honour and Civilization dominating Conflict, it could also suggest forceful repression.

The third song, to Charles, engaged more closely with reality. The 'quar'ling winds' have fled, 'to reconcile themselves on shore'. An apparent strategy is praised:

> If it be Kingly patience to outlast
>    Those stormes the peoples giddy fury rayse,
> Till like fantastic windes themselves they waste,
>    The wisedome of that patience is thy prayse.

The effect is to make him seem rather passive; nevertheless, criticism and discontents are diminished into 'murmurs':

> *Murmur*'s a sicknesse epidemicall;
>    'Tis catching, and infects weake common eares;
> For through those crooked, narrow Alleys, all
>    Invaded are, and kil'd by Whisperers.

The corridors and corners of the City and its taverns, Whitehall and Parliament, echo 'the natural gates and alleys' of the ear and body of poisoned King Hamlet, poisoning the body of the country. The Chorus praise the King's clemency, and conclude:

> Hee's fit to governe there, and rule alone,
>     Whom inward helps, not outward force, doth raise.

Whilst decrying outward force, the Chorus emphasize that the King should 'rule alone', without Parliamentary interference.

However, he is not alone for long. As the printed introduction has it, 'the Queen is sent down from Heaven by Pallas as a reward of his prudence for reducing the threatening storm into the following calm'. In a brilliant cloud of various colours, with bright mists and 'exhalations', and escorted by her entourage of ladies, the Queen descends, a star or planet ruling the night and surveilling all below –

> For through the Casements of her Eyes
>     Her Soule is ever looking out,
> And with its beames she doth survay
>     Our growth in Virtue, or decay …
>     The valiant take from her their Fire!

The valiant might have been impressed by how she and her ladies were dressed, in Amazonian costumes of carnation colour embroidered with silver, with plumed helmets and baldrics for their swords. As it happened, the Queen was four months' pregnant, but the costumes would have partially concealed this. The militaristic effect of the warrior-woman costume is remarkable; Charles's relatively moderate, placatory strategies are undercut by her more severe and aggressive appearance (in accordance with her more combative recent activities – no lover, she, of concessions to Parliament).

The King and Queen then dance, against a backcloth of magnificent buildings, a grand bridge – symbolizing the bridge-building hopes of the masque – and a great city; the heavenly spheres and deities appear, together with the figure of Harmony. Roy Strong, again:

The final scene is perhaps the most eloquent and touching of all those devised for the Stuart masques ... celebrating through architecture and engineering a glory that reality was shortly to deny ... Everything Jones believed in was woven together in this single emblematic stage scene: the cosmic harmony of the universe is overtly linked with the classical architecture below, which, built according to Renaissance canons, reflected the harmony of the heavens. All symbolized the harmony of the King's love for the Queen and their mutual love for their people.[27]

That was the idea, anyway; how many of the uncommitted spectators were persuaded, is questionable. Strong cites one member of the Court remarking, 'I was wise enough not to attend,' thereby testifying less to the dangerous efficacy of apparition and harmony than to their total irrelevance.'

After their final dance, the fifth song advises them, in effect, to dance while they may:

> Time never knew the mischiefs of his haste!
> Nor can you force him stay
> To keepe off day:
> Make then fit use of Triumphs heere;
> It were a crime 'gainst pleasant youth to waste
> This night in overcivill feare ...

The Chorus 'of all' sing the final song to the King and Queen, accompanied with celestial effects:

> So musicall as to all Eares
> Doth seeme the musick of the Sphears,
> Are you unto each other still,
> Tuning your thoughts to eithers will.
>
> All that are harsh, all that are rude,
> Are by your harmony subdu'd;
> Yet so into obedience wrought,
> As if not forc'd to it, but taught ...

Nicoll waxed sentimentally lyrical: 'Thus the masques ended their career in a blaze of splendour amid the heavens, music from the enskied deities sounding in swan notes beautiful and sad.'[28] All very lovely – but: the words were, 'As if'. It was all 'as if', rhetorical gesturing. The opposition would prove to be neither taught, nor, despite military action, forced into obedience. Inigo Jones's 'invention' and Lewis Richard's music were celebratory of royalist fantasy, but Davenant's words, however flattering, could not entirely filter out glimpses of difficulties and reality. The magnificent masque concluded with two small, glittering figures gracefully capering together in the flickering candlelight, apparently uncomprehending of the impending storm. The calm evoked did not last long. When Parliament was summoned shortly after, it would not be appeased or cowed.

Around the turn of 1640/1, Davenant even wrote 'To the Queen',[29] attempting to persuade her to moderate the King's obduracy. She was to soften his hardness, like that of an old gold coin or medal, which she would polish to 'a yieldingness /That shews it fine but makes it not weigh less'. He tells her, 'You are become (which doth augment your state) / The Judges Judge, and Peoples Advocate; /These are your Triumphs ...' It was a desperate, but, he must have suspected, futile effort: throughout the Civil War, Henrietta Maria was even more intransigently opposed to compromise with Parliament than was Charles himself. Now there was nothing for it, but to fight it out when the time came.

# Chapter 7

# Times of Humiliation (1640–1645)

In the autumn and winter of 1640/1, the King's efforts against the Scottish insurgents were not going well. The clash at Newburn Ford on 22 August 1640 had been a notable defeat and even rout for the English forces – incidentally wrecking Sir John Suckling's military reputation and personal finances – provoking resentment among the English officers. Meanwhile, down south in London, Parliament was becoming ever more aggressive, and on 18 December voted to impeach Archbishop Laud for treason; the Scots were demanding the end of episcopacy in England, and mobs took to the streets demanding the head of 'Black Tom Tyrant', the Earl of Strafford. (Charles had promised him that he would 'not suffer in life, honour or fortune' when he came to London; now he was sent to the Tower; his trial – attended by the King and Queen – began on 22 March 1641.) In the face of Scottish threats, in early March Parliament voted to divert to the Scottish army £10,000 originally intended to pay English soldiers, still waiting for their wages. The effect on the army was predictable.

Not only did the English officers feel dishonoured by what had happened at Newburn, but discipline had been affected by lack of both money and of sympathy from English merchants and justices. In March 1641, a group of officers in York drew up a memorial to the Lord General, the Earl of Northumberland:

> First wee complayne as gentlemen that by the long neglect of sending our paie wee have bene enforced contrary to our disposicion, and the qualities of our former lives, to oppresse a poor countre, and live upon the curtesie and at the discretion of strangers, which both they and wee are weary of.[1]

It was not just lack of pay and respect that they complained of: they wanted to have another go, and redeem themselves against the Scots.

The letter was entrusted to a Captain John Chudleigh, who, however, did not go straight to Northumberland, but, instead, rode into Whitehall to meet 'Davenant the poet.' On reading the letter, Davenant told him that this was 'a matter of greater consequence than he imagined', telling him, furthermore, that 'Parliament was so well affected to ye Scotts, as yt there was no lyklihood the army should have satisfaction so soone as they expected it'. He now took Chudleigh to see Henry Jermyn and Sir John Suckling, who immediately grasped the implications of the letter: the army might be drawn south into the struggle against Parliament and for the saving of Strafford. Jermyn wanted to show the letter to the Queen, and offered to take Chudleigh to her, but he backed off from that.

Meanwhile, another conspiracy, led by Henry Percy, brother of Northumberland, was afoot: the idea was to replace Northumberland by the Earl of Newcastle as commander-in-chief, with Colonel George Goring (for whose supposed death Davenant had earlier written an elegy), noted more for courage than acumen, as lieutenant-general. The army would occupy the capital, and Parliament be forced to back down. The bishops' position and functions would be preserved, Strafford saved, and the King's revenues improved. There was talk of taking the Tower of London. Then, probably on 29 March, the King organized a meeting to bring the two groups together (but excluding the lightweights Suckling and Davenant). It was all too 'sharpe and high' for Percy, who saw it as dishonourable and illegal, and the machinations ground to a halt. Later, the King was reported to have said that 'these ways were vain and foolish, and would think of them no more', but some believe that he was a participant in a scheme to bring the army south. Now Goring told 'the mayn of the business' to his brother-in-law, Lord Dungarvan, and word rapidly leaked out. On 6 April, the Commons voted that no one was to move the King's army or the Yorkshire trained bands 'without special order of his Majesty with the advice and consent of both Houses of Parliament'. The army officers backed off. There were still plans to get Strafford out, to take the Tower, or to get the Queen away to Goring's base at Portsmouth, but they all fizzled out.

On 5 May, Lords and Commons met for a report on 'the late discovered Plot', later described as 'the greatest treason ... that was in England since the powder plot'. The leaders of the plots were sent for: Henry Percy, Henry Jermyn, Sir John Suckling, Colonel William Billingsley – who had been in charge of recruitment – and William Davenant. The next day, Northumberland signed an order for the ports to be blocked and the men brought in for questioning. Despite that, by then the five had fled. Four got away to Dieppe from Portsmouth, where Goring was Governor, who, despite having revealed the conspiracy, now approved the royal warrant licensing Jermyn to travel abroad and approved Suckling's lack of a passport; Davenant, however, having tried to get away through Kent, was captured at Faversham with Elias Wallen, his servant. The wits knew how he had been recognized:

> Soon as in *Kent* they saw the Bard
> (As to say truth, it is not hard,
> For *Will* has in his face, the flawes
> Of wounds receiv'd in Countreys Cause:)
> They flew on him, like Lions passant,
> And tore his Nose, as much as was on't;
> They call'd him the Superstitious Groom,
> And Popish dog, and Curre of *Rome*. ...[2]

As Aubrey wrote, ''Twas surely the first time that Wills Religion was a Crime.' There is no evidence that he had become a Roman Catholic, but his position as servant-poet to the Queen made him suspect.

Davenant was imprisoned, and examined by Parliament on 18 May (after Strafford's execution – for all Charles's promises and prevarication – on 12 May) and several times later, and there was expectation that he too would be executed. As nothing happened, and there was little evidence that he had been a serious threat, he had time to have printed a 'Humble Remonstrance' addressed to the Commons, properly humble enough but still with his characteristic touches of humour.[3] He begins with – he hoped – disarming cheeriness:

I humbly beseech you to conceive, that I have absented to appeare before this honourable Assembly [euphemism for attempting to run away abroad], rather from a befitting bashfulnesse, as being an ill object [a joke about his appearance], then of an outward sence of guilt, as being a delinquent. I did believe, if I were layd aside a while, my Cause would be forgotten, because I knew nothing stronger but suspicions and mere opinions can be brought against me. ...

(Suspicions and opinions had done for more serious men than him; now he moved on to The Patriotism Defence):

> unless I may particularly suffer for the old infirmity of that Nation which hath ever been bred with liberty of speaking; and the very Mechanicks of *Spaine* are glad they are *Spaniards*, because they have liberty; and thinke, when over-speaking becomes dangerous, that then they chiefly lose the liberty of Subjects.

(You would not want to be worse than the Spanish.) What he may have said was only loose words, over a few drinks at dinner,

> not words made in dangerous principles or maxims, but loose Arguments disputed at Table perhaps, with too much fancy and heat. I have perhaps committed errours, but never irreverently or maliciously against Parliamentary government.

He admits his friendship with 'Master *Iarmin* and Sir John *Suckling*,' but does his best for them as he knew them – after all, if they were innocent, then so was he – suggesting

> they were strangely altered, and in a very short time, if it were possible they could design any thing against your happy and glorious proceedings, who ... have so often extold the natural necessity of Parliaments here, with extreame scorne upon the incapacity of any that should perswade the King he could be fortunate without them. And it is not long since I wrote to the Queens Majesty in praise of her inclination to become this way the Peoples advocate, the which they presented to her ... for the Arguments sake ... now mentioned in hope it may be accepted as a Record of my integrity to the Commonwealth.

Here he refers hopefully to his recent poem to the Queen, but earlier he had expressed support for absolute royal rule, with Parliament merely obedient and consultative;[4] but times had changed.

In the meantime, he repeats that his failure to appear 'did rather proceed from a reverend awe your displeasure bred in me', and concludes by imploring them to 'leave me to posterity as a marke of your compassion, and let not my flight or other indiscretions be my ruine, though contrary to *David*s opinion [1 *Samuel* X], I have fled from Divine power, which is yours by derivation [for some, flattery can never be too gross], and chose to fall into the hands of men, which are your Officers that apprehended me'.[5]

The grovelling apparently found favour, with Parliament, who released him in July on bail of £4,000 – £2,000 of his own, and £1,000 each from friends. As for the others, the Commons still considered them guilty of high treason. In Paris, Percy and Suckling were having a hard time of it, receiving little sympathy from the ambassador there. Then, Suckling, Davenant's old friend, having, as Aubrey recorded, 'come to the bottome of his Found, reflecting on the miserable and despicable condition he should be reduced to, having nothing left to maintaine him, he … tooke poison, which killed him miserably with vomiting', aged 33.

Davenant was not the only one to feel his loss, while his own position was certainly somewhat precarious at this critical time for the Royalist cause. His poetic silence was noticed: one writer linked them in 1642, in *An Elegie upon the Death of the Renowned, Sir John Sutlin*:

> Dead to thir Country both; the one's not here,
> Th'other present, dares not speake for feare.
> Which of the two is surest slave to death,
> One breathes not, th'other dare not use his breath.[6]

Sadly, but wisely indeed, Davenant failed to provide an elegy on the death of his friend. For himself, he had been let go, and lived quietly in London for a while, until the King, after his spectacular and disastrous attempt to arrest the Five Members of the Commons in January 1642, withdrew to Nottingham, to raise his standard, and the Queen went south to the Continent, to drum up money and support; Davenant got away with her.[7]

Parliament now prepared the people for what was to come, and on 2 September announced that 'While these sad causes and set Times of Humiliation doe continue, Publike Stage Playes shall cease and be forborne … to appease and avert the Wrath of God … publike Sports doe not well agree with publike Calamities, nor publike Stage-playes with the Seasons of Humiliation … Spectacles of pleasure too commonly expressing lacivious Mirth and Levitie.' Their occupation gone, many actors, especially the King's servants, sold off their costumes and equipment and enlisted on the royalist side. (In 1644, the Globe playhouse was pulled down 'to make tennements in the room of it.')[8]

Sir William Cavendish, Earl of Newcastle, more noted for his horsemanship than his military skills, was appointed Lord General of the King's army, with Davenant's friend, Lord Goring, the General of Horse. Davenant himself was in Amsterdam, pawning the Queen's jewels,[9] to great effect, but soon found himself sent up to join Newcastle, as a result of her letter of 11 October to the Earl:

> I beg you not to make any promise in the army that you are raising, for the place of the master of artillery, for I have it in my thoughts to propose you one whom I think very fit for it, and with whom you will be satisfied.[10]

A contemporary described Newcastle as 'a gentleman of grandeur, generosity, loyalty and steady and forward courage ... he had a tincture of a Romantick spirit, and ... somewhat of the Poet in him, so as he chose Sir William Davenant, an eminent good Poet, and loyall Gentleman, to be Lieutenant-generall of his Ordinance',[11] – not that he had any real choice in the matter. Perhaps Davenant's youthful scheme for exploding Dunkirk had something to do with this, or simply that Henrietta Maria wanted someone there she could rely on. In any case, he was appointed Lieutenant of the Ordnance, ostensibly under the Earl's 18-year-old son, Lord Mansfield, though, more experienced and capable, Davenant would have been chiefly responsible. After slipping into England past Parliamentary patrols and then through probably hostile country, he joined Newcastle's staff at York that October. He was fortunate to avoid the dreadful battle of Edgehill on 23 October 1642, when over 6,000 men were killed, the Royalists claiming victory as Essex's army pulled back to block the way to London.

The King withdrew to Oxford on 29 October, when his company 'came in their full march into the towne, with about 60 or 70 cullours borne before them which they had taken at the saide battell of edgehill from the parlament's forces', wrote the historian Anthony Wood – as though it had been a real victory. Their triumphant procession (minus several hundred lying dead at Edgehill) marched along Cornmarket, past the

Davenant tavern, to Carfax, where the mayor and townsmen 'presented [the King] with a summe of money, as I heard'. The Queen had been busy on the Continent; by early that year, with selling and pawning jewels, she raised loans totalling about £180,000. She herself got back to England in late February, landing at Bridlington, narrowly escaping a fierce bombardment there by Parliamentary ships, which she described in a letter to the King as though it had been a misjudged royal entertainment: 'The balls were whistling upon me in such style that you may easily believe I loved not such music.' In York, she briefly had her own little court, and on 25 March 1643, Davenant presented her with 'A New-years Gift'.[12] Tactfully making no reference to their current circumstances, the poem deploys Catholic references as he makes 'Confession' of his 'old years crimes', which were his conventional praises of her in 'The Poets dull and common way', comparing her to the moonlight, birdsong or flowers, 'Or what doth please the Peoples sence, /Or what by rasher Fame is taught'. In this unreliable, contaminated situation (literary or political) she is removed to an almost solipsist isolation, where she can be likened only to herself, unique and incomparable (except, perhaps, to the Virgin Mary).

Aubrey relates a story, presumably told him by Davenant, of how, when in York, Davenant was made responsible for 'two Aldermen of York his Prisoners, who were something stubborne, and would not give the Ransome ordered by the Councell of Warr' (they were, after all, Yorkshiremen). He 'used them civilly and treated them in his Tent, and sate them at the upper end of his Table à la mode de France'; but after a while he found this rather too expensive, and hinted that they might escape, 'which they did; but having been gon a little way they considered with themselves they ought to goe back and give Sir William their Thanks; which they did', before eventually getting away. (In his preceding sentence, Aubrey reported that he had heard Robert Davenant say that 'for service there was owing to [William] by King Charles the First 10,000 pounds'; neither King Charles recompensed him, then or later.)

That summer, the Queen set off to join the King at Oxford, escorted by a substantial force of 3,000 foot, 1,500 horse, 150 wagons and a train of artillery, which might have been useful elsewhere; on the way she lodged at Shakespeare's house, New Place, in Stratford, still occupied by his eldest daughter, the widowed Susanna Hall. She would not have been welcome at the great house at nearby Charlecote Park, a household of puritan Parliamentarian sympathizers. On 13 August she wrote to the Earl of Newcastle that Davenant had joined her in Oxford: 'I have not yet spoken to him. On his return, he will inform you of many things which cannot be written, but I will not fear to write.' For Davenant, probably staying at his sister Jane's tavern in Cornmarket; it must have been a curious experience, combining his childhood home and family, courtiers and former actors he had known in London. The Cavaliers behaved predictably: one Sunday evening in October, Prince Rupert with a band of Hooray Henries 'danced through the streetes openly with musick before them', and went into a college to see a play, 'followed by a pack of women, or Curtizans it may be supposed, for they were hooded and could not be knowne'.[13] Parliamentarian journals reported on such goings-on, anticipating how

> in time they will go neere to put downe all *preaching* and *praying*, and have some *religious Masque* or play instead of Morning and Evening Prayer, it has been an old fashion at Court, amongst the Protestants there, to shut up the *Sabbath* with some wholesome Piece of *Ben Johnson* or *Davenant*, a kinde of *Comicall Divinity*.

Soon after this, Davenant did not return north, as originally expected, but joined the King at the siege of Gloucester. There, in September, being then 'in great renown for his loyalty and poetry', as Wood puts it, he was knighted by Charles. His efforts at money-raising on the Continent, or experience with the artillery, or even with the mining operation against the eastern gate of the city (memories of his 1628 plan to blow up Dunkirk) might have helped, though the King might simply have given a (cheap) present to one of his wife's favourites. The siege did not go well; a relieving force under the Earl of Essex got in; both armies withdrew, and engaged again at the bloody battle of Newbury (which Charles might have won, but for insufficient gunpowder for his artillery).

The King withdrew again to Oxford, where Parliamentary mockery of Court conduct continued; George Wither wrote how 'the queen will not have so many Masks at Christmas and Shrovetide this yeare as she was wont to have other yeeres heretofore; because *Inigo Jones* cannot conveniently make such Heavens and Paradoxes at *Oxford* as he did at

*White-hall*; and because the Poets are dead, beggared or run away'.[14] Davenant had not run away, but gone back to the Continent on his fund-raising efforts. Over eighteen months, his little ships repeatedly broke the Parliamentary blockades, bringing in quantities of essential arms and ammunition, so effectively that one news-writer in Rotterdam described '*Davenet* the Poet (now knighted)' as particularly active there as the King's chief agent,[15] and in March 1644 Parliament passed a resolution accusing him of high treason, and ordered articles of impeachment to be drawn up.[16] Nevertheless, he was soon back again in Oxford with dispatches from Newcastle, and with the Queen, and at some time between 25 March and 17 April wrote, 'To the Queen; Entertain'd at Night. In the Year 1644.'[17] In the circumstances, it could not have been much of an entertainment. The poem begins sadly enough:

> Unhappy Excellence, What make you here?
>   Had you sin enough to be afraid,
> Or we the vertue not to cause that feare,
>   You had not hither come to be betray'd.

The verse may refer to a recent Parliamentary victory at nearby Alresford, which prompted the pregnant Henrietta Maria to leave Oxford on 17 April for greater safety in the West Country – she and Charles were never to meet again. The poem itself – it was to be his last poem to her – provides a bitter review of the current socio-political situation, as it imagines dispensing the Queen's virtues throughout the land. With the Royalists less confident, he writes how

> Your patience, now our Drums are silent grown,
>   We give to Souldiers, who in fury are,
> To find the profit of their Trade is gone,
>   And Lawyers still grow rich by Civill War.

Apart from all the legal actions consequent upon the fighting, Davenant was hard at work getting munitions through, with help from royalist sympathizers, though still having trouble getting matériel through, with his ships getting captured at sea, and especially with Dutch Republic officials sympathetic to the Parliamentary cause preventing his ships from sailing. At Rotterdam, the government sold him a frigate for £2,500, but would not let it leave harbour.

After the defeat at Alresford, Oxford seemed insecure, but Charles was planning – against Prince Rupert's advice – a drive south-west, risking a possible Parliamentary advance. Rupert moved north, but paused at Chester, uncertain whether to return south to help the King or to assist the Royalists at York. On 13 June 1644, Davenant took it upon himself to write to him,[18] urging him to support the desperate forces there suffering from 'want of victualls [and] the Enemies continuall assaults': if the King himself had to withdraw northward, he would 'hardly be follow'd by those Armys which consist of Londoners; for it was never heard that any force or inclination could leade them so farre from home', whilst if Rupert were 'invited towards the King', he would lose 8,000 foot soldiers in York, as well as other forces in Newcastle and Hartlepool and other invaluable resources, the whole constituting 'a much greater Army than ever the South will be able to rayse in his Ma[ties] behalf'. In addition, they would lose 'the 3 great mines of England (Cole, Allum and lead) immediately in the Enemys possession and a constant treasure,' as 'they having the advantage of the sea will make those Mines a better maintenance to their cause than London hath binne'. With his quartermaster experience, he knew the importance of adequate supplies.

In the event, Rupert chose to go north, as Charles got his own forces out of Oxford, slipping between two Parliamentary armies, over to Worcester. He was then pursued through the Cotswolds, before managing a narrow victory at Cropredy Bridge, just north of Banbury, on 29 June. After a hurried march across the Pennines, Rupert relieved York on 1 July, and then, despite his own forces' weariness, engaged Sir Thomas Fairfax and Oliver Cromwell at Marston Moor, a few miles to the west, early on 2 July. The battle lasted all day – some 45,000 soldiers took part in the largest battle of the war – and despite some successes by Goring against Fairfax's cavalry and brave resistance by Newcastle's forces, Cromwell's cavalry carried the day, triumphing at last in mist and twilight. Thousands were killed, and bodies strewed the roads and fields on the way to York, which the Parliamentarians soon took. An early report claimed that 'Davnant the Poet' had been killed, but he was almost certainly not at the battle. His commander, Newcastle, to protect his own dignity, fled to Scarborough and then on a fishing boat to Hamburg, and eventually to Paris. Parliamentarian pamphleteers mocked 'the brave Marquess of *Newcastle*, which made the fine plays, he danced so quaintly, played a part a while in the North, was soundly beaten, shew'd a pair of heels, and exit *Newcastle*'.[19]

Though the Royalists' ascendancy in the north was now lost, it was not immediately apparent that this battle was the turning point in the war. The Queen sailed again for France, accompanied by ever-faithful Jermyn, and the King led a campaign through Devon and Cornwall, in pursuit of the Earl of Essex. Davenant was with him, ready to renew his activities as gun-runner and message-bearer. In mid-August he was at Boconnoc, near Lostwithiel, when Sir Hugh Pollard wrote anxiously to the Governor of Dartmouth:

> I join with Sir William Davenant in desiring you to let him know whether you have any ship or bark in your harbour that will transport him into France; that secrecy and speedy answer is likewise desired, and I am sure when you consider whose business he carries with him, you will need no quickening to afford him all the accommodation you possibly can … upon notice from you, Sir William will be instantly with you.[20]

To and fro he went, on his import-export business. In a letter from Paris, Jermyn wrote,

> This bearer, Sir William Davenant, is infinitely faithful to the Kings cause; he hath been lately in Holland, so that he met there with the knowledge of our treaty [the Queen's plan to marry off her son in exchange for military aid from the Dutch] … Pray if Davenant have need of your favour in anything use him very kindly for my sake.[21]

In December 1645, a Parliamentary agent in Paris wrote of 'Sir William Davenant, the poet – now the great pirott – and he that was the agent in projecting and bringing up the northerne army three years since', and suggested that he should be 'put into the exceptions for life. No man hath don you more hurt, and hath been a greater enemy to the parliament'[22] – that is, if captured, he should have no pardon. 'In all, Davenant is said to have succeeded in delivering more than £13,000 worth of arms and ammunition.'[23]

Yet it was all in vain, as Parliament pushed on; the army was reorganized, with Sir Thomas Fairfax in overall command, and Cromwell the General of Horse. In January 1645, Archbishop Laud was executed. That summer, the great wooden Masquing Hall in Whitehall was pulled down; in Oxford, the actors who had rallied to the King's cause now went down to London to make their peace there, in hope, as the *Mercurius anti-britanicus* put it, 'they shall returne to their old and harmlesse profession of killing Men in Tragedies without Manslaughter,'[24] (though it was not time for that yet). In October, when Parliamentary soldiers seized Basing House, the seat of the royalist Marquis of Winchester, they ripped out the expensive furnishings and 'popish ornaments' and took away the owners' silk clothes; Inigo Jones, now aged 73, was carried away naked in a blanket, having lost his clothes. More important was the battle of Naseby, on 14 June, when some 30,000 men took part; again, as at Marston Moor, the effect of Cromwell's cavalry was crucial; again, there was heavy slaughter, with bodies scattered across miles of countryside. This was the last major battle of the war, and was decisive.

The Royalist cause was collapsing. In the West Country, Lord Goring, appointed in command of the forces there, was dissolving with drink, laziness and bickering; he failed to prevent Parliamentarian forces from relieving Taunton, and was heavily defeated at Langport in July, before abandoning Bridgwater. In November, pleading ill health, he was escorted by Davenant to Le Havre, and then Rouen and Paris.[25] A proposal by the Queen for Davenant to escort a force of several thousand troops from France to Newhaven and Dartmouth predictably fell through.[26] Late in April 1646, with his base in Oxford threatened again, Charles, his hair cut short and in disguise in plain black clothes, slipped away, and, after giving up on possible escape routes to the Continent, on 5 May gave himself up to the Scots at Southwell, near Newark. Sir William, after all his efforts, now had to resign himself to staying at the Court of Queen Henrietta Maria, with Jermyn and young Prince Charles, at St Germain-en-Laye, near Paris, and finding something to do.

# Chapter 8

# The Art of the Heroic (1645–1650)

Here Davenant began work on his project to achieve status as an author (as distinct from a mere playwright or Court panegyrist) with what he thought of as an 'Heroick poem', or epic. He worked at it intermittently from 1645, undertaking extensive reading, and discussing it with his fellow exile, the mathematician/philosopher, Thomas Hobbes, himself working on his political philosophy, the *Leviathan* (published in London in 1651), who kindly read it and replied to his published preface. There were several serious interruptions. When, in 1647/8, his patron, Jermyn, and Lord George Digby fell out and were to have a duel, Davenant bravely offered himself as Jermyn's second, which would have opposed him to the other second, Sir Kenelm Digby (who would have known more about swordplay); fortunately, it came to nothing. Later, another courtier, Sir Balthazar Gerbier, accused 'Davenant the poet' of spreading lies about him; another instance of 'something of nothing'.[1]

Remarkably, in a letter of 14 August 1646 from St Germain to the English ambassador, Sir Richard Browne, he wrote,

> I understand that I have 2 children newly arrived in Paris, which a servant of my wives hath stolne from an obscure Country education in which they have continued during this Parliament neere London.

It is not clear who these children were, if they were indeed his offspring. They were unlikely to be from his wife, Mary: his son, William, would now be 22 and daughter, Mary, 4; who these two are is unknown. He continues:

> I shall desire you will be pleased to contribute a little of your care toward the provision of such necessarie things as shall refine their Bodys, and for their minds, I will provide a Magician of mine owne.

Mrs Porter tells me Mistresse Sayers will upon your intreaty take this paynes: and I will intreat you to give her mony to furnish them cheap and handsomely which upon sight of your hand shall be returned to you by /Your most humble and affectionate servant / Will: Davenant. [2]

His reaction is notably cool. They are to be looked after cheaply; Mrs Sayers appears to have been a cook/housekeeper; and we hear no more of them.

He was to show more concern about the condition of his dear patron, Endymion Porter, who had lost all his money in his king's service – most of his property confiscated by Parliament –a nd had arrived in France in 1645 almost destitute. In a letter, Porter wrote,

I am in so much necessity, that were it not for an Irish barber that was once my servant, I might have starved for want of bread. He hath lent me some money that will last me for a fortnight longer …
I am so retired into the streets of a suburb that I scarce know what they do at the Louvre, and I want clothes for a Court, having but a poor riding suit I came out of England in. Here in our Court no man looks on me, and the Queen thinks I lost my estates for want of wit rather than from loyalty to my master.[3]

He could do no more for her, so she had no interest in him. He fell ill, and Davenant expressed concern in a letter; when he recovered, briefly, Davenant wrote a poem, 'To all Poets /upon the recovery of Endimion Porter',[4] urging them to cheer the invalid: 'Arise! bring out your Wealth! perhaps some Twiggs /Of Bay and a few Mirtle Sprigs /Is all you have.' The poem suggests the exiles' financial difficulties, while advising them to recuperate their own spirits in a wine cellar. About this time, he wrote a curious poem, 'The Dreame',[5] to George Porter, Endymion's disreputable eldest son, who had recently gone over to the Parliamentary side. Ostensibly a love-dream poem, it is about fidelity. In it, the narrator dreams that his beloved is dead, and thinks that he is free from 'Loves Monarchy', with independent choice and power. Soon, however, he finds 'the vanity of being free /Bred the discretion to be bound', just as 'dull Subjects see too late /Their Safety in Monarchal Reign, /Finding their freedome in a State /Is but proud strutting in a Chaine'. In a 'free State' are many snares, and lovers (people) find 'the harm of liberty', and, led to jealous conflict, repent. The sentiment is Hobbesian: submission to authority, or civil war. The dreamer awakes to find Clarinda alive after all; perhaps George will regret his desertion, and want to return.

Then, that autumn, Henrietta Maria sent her servant Davenant on a mission to the King in Newcastle, to carry a letter urging him to make a token acceptance of the Scots' Covenant. Chancellor Hyde, in his *History* (IV) later wrote that Davenant was 'an honest man and a witty, but in all respects inferior to such a trust'. As the Queen knew, Davenant was experienced at getting in and out of the country, and would say what she wanted said. After a long and difficult journey, he at last met the King, himself weary from long pressure from being harangued, argued with and preached at. Though Davenant – like the Queen and others, including Jermyn – advised him to compromise, Charles refused this derogation of royal authority. As God's choice, by Divine Right, he could not become only a 'titular king', as he wrote to the Queen, with the power of government instituted in Parliament, and the supreme power in the people, to whom kings ought to give account. To compromise, was to accept that his whole principle of rule, of life, was only an idea, a fiction. He could not do it. Hyde wrote that the King spoke to Davenant very severely, 'whereupon the poor man, who had in truth very good affections, was exceedingly dejected and afflicted, and returned into France, to give an account of his ill success to those who sent him'.[6]

The dejection, if any – there is no evidence that the King was hostile to him, then or later – was more likely due to his realization of the probable consequences of the King's intransigence. On 30 January 1649 the King was executed, and his son, Charles, became the king in exile. In August, Endymion Porter, dear friend and patron, having compounded with Parliament, died in poverty in London.

Davenant was lodging with Jermyn; this was probably when he settled to work on his 'heroic poem', but once again was interrupted. That September, the new King Charles appointed him Treasurer of Virginia, to bring in fresh workers, before instead naming him Lieutenant-Governor of Maryland, to replace Lord Baltimore, a Catholic who nevertheless did 'visibly adhere to the Rebells of England'. Later, in June 1650, he was appointed to the Council of Virginia, to build forts there 'for the better suppressing of such of Our subjects as shall at any time rebel against Us or Our Royall Governor there',[7] but Davenant did not know of that change of plan at that time.

Before getting on with this, he took the precaution – and in the pride of authorship – of publishing his *Preface* to his proposed heroic poem. As a major effort and important contribution to seventeenth-century literary theory, which aroused considerable discussion at the time, it seems appropriate to consider it now, as at the time of its publication, before returning to his later adventures. Addressed to his *'much Honour'd* FRIEND Mr HOBS' (whose influence is apparent throughout) in the 1673 folio edition of his *Works*, the Preface (included in Gladish's edition), on which he spent much effort, is intended as a defence of writing such a poem in those times. He sees it as part of a general moral responsibility to engage in public life. His object is moral influence; for this reason, he has set his story abroad, and in the past, in the belief that readers will find this more appealing and impressive. It is fiction, in the interest of truth: 'Truth narrative, and past, is the Idoll of Historians (who worship a dead thing) and truth operative, and by effect continually alive, is the Mistresse of Poets, who hath not her existence in matter, but in reason.'

He has drawn, cautiously, from Courts and Camps, as 'the most effectual Schooles of Morality', though the people at large suspect both:

> They look upon the outward glory or blaze of Courts, as Wilde beasts in darke night might stare upon their Hunter Torches (whereby they shine) as that consuming glory in which the people think their glory is wasted (for wealth is their liberty and lov'd by them to jealousy [i.e. people resent their taxes being consumed by the Court's shows] ... yet Courts ... are not the Schooles are bred to oppression, but the Temples where sometimes oppressors take sanctuary.

The Courts are seen as predatory, while the people are guilty of what are now called 'the politics of envy'. The army is discussed only briefly, as not 'the Schooles of wicked Destroyers'. His writing is intended for 'the most necessary Men', who are made so by inheritance or ability. 'The common Croud (of whom we are hopelesse) wee desert; being rather to be corrected by Lawes (where precept is accompany'd by punishment) then to be taught by Poesy' – but they might want to imitate the moral 'necessary men'.

His subjects will include Love and Ambition, 'too often the raging Feavers of great minds. Yet Ambition (if the vulgar acception of the Word were corrected) would signifie no more then an extraordinary lifting of the feet in the rough ways of Honour over the impediments of Fortune'. (As in the career of an Oxford vintner's son.) Love is distinguished from Lust as 'the most acceptable imposition of Nature, the cause and preservation of Life and the very healthfulnesse of the minde as well as of the body'. He insists: 'They who accuse Poets as Provokers of Love, are Enemys to Nature; and all affronts to Nature are offences to God.'

As to the poem itself, he summarizes its structure as that of the five acts of a play, and defends his four-line stanza form (later adopted by Dryden, for his *Annus Mirabilis*) as providing flexibility and variety. In the course of composition, he has 'mov'd with a slow pace ... nor have I refrayn'd to be oblig'd to men of any Science, as well mechanical as liberal'. He has put in the work. '*Witte* is the laborious, and the lucky resultances of thought, having towards its excellence ... as well a happinesse as care ... *Witte* is not only luck and labour, but also the dexterity of thought; rounding the world, like the Sun, with unimaginable motion; and bringing swiftly here to the memory universall surveys.'

He discusses why he has taken 'so much paines to become an Author ... Men are chiefly provok'd to the toyle of compiling Bookes, by love of Fame, as often by officiousness of Conscience, but seldom with expectation of Riches'. He admits, 'the desire of Fame made me a Writer; I next declare why in my riper age I chose to gain it more especially by an Heroicall Poem ... by most allow'd to be the most beautifull of Poems'.

The value of such poems as his is, in effect, political. In the context of the present situation of wars in England, Ireland and the Continent, part of the problem is how to manage 'the Will of the People', unsettled by continuous politico-religious dispute, 'more unquiet then in former Ages; so disobedient and fierce, as if they would shake off the ancient imputation of being Beasts by shewing their Masters they know their own strength'. 'Statesmen' and 'makers of laws' are most to blame: the former (rulers) have imposed 'new Lawes presumptuously without the consent of the People' without adequate propaganda (as, for example, Charles's Ship Money taxes), or force; the latter (he probably has in mind the Parliamentary opposition of the 1640s) 'more civilly seem to whistle to the Beast, and Stroak him into the Yoak, [when] the People (with too much Pampering) grow soon unruly and draw awry'. While force is necessary to control the people, a better way, he suggests, is by persuasion, whether by entertainment, distraction or other (mis)information. 'None are so fit aides to this important worke as Poets ... the persuasions of Poesy in stead of menaces are Harmonious and delightfull insinuations, and never any constraint' so that morality, that is, order, 'is sweetened and made more amiable by Poesy'.

Ultimately this is an instrumental and authoritarian theory, which Hobbes would have commended, of the arts generally being used to manipulate and more easily control people, the to-be-governed of any class. He insists, 'The lastingnesse of government is the principall Worke of Art,' (though he may not have been so emphatic later).

For all that, the publication of the Preface without the poem inevitably attracted mockery from both exiled courtiers and other writers, then and later. In 1653, *Certain Verses Written by Several of the Author's Friends*[8] (with friends like these) – chiefly the Duke of Buckingham and Sir John Denham – had fun at his expense:

> A Preface to no Book, a Porch to no house:
> Here is the Mountain, but where is the Mouse?
> But, oh, America must breed up the Brat,
> From whence 'twill return an Indian rat,
> For Daphne, alas, is gone from among us,
> With thirty two slaves, to plant *Mundungus*.     [tobacco]

('Daphne' is not to suggest any sexual ambiguity, but to combine his name with that of the nymph, Daphne, metamorphosed into laurel, the garland of the Poet Laureate.) Aubrey recorded that when *'Gondibert* came forth, Sir John [Denham] askt the Lord Primate [of Armagh, Archbishop Ussher] if he had seen it. Said the Primate, Out upon him, with his vaunting Preface, he speakes against my old friend Edmund Spenser'.

To return to the events surrounding Davenant's transatlantic expedition: having received his instructions from Charles, possibly in person, Davenant set about obtaining men for the colonies. Aubrey relates his

Ingeniose Designe to carry a considerable number of Artificers (chiefly Weavers) from hence [France] to Virginia; and by Mary the queen-mother's meanes, he got favour from the King of France to goe into the prisons and pick and choose. So when the poor dammed wretches understood what the designe was, they cryed *uno ore* [as one], *Tout tisserans*, i.e. We are all weavers. Will picked 36, as I remember, if not more.

He stopped off in Jersey to get supplies and more convict colonists from the Governor, Lord Carteret (responsible for renaming the New Netherlands, New Jersey), and, with Thomas Cross as his secretary and a couple of Books of *Gondibert* in manuscript, set sail on 24 April. Very soon, however, they were captured by the privateer frigate *Fortune*, commanded by Captain Green. Green and his men were no doubt delighted to have seized such a rich cargo of stores designed to restock a settlement; they forced all the crew and passengers to strip, finding two Capuchin friars with crosses and chalices, papers intended for Maryland, the remaining convicts ('the Slaves, I suppose, they sold,' wrote Aubrey), and, of course Davenant, a real bargain. Green kept him awhile on the *Fortune*, to get the best terms, then transferred him to Cowes Castle on the Isle of Wight. 'We have not heard from Sir W. Davenant since he left us,' wrote Cowley, from Paris, in May; then, in July, Hyde wrote to him, 'I am exceedingly afflicted for the misfortune of poore will Davenant. I beseech you lett me know wt is become of him, for I heare no more then yt he was taken prisoner and carried to ye Isle of Wight.' With his wartime record, Davenant was a real cause for worry.

In Cowes, Davenant had nothing to do but tinker with his *Gondibert* manuscripts, while the Parliamentarian Council of State considered what to do with him, 'he having been an active enemy to the commonwealth'. Although some provision had been made for Royalists prepared to submit and live quietly, Davenant was not thought suitable for this. In early July, his name was included in a list of those to be brought to trial. As Aubrey reported, 'He expected no mercy from the Parliament, and had no hopes of escaping his life.' When his case came up in Parliament, twenty-seven voted for him and twenty-seven against; fortunately, the Speaker voted for him. The newssheet *Mercurius Politicus* reported that 'some *Gentlemen*, out of pitty, were pleased to let him have the *Noes* of the House, because he had none of his own'. His reputation as a humorous, somewhat comic figure might have helped. Then the opposition hardened, and, with others, he was ordered to be tried for their lives for 'all Treasons, Murthers, felonies, Crimes and offences', which put him in extreme peril. Some popular sympathy (perhaps from former theatre-goers) remained, and the newssheet expressed the hope that 'Will D'Avenant may not dy, till he have finished his own *Monument*'.[9]

Bureaucratic indolence and delaying tactics by friends may have helped; nothing much seemed to be happening. Nevertheless, in his *Postscript* to *Gondibert*, dated from Cowes Castle on 22 October 1650, he wrote, in undaunted spirit,

> 'tis high time to strike Sail, and cast Anchor (though I have run but halfe my course [of *Gondibert*]), when at the Helme I am threatened with Death; who, although he can visit us but once, seems troublesome; and even in the Innocent may beget such a gravity, as diverts the Musick of Verse ... I shall ask leave to desist when I am interrupted by so great an experiment as Dying ...

In the circumstances, his tone here is remarkable, a kind of wry insouciance, as he acknowledges that, in a few weeks, he might be killed; it seems quite brave, almost heroic. On 7 November, he was taken to the Tower. With, as Aubrey wrote, no expectation of mercy from Parliament, he took the precaution of making arrangements for the preservation of his 'Heroick Poem', and, that December, two Books and a third achieved publication in London, and two further editions in quarto and octavo in 1651. He also took the chance to petition the Council of State, acknowledging that he had been the King's servant under Lord Newcastle in the wars, but had left the country. He admitted his attempt to leave for a new life in America (as one might), but his ship and goods had been taken away from him. He had done no more against Parliament than many had done who had been allowed to compound for their activities; now he had lost his fortune, such as it was, and hoped only for his life.[10]

There was some growing sympathy for him. James Howell, himself newly at liberty, wrote verses against 'Some, Who Blending Their Brains Together, Plotted how to Bespatter ... Sir Will Davenant, Knight and

Poet', and there was no general wish to execute the noseless laureate. Aubrey, and possibly Davenant, thought that 'the two Aldermen of York aforesaid, hearing that he was taken and brought to London to be tried for his life', came all the way to London 'to try what they could to save Sir William's life, who had been so civill to them and a meanes to save theirs', and petitioned Parliament for him. Aubrey also wrote that Colonel Henry Marten saved him in the House: 'when they were talking of sacrificing one, then said Henry that in Sacrifices they always offered pure and without blemish: now yee talke of making a Sacrifice of an old rotten rascall.' (The kind of humorous story that Aubrey liked.) While some are doubtful about this,[11] Davenant himself wrote to Marten: 'I would it were worthy of you to know how often I have profess'd that I had rather owe my libertie to you then to any man, and that the obligation you lay upon me shal be for ever acknowledged.'[12] There is also a story, from Alexander Pope, via the actor Thomas Betterton, that John Milton, then Parliament's Latin Secretary, intervened on behalf of his fellow poet: it is possible, as they had common acquaintance, including Henry Lawes and the Lawrence family; they may also have met briefly in 1637. With all this, and a general political relaxation, Davenant was spared execution, but had to spend dreary years in the Tower.

When *Gondibert* was published, it had commendatory poems by his friends Edmund Waller and Abraham Cowley, who picked up on its distinctive features: the absence of mythological figures and emphasis on love rather than personal ambition. Waller praised the 'matchlesse Book ... in /Which no bold tales of *Gods* or *Monsters* swell, /But humane Passions, such as with us dwell. /Man is thy theame, his Vertue or his rage'. Henry Vaughan[13] marked the poem's context –

> Well, we are rescued! and by thy rare pen
> Poets shall live, when *Princes* die like men.

He praised the absence of '*giants* and *enchantments*' which 'made thy *fire* /Break through the *ashes* of thy aged *Sire* [blind Homer, father of epic, mentioned in the Preface] /To lend the world such a convincing light /As shows his *fancy* darker than his sight', and concluded that the characters' virtues are 'inherent' in the author, as

> All confess thee (as they ought to do)
> The prince of *poets*, and of *lovers* too.

Other writers thought well of it. In the Restoration, Lady Margaret Cavendish, poet and wife of his former commander, the Duke of Newcastle, wrote: 'of all the Heroick poems I have read, I like Sir *W.D.s* as being Most, and Nearest to the Natures, Humours, Actions, Practice, Designs, Effects, Faculties, and Natural Powers, and Abilities of Men or Human Life.' That seems to cover everything.

Set in a once-upon-a-time medieval Lombardy, the poem is more like a romance, in dwelling upon love, rather than like conventional epic that provides foundational myths and heroic achievements. As its modern editor comments, it provides 'an anthology of seventeenth-century commonplaces, often put very wittily and often quite lyrically'.[14] He points to the various 'set pieces': the love lyric, the prospect poem, the character sketch, the literary curse, the description of a painting. (Hobbes, in his reply to the Preface, praised 'The Hunting, The Battel, the Citee Morning, The Funeral, The House of Astragon, the Library and the Temple'.)

The first set-piece is the account of a stag hunt in a forest near Verona. The theme here is, as often in Davenant, human savagery contrasted with animal behaviour:

> Tyrranique Man! Thy subjects Enemy!
> And more through wantoness then need or hate...
>      ... now the Monarch Murderer comes,
> Destructive Man! Whom Nature would not arme,
>      ... but Art Armes all,
> From single strife makes us in Numbers fight,
> And by such art this Royall Stagg did fall. (I.ii.31–5)

The royal stag is King Charles.

In the story, old Aribert, King of Lombardy, has an only daughter Rhodalind; Prince Oswald wishes to marry her and so inherit the throne, but she and her father prefer Duke Gondibert. After a battle and duel in which Oswald is killed and Gondibert wounded, Gondibert is taken to the House of Astragon, a wealthy philosopher, near Verona. Book II opens with a description of morning in the city; after an over-researched account of Veronese architecture, Davenant does what he does best: realist images of urban life: 'When from their Dwellings busy Dwellers meet',

> From wider Gates Oppressors sally there;
> Here creeps th'afflicted through a narrow Dore,
> Groans under wrongs he has not strength to bear,
> Yet seeks for wealth to injure others more,
>
> And here the early Lawyer mends his pace;
> For whom the earlier Client waited long;
> Here greedy Creditors their Debtors chace,
> Who 'scape by herding in th'indebted Throng.
>
> Th'advent'rous Merchant whom a Storm did wake,
> (His Ships on *Adriatick* Billows tost)
> Does hope of Eastern windes from Steeples take,
> And hastens there a Currier to the Coast.
>
> Here through a secret Posterne issues out
> The skar'd Adult'rer, who out-slept his time;
> Day, and the Husbands Spie awhile does doubt,
> And with a half hid face would hide his crime.
>
> There from sick mirth neglectful Feasters reel,
> Who cares of want in wines false *Lethe* steep.
> There anxious empty Gamsters homeward steal,
> And fear to wake, ere they begin to sleep.
>
> Here stooping Lab'rers slowly moving are;
> Beasts to the Rich, whose strength grows rude with ease;
> And would usurp, did not their Rulers care
> With toile and tax their furious strength appease. [II.i.14–23]

Social criticism, as of the wealthy oppressing the feared workers, is apparent, if carefully qualified. More overt social criticism is safely transferred to radical orators attacking Church hypocrisy and exploitation.

One is quoted at greater length than would be sufficient for merely narrative purposes:

> We know, though Priests are Pensioners of Heav'n,
> Your Flock which yeilds best Rent, is this dull Crowd;
> The Learn'd examine why their Fleece is giv'n.
>
> Though by the Rich first shorn, to you they bear
> A second tribute, and by zeal support
> Temples, which Kings for glory raise, and where
> The Rich for fame, the Learn'd as Spies resort.
>
> Temples are yours, not God's lov'd Palaces;
> Where Off'rings make not his, but your own Feasts;
> Where you most wisely live, because at ease,
> And entertain your Founders as your Guests.
>
> With ease you take, what we provide with Care …
>
> The antient Laws liv'd in the People's voice:
> Rites you from Custom, not from Canon draw;
> They are but fashions of a graver choice,
> Which yeild to Laws, and now our voice is Law. (II.i.50–9)

Popular resentment seems justified, but feared. A notably weaker defence of the Church follows:

> Your splendid Pomp, by which your Pow'r indures,
> Though costly, costs much less then Courts or Lawes;
> And more then both, Religion us secures;
> Since Hell (your Prison) more then dying awes. (II.i.66)

He goes on to attack familiar targets: excuses for war ('Number gives strife th'authentick name of War'), questioning,

> How vain is Custom, and how guilty Pow'r?
> Slaughter is lawful made by the excess;

> Earths partial Laws, just Heav'n must needs abhor,
> Which greater Crimes allow, and damn the less – (II.i.73–5)

and Court corruption: 'Court's hectick Feaver, Faction (which does raign /Where Luxury, the Syre of Want, does sway).' (II.ii.35)

Such social criticism is rare in the poetry of the time, and would not have been welcome in the governing classes. In Act II, v, he describes The House of Astragon, a centre of fictional pre-Renaissance scientific enquiry. Astronomers

> with Optick Tubes the Moons scant face
> (Vast Tubes, which like long Cedars mounted lie)
> Attract through Glasses to so neer a space
> As if they come not to survey, but prie.

The hint of criticism is developed:

> Since Opticks first were known to *Astragon*,
> By whom the Moderns are become so skill'd,
> They dream of seeing to the Maker's Throne.

Astragon has developed the theory of the non-geocentric universe, which Davenant defends (somewhat uncertainly):

> Man's pride (grown to Religion) he abates,
> By moving our lov'd Earth; which we think fix'd;
> Think all to it, and it to none relates;
> With others motion scorn to have it mix'd.
>
> As if 'twere great and stately to stand still
> Whilst other Orbes dance on; or else think all
> Those vast bright Globes (to shew God's needless Skill)
> Were made but to attend our little Ball. (II.v.15–20)

The analogy calls to mind (perhaps unfavourably) Charles and his attendant courtiers at a masque. The visitors are shown other areas of scientific study, a museum of '*Skelitons* of ev'ry kinde' and a great library, where the Bible introduces another favourite theme, criticism of religious debate:

> But here, the Souls chief Book did all precede:
> Our Map tow'ds Heav'n; to common Crowds deny'd;
> Who proudly aim to teach, ere they can read,
> And all must stray, where each will be a Guide.

Volumes of religious theorizing remain unread (with a favourite image),

> For a deep Dust (which Time does softly shed,
> Where onely Time does come) their covers beare;
> On which, grave Spyders, streets of Webbs had spread ... (II.v.52)

(As ever, fixed authority rather than uncertain freedom.)

Returning to the story: convalescent Gondibert now (Canto vii) meets Astragon's only daughter, Birtha (echoes of Prospero and Miranda), a 'Country Maid' of great beauty, virtue and gormless ignorance, who had never seen Courts or cities, and 'thinks that Babes proceed from mingling Eies, /Or Heav'n from Neighbourhood increase allows', or possibly '(as she hears) from Mothers pain ... yet that she will sustain, /So they be like this Heav'nly Man she loves.' (vii. 6–7, 45–6) They fall in love, instantly. Meanwhile, a political destiny threatens Gondibert, after his defeat of Oswald. Astragon warns him that, as victor, he may have to marry Rhodalind. Though he rejects military glory, he insists:

> I here to *Birtha* make
> A vow, that *Rhodalind* I never sought,
> Nor now would with her love her greatness take.
>
> Loves bonds are for greatness made too straight;
> And me Ambition's pleasures cannot please ... (III.ii.74–5)

Nevertheless, his lieutenant and friend, Goltho (who secretly also loves Birtha – as usual) insists that '*Birtha* (a harmless Cottage Ornament) / May be his bride that's born himself to serve; /But you must pay that blood your Army spent, /And wed that Empire that our wounds deserve'.

(vii.57) (Davenant had observed how military events could force rulers' actions.)

King Aribert now proclaims Gondibert his successor, and that he is to marry Rhodalind, and summons him to attend Court, with his attendants Goltho and Ulfinore (though Astragon encourages Birtha to follow, in secret, as Rhodalind's maid). As Golitho and Ulfinore are riding through the western gate of Verona at sunset (III.vi.), their attention is distracted,

> For a black Beauty did her pride display
> Through a large Window, and in Jewels shon,
> As if, to please the World, weeping for Day,
> Night had put her starry Jewels on. (vi.31)

(Perhaps too many jewels here.) Aubrey wrote that this episode derived from Davenant's 'unlucky mischance' with the 'Black handsome wench … which cost him his Nose'. In any case, in this last part of the poem, the writing lifts, to provide livening entertainment.

> The Beauty gaz'd on both, and *Ulfinore*
> Hung down his Head, but yet did lift his Eies,
> As if he would fain see a little more:

For much, though bashful, he did beauty prise.

> *Goltho* did like a blushless Statue stare;
> Boldly her practis'd boldness did out-look …

> She, with a wicked Woman's prosp'rous Art,
> As seeming modesty, the Window cloz'd;
> Wisely delay'd his Eies, since of his Heart
> She thought, she had sufficiently dispos'd. (32–4)

However, her 'little Page /Clean and perfum'd', nips down to fetch Goltho in. They go up to her luxurious bedchamber, where she urges Ulfinore to go away, which he refuses to do, remembering 'Tales, to forward Youth / In winter Nights by Country Matrons told

> Of *Witches Towns*, where seeming Beauties dwell,
> All hair, and black within, Maids that can fly!
> Whose Palaces at Night are smoaky Hell,
> And in their beds their slaughtered Lovers lie.
>
> And though the Sun now setting, he no Lights
> Saw burning blew, nor steam of Sulphur smelt;
> Nor took her two black *Meroes* [Moorish] Maids for Sprites;
> Yet he a secret touch of horror felt. (55–7)

He goes on to warn Goltho:

> You'll stay, and have your sleep with Musick fed,
> But little think to wake with *Mandrake*s grones,
> And by a Ghost be to a Garden led
> At midnight, strew'd with simple Lovers bones.
>
> This *Goltho* is enchantment ...
> Let's goe! Before our Horses learn to fly,
> Ere she shew cloven feet, and they get wings. (63)

The two men get away to the Duke's Palace. And there, after this cheering episode, not obviously furthering the plot, but perhaps thought of as one of the pleasant 'Meanders' he had mentioned in his *Preface*, the poem ceases, interrupted, as he wrote in the following *Postscript*, by the possibility of so 'great an experiment as Dying'. There is no evidence that, perhaps wisely, he made any further efforts.

When Henry Herringman published Davenant's *Works* in 1673, he included two poems, 'The Philosophers Disquisition, directed to the dying Christian', and 'The Christians Reply', which he indicated were originally intended to form part of *Gondibert*, though it appears that at some time Davenant made some slight alterations so that they could be read as a self-sufficient pair. Manuscript versions include verses suggesting that the ailing Astragon chose a disciple, Thenour, to look into the fear of death and 'to reveal such doubts as growe /Still dark, & make truths progress slow'.[14]

*The Disquisition* (90 stanzas long), belongs with other contemporary debates between traditional injunctions not to question God's work, whether in the Bible or Nature, and the growth of religious conflict and of rationalist thinking.[15] The first part considers the limitations of human understanding and knowledge; nevertheless, the pursuit of knowledge is essential and virtuous:

> If Knowledge must, as evill, hidden lie,
>    Then we, its object, Nature, seem to blame;
> And whilst we banish Knowledge, as a Spy,
>    We but hide Nature as we cover shame.

The Edenic allusion is developed:

> In gathering Knowledge from the Sacred Tree,
>    I would not snatch in haste the fruit below;
> But rather climbe, like those who curious be,
>    And boldly taste that which does highest grow.' (stanza 20)

The central section of the poem (24–59) concentrates on the conflict of Faith and Reason (again, submission or independent uncertainty). On one hand, 'Where Men have several Faiths, to find the true /We only can the aid of Reason us', (25) but 'Faith claimes that Reason should submit' to Faith. 'So Reason, though she were at first Fayths Guide /To Heav'n, yet waites without, when Faith goes in'. (39) The human plight is such, that

> Our Soules but like unhappy strangers come
>    From Heav'n, their Countrey, to this Worlds bad Coast;
> They Land, then strait are backward bound for home;
>    And many are in stormes of passion lost!

> They long with danger sayle through lifes vext Seas,
>    In Bodies, as in Vessels full of leaks;
> Walking in veines, their narrow Galleries,
>    Shorter then walks of Seamen on their Decks. (47–8)

Faith rejects Reason and steers towards Heaven: 'In Reasons place, Tradition doth her lead; /And that presumptuous Antiquary makes / Strong Lawes of weak Opinions of the Dead ... and weares out Truths best Stories into Tales.' (51–2)

Mankind is constantly frustrated, 'at once ... bidden and forbid'. (65) This leads to some of the Frequently Asked Questions About Christianity, that Milton's *Paradise Lost* was soon to grapple with. 'If, as Gods Students, we have leave to learne /His Truths, Why doth his Text oft need debate?' (68) Why did God not express himself directly? More pertinently, why did God originally permit sin? 'Why did not Heav'ns prevention Sin restraine? /Or is not Pow'rs permission a consent? /Which as in Kings as much as to ordaine; /And the ordain'd are free from punishment.' (75) The doctrines of eternal punishment and predestination are particularly troublesome:

> That we are destin'd after Death to more
>     Then Reason thinks due punishment for Sins,
> Seems possible, because in life, before
>     We know to sin, our punishment begins.
>
> Why else do Infants with incessant cries
>     Complaine of secret harme as soon as born? (86–7)

Indeed,

> Doth not belief of being destin'd draw
> Our Reason to Presumption or dispaire?
> If Destiny be not, like humane Law,
> To be repeal'd, what is the use of Prayer? (88)

*The Christians Reply*, only ten stanzas long (perhaps because he is dying) ignores these questions. Faith is 'Religion's trembling Guide', which should be 'by Reason councell'd, though not sway'd'. It concludes by celebrating 'harmless Death! Whom ... all the Good embrace, who know the *Grave*, /A short dark passage to Eternal Light'.

It seems unlikely that Astragon would have felt greatly comforted.

# Chapter 9

# Entr'Acte

In 1652, after more than two weary years of imprisonment, largely neglected by Parliament, Davenant was asked – as 'Davenant the Poet' – to write some commendatory verses for slender volumes by other poets. Now, in 'To Mr. Benlowes, on his Divine Poem',[1] (*Theophila, or Loves Sacrifice*, thirteen cantos celebrating the progress of the soul, published 1652) he took the occasion, in his middle years, to look back at a life spent writing for, and living off, a Court the values of which he had never really shared, and that itself seemed unlikely to be renewed. His poem is signed, 'Will D'Avenant. Tower, *May* 13th 1652'; in it, he contrasts Edward Benlowes's religious raptures with the careers of Court poets, notably, though not explicitly, his own. He admits,

> Though Poets are, like Eaglets, bred to soar,
> Gazing through Stars at Heav'ns Misterious Pow'r,
> Yet I observe they quickly stoop to ease
> Their Wings, and Pearch on Palace-Pinacles.

As a young, middle-class man on the make, he had not been independently minded or poetically ambitious, but had quickly attached himself to the Court, writing flattering verses to anyone who might do him some good. He goes on to remark how Court poets

> From thence more usefully they Courts discern;
> The Schools where Greatness does Disguises learn.

The plays he wrote consistently show Court life as one of corruption, deception and betrayal, where his actors, in effect, portray actors. Court and Stage mirror each other:

> The Stages where she [Greatness] acts to vulgar sight
> Those parts which States-men as her Poets write;
> Where none but those wise Poets may survay
> The private practice of her publick Play.

The Great – monarchs, their women, great nobles – are advised, or, rather, manipulated in their performances, by 'statesmen', senior courtiers, rather as playwright Davenant deployed his characters,

> Where Kings, Gods Counterfeiters, reach but the skill,
> In study'd Scenes to act the Godhead ill.

Kings – such as Charles – might expect to be described as God's deputies, representatives or agents, but not as fakers, counterfeiters, bad actors, who do harm,

> Where Cowards, smiling in their Closets, breed
> Those wars which make the vain and furious bleed.

The villainous Machiavels of Jacobean drama walk on as the conniving courtiers, smiling in their closets, safely urging others into war, where the fierce captains and colonels are dismissed as vain and furious. He goes on, from his implicit comment on Charles I's Court (though he had also had some brief observation of Louis XIV's) apparently to disparage royal inadequacy and royal succession (even the Stuart principle of the Divine Right of Kings), noting how

> as successive Kings scarce seem to reign,
> While lazily they Empires weight sustain;
> Thinking because their Pow'r they Native call,
> Therefore our duty too is Natural;
> And by presuming that we ought obey,
> They loose the craft and exercise of sway.

He had in the past hinted that Charles needed to make more effort to persuade, and to earn loyalty.

Remarkably, these last lines are in fact not openly directed at the monarch(s), but are part of a surprisingly lengthy account of the power of women over men, especially of Court Beauties over courtiers:

> Where Beauty playes not merely Natures part,
> But is, like Pow'r, a Creature form'd by Art.

The Great and the Beautiful are both artificial constructions, their power derived from skilful performances and manipulation by themselves and their acolytes, rather than from merit:

> So harmless Beauty (which has now far more
> Injurious force then States or Monarchs Pow'r)
> Was by consent of Courts allow'd Arts ayd …
> Twas Art, not Nature, taught excessive Pow'r;
> Which whom it lists does favour or devour:
> 'Twas Art taught Beauty the Imperial skill,
> Of Ruling, not by Justice, but by Will.

Likewise, any 'Native Beauty' who neglects technical and courtly arts will soon lose her influence and reputation as a 'Beauty'. The analogy between the reigns, and ends, of royalty and beauty is drawn tightly:

> Soon then, when Beautie's gone, she turns her face,
> Asham'd of that which was e'rewhile her Grace;
> So, when a Monarch's gone, the Chair of State
> Is backward turn'd, where he in glory sate.

All this, he suggests, has been the concern of Court poets:

> The secret Arts of Love and Pow'r; how these
> Rule Courts, and how those Courts rule Provinces,
> Have bin the task of ev'ry Noble Muse.

The powerful have not only used such writers in publicizing their achievements more widely,

> Whose Ayd of old nor Pow'r nor Love did use
> Meerly to make their lucky Conquests known,

but learned to use their writings to influence and control their subjects:

> But they by studying Numbers rather knew
> To make those happy whom they did subdue.

As he wrote in the *Preface*, 'the persuasions of Poesy in stead of menaces are Harmonious and delightfull insinuations', and 'The lastingnesse of government is the principall Worke of Art'. He does not sound so happy about that now. The flattering writers used the Court to make a living; in turn, the Court used them to secure their position over those 'they did subdue'. ('Subdue' cannot wholly avoid suggestions of 'oppress' or 'crush'.) The conniving writers – such as himself – were also responsible; which leads Davenant to the contrast with the spiritually minded Benlowes, whom he cannot emulate.

Now he looks back with mixed feelings on a career that had brought him worldly success, a knighthood and moderate wealth (now gone). A former Court poet in Parliamentary hands might do well to criticize Court practices in a poem for a 'Moral Poet' – which would not make his retrospective self-evaluation insincere. For the last third of the poem he is properly polite to Benlowes.

His time in the Tower dragged on, as he struggled to escape the cobwebs of bureaucratic delay. In November 1651, Colonel John Bingham, Governor of Guernsey, wrote hoping to arrange a prisoner exchange;[2] on 7 October 1652, the Council of State ordered his release, and Davenant wrote a letter of thanks to Bulstrode Whitelocke, an old friend from Inns of Court days and now a member of the Council.[3]

It now appears that Mary, his first wife, had died at some unknown date, presumably during the war (it does not appear to have been a close marriage, and in *Gondibert* he wrote that marriage 'is too oft but civil warre'); he now took the occasion to marry Anne Cademan, the widow of Sir Thomas Cademan, the doctor who had treated him for his bout of venereal disease. Sir John Denham later wrote, unkindly, how 'Her beauty, though twas not exceeding, /Yet what in Face and shape was needing, /She made it up in Parts and Breeding'. Perhaps more important at the time, with her came jewels worth £600, which he pawned, and £800 from the estate of her first husband, Thomas Cross. Her breeding had also produced four stepsons, including Thomas Cross whom Davenant had been going to take to America as his secretary.

Shortly after this, he was again arrested for debt. On 1 February 1654, Bingham again wrote on his behalf, pointing out that while he was 'in prison on bail … to return to the Tower when demanded', there was little he could do to recover his debt, and asking for his release, 'as his sufferings, contrary to the articles of war, have been grea'. Davenant himself appealed to Oliver Cromwell as Lord Protector, for a pardon, so that he might 'live as a faithful subject'. Pardon was approved on 22 July, and Davenant was at last released, on 4 August 1654.

# Chapter 10

# How Daphne Pays His Debts (1654–1659)

A fter his release from the Tower, he and Anne probably moved into the Cademans' house in Tothill Street, Westminster, before moving to Holborn. The city was grimmer than he had known it, with theatres and traditional festivities banned and sexual activity strictly policed (as he was later to recall in *The Law against Lovers*, his adaptation of *Measure for Measure*) – adultery was, in theory, punishable with the death sentence. In his earlier poem, 'To the Queen returning to London', the city was smoky and dirty; now, he wrote, 'London is smother'd with sulph'rous fires; /Still she wears a black Hood and Cloak /Of Sea-coal smoak, /As if she mourn'd for Brewers and Dyers.'[1] Looking around, he must have sensed the general, if repressed, desire for entertainment, especially for theatre. A poem by Aston Cokaine, *A Praeludium to Mr Richard Bromes Plays*, in 1653, looked forward to a time when

> ... we shall still have *Playes*! And though we may
> Not them in their full Glories yet display;
> Yet we may please ourselves by reading them,
> Till a more Noble Act this act condemn...
> Davenant and Massinger and Sherley then
> Shall be cry'd up againe for Famous men ...[2]

They could well have attended such few theatrical performances as were available, perhaps at the Red Bull in Clerkenwell. Soon, however, his new wife, Anne, (not in her first youth) died in March 1655, perhaps killed off by the noxious atmosphere of the city. Nethercot comments on his reaction: 'Whatever the precedent circumstances, her loss did not occasion her practical husband any prolonged fit of mourning. D'Avenant, in spite of being a Cavalier poet, never regarded the marriage relationship with even an ephemerally sentimental or romantic eye.'[3] One might remark that it was more the Cavalier upper classes (of which Davenant was not a member) who married for status or wealth; early deaths and frequent re-marriages (this was her third) were common occurrences at that time. Whatever he may have felt, the ever-resilient Davenant was soon literally taking steps to remedy his situation, setting off on 10 August (with official permission) to France, initially to wait on Henrietta Maria, the Queen Mother, but chiefly to visit Anjou, to court and marry a young widow whom he must have known a few years before in Paris, Henrietta-Maria du Tremblay (probably a Catholic, like Anne), who was presumably to provide him with money as well as two more stepsons.

They moved with his daughter and other stepsons into Rutland House, near Charterhouse Yard, the former home of the Earl of Rutland (father-in-law to the Duke of Buckingham), for whom he had written an elegy back in 1632; it had been seized from the Catholic Dowager Countess by the new government, but was now leased to him. The couple may have been back in London by 14 September 1655, when soldiers raided the Red Bull Tavern Theatre and seized the properties and costumes of the actors, and the audience members who could not pay the fine of five shillings. *The Weekly Intelligencer* concluded that 'the Tragedy of the Actors, and the Spectators, was the Comedy of the soldiers.' A ballad commented:

> The poor and the rich,
> The whore and the bitch,
>   Were every one at a losse,
> But the Players were all
> Turn'd (as weakest) to the wall,
>   And 'tis thought had the greatest losse.

Undeterred, Davenant pushed on with his theatrical ambitions, and even put on a few pieces in halls here and there,[4] as is suggested by a ballad of March 1656, entitled, *How Daphne pays his Debts*.[5] The ballad mocked the financial failure of *Gondibert*:

> Quoth he, I now have made my book,
> A fam'd Heroick Poem,
> For which I'm promis'd so many pounds,
> That I know not where to bestow 'em ...

> But when this *book* it did come forth,
> As some have given a hinting,
> The gains of his pitifull *Poetry*
> Scarce paid for paper and printing ...

Creditors pursued him:

> At the months end they come again,
> Molesting him like Devils,
> *Well, now I'le pay you all*, quoth he,
> *I must be master o'th'Revels*,
>
> *The State hath promis'd this to me ...*

He was pipped to the post for this, but, undeterred, set up a new venture:

> *Already I have hir'd a house,*
> *Wherein to sing and dance,*
> *And now the ladies shall have Masques*
> *Made a la mode de France.*

The ballad provides some information:

> Now in these houses he hath men,
> And cloathes to make them trim;
> For six good friends of his laid out
> Six thousand pounds for him.

Whether or not it was as much as this, which seems exaggerated, he and one William Cutler and some others banded together to finance 'a structure for representational shows', near Charterhouse Square, but the plan fell through. Instead, he used his own home, Rutland House, and on Friday, 23 May 1656 he put on *The First Days Entertainment at Rutland House, by Declamations and Musick, after the manner of the Antients* (*Dramatic Works* Vol. III). This 'Entertainment' – not to be confused with a play! – was put on in what an official report called 'a clap-board scene' in a narrow hall, with a stage at the end and musicians set above in a curtained gallery, with a purple and gilt curtain and two side platforms for

the audience of 150, rather like a college chapel. A Prologue apologized
for the seating arrangements:

> though you cannot front our cup-board scene,
> Nor sit so eas'ly as to stretch and lean,
> Yet you are so divided and so plac'd,
> That half are freely by the other fac'd ...
> Think this your passage, and the narrow way
> To our Elizian field, the *Opera*.

('Opera' was a fairly uncommon word in England at the time; in his
diary, John Evelyn records going to one in Italy in 1644.) The curtain and
painted backcloth might have reminded some of the audience of masques;
the musical performers were distinguished, including Henry Lawes and
'Captain' Henry Cooke, who had been a chorister in the King's chapel.
Episodes were punctuated by songs, the lyrics by Davenant, of course. The
main feature was a debate between Diogenes and Aristophanes, seated,
and dressed as it was thought Ancient Greek philosophers might dress,
who spoke respectively against and for 'public entertainment by moral
representation'. Unexciting as this might seem, it was crucial: whether
drama might provide moral entertainment, and what form it might take.
Diogenes attacked the use of imitation, the deceitful arts of music, poetry
and stage scenery ('which is, to be entertain'd with the description of
motion, and transposition of Lights'), and Aristophanes defended them
all, in turn attacking Diogenes:

> This discontented Cynick would turn all time into midnight, and all
> Learning into melancholy Magick. He is so offended at mirth, as if
> he would accuse even Nature her self to want gravity, for bringing in
> the Spring so merrily with the Musick of Birds.

The episode concluded with a song, asserting, 'The Poets they are wise'
and suggesting,

> Can Age ere do them harm
> Who chearfully grow old?
> Mirth keeps their hearts still warm.
> Fooles think themselves safe in sorrow and cold.[6]

More obviously entertaining was a debate between a Parisian and a Londoner as to the defects of the other's city (his wife may have contributed here). The Parisian, speaking in comic broken English, criticizes London's dark, narrow streets, 'where the Garrets ... are so made, that opposite Neighbours may shake hands without stirring from home', as well as the bad food and drink, the football played in the streets and the severe treatment of children, to whom 'you are so terrible', and teach only 'Bashfulness', 'as if youth were a crime, or, as if you had a greater quarrel to Nature then to the Devil'. The Londoner denounces the French tall, cramped houses and flea-ridden beds, and French cooks, 'Embroiderers of Meat who (though by education cholerick and loud) are ever in profound contemplation; that is, they are considering how to reform the mistakes of Nature in the original composition of Flesh and Fish ... at Feasts, when I uncover a Dish, I think I feed on a very *Epigram.*' The episode concludes with a song about London's 'sulph'rous fires' cooled by the Thames, contrasted with the non-tidal Seine and lack of a 'Ship at Sea'. It all seemed to have gone quite well. One evening in 1664, when his young French wife (née Elizabeth de St Michel) was unwell, Pepys read to her, 'with great mirth', 'Sir W. Davenents two speeches in dispraise of London and Paris', to cheer her up.

The authorities having condoned this exercise, which ran for several days, Davenant could now venture further; but always he had to be sure to be on good terms with those with influence. In November 1656, the daughter of the Puritan statesman, Henry Lawrence, got married and Davenant soon wrote an *Epithalamium.*[7] This poem, by a noted royalist Court poet writing for Parliamentarian grandees of the new Commonwealth, circles around some very sensitive political metaphors and recent history. Thus, the bridegroom becomes a king, crowned by his bride, who

> though she cannot well depose
> The sov'raign Prince whom she has chose,
> Yet she awhile can kill him with a frown.

As 'Loves King and Queen' they have their court, attended by the poet as priest of the marriage god, Hymen. He warns them not to be too extreme or exalted in their love,

For *Hymen*'s Common-weale cannot dispense
In private with Monarchick excellence.
When singularly good you strive to be
   Then will the marry'd Populace
   Cry, Libertie! And soon deface
Your vertue to preserve their Vices free.

Excess of any kind by rulers provokes resentment – 'an excessive purity of Love /Unarmes you to invite offence.' Perhaps his point is, that a new royalty has arrived.

A year later, in December 1657, when he was busy buttering up influential Parliamentarians for his next theatrical plans, he included in the Stationers' Register an extremely lengthy eulogy addressed to 'My Lord Broghill'. This was Roger Boyle, then Baron Broghill, who had initially campaigned in Ireland for the Royalist cause, and then under Cromwell. Whether this poem ever appeared publicly is not known – it seems unlikely, in view of the developing political situation. Indeed, with the Restoration, Boyle went back to the Royalist camp and again dealt with Irish rebels (possibly different ones), and was rewarded by Charles II with the Earldom of Orrery. In the posthumous volume of Davenant's verse, *Poems on Several Occasions* (1672) appeared 'Poem to the Earl of Orrery',[8] substantially the same poem with a different title and tactful changes to remove any anti-royalist passages and insert anti-puritan passages, unthinkable in the first, pre-Restoration version. The Orrery version will be discussed later; but in either version, Davenant pointedly insists that 'the most important Things (which are /Empire and Arts) require 'Heav'ns special care' – perhaps especially Boyle's. 'The Muses' are essential, especially in the theatre.

With a specific instance of theatre in mind, on 3 September 1656, he wrote to his old friend Bulstrode Whitelocke, now risen to Lord Commissioner of the Treasurer, with the script of his new venture: 'My Lord, when I consider the Nicety of the Times, I fear it may draw a Curtain between your Lordship and our Opera; therefore I have presumed to send your Lordship, hot from the Presse, what we mean to represent, making your Lordship my supreme Judge.'[9] The piece was approved, as Whitelocke dryly noted, 'notwithstanding the nicety of the Times', and Davenant could go ahead.

This was what was to be one of his most important, and most successful, theatrical enterprises, what Dryden later called the first English opera, *The Siege of Rhodes: A Representation by the Art of Prospective in Scenes, And the Story Sung in Recitative Musick.* (*Dramatic Works*, Vol. III). He again used part of his own house, Rutland House, but what had been just sufficient room for his earlier effort, now proved distinctly cramped for his new scenery, cast and musicians. In his printed prologue, dated 17 August 1656, he apologized for the 'narrowness of the room', complaining that

> It has been often wisht that our Scene (we having oblig'd ourselves to the Ancient Dramatic distinctions made for time) had not been confin'd to eleven foot in height, and about fifteen in depth, including the places of passage reserv'd for the Musick. This is so narrow an allowance for the fleet of Solyman the Magnificent, his army, the Island of *Rhodes* and the varieties attending the Siege of the City, that I fear you will think we invite you to such a contracted trifle as that of the *Caesars* carved upon a pin.

Despite these constrictions, Davenant invested in quality ('O costly *Opera!*' he remarked in his Lawrence epithalamium). He had been accustomed to elaborate scenery in masques and French staging; now, perhaps for the first time in English theatre, there was pictorial scenery with painted backcloths and scene changes. Design was by no less than the former assistant and successor to Inigo Jones, John Webb; music was of major importance, again provided by distinguished musicians – Henry Lawes, Charles Coleman and others generally familiar with the fashionable Italian style. He apologized for the limited cast (seven in the original version; a few more were available later), some of whom did double duty as musicians and performers in the Entries. Coleman played the hero, Alphonso, and his wife Catherine played the heroine, Ianthe – so becoming the first identified woman to act upon an English stage. The dialogue, in rhyming lines of varying length, rather like contemporary Italian libretti, was performed largely in recitative, with each scene – or Entry – concluding with a chorus, often quite cheery. After the initial success in Rutland House, Davenant was able to transfer to the production, including the expensive scenery, to the Cockpit Theatre in Drury Lane (dismantled in 1649 but refitted two years later), again perhaps through the good offices of Whitelocke.

The story was based ultimately on the siege of Rhodes by the Turkish Sultan, Solyman the Great, in 1522, when a multi-national Christian force of some 600 resisted many thousands of Turks. In the sixteenth and seventeenth centuries there was great and apprehensive interest in the Ottoman Empire, then at its peak and extending through the Middle East, the Levant and the Barbary Coast and northwards as far as the walls of Vienna. Turks and Moors figured in scores of plays, such as *The Jew of Malta*, *Titus Andronicus* and *Othello*. A major source of information was *The Generall Historie of the Turkes*, by Richard Knolles, of 1603, together with Thomas Artus's *Continuation de l'Histoire des Turcs* of 1612. Davenant's plays – for the success in 1656 led to a Part II in 1661 – dealt with the war and heroic military material well enough, but the main dramatic interest was in a familiar Cavalier topic, the relationship between Love and Honour. An important element also – not for the first time in Davenant – was consideration of the uncertain relationship between ruler and ruled, and the need for rulers to be responsive to popular wishes.

An earlier version and source of the heroic-romantic story is Thomas Kyd's tragedy of 1592, *Soliman and Perseda*. There, Erastus and Perseda are lovers in Rhodes, but become separated; he joins the Turks, befriends Soliman and helps in the attack on Rhodes. When Perseda is brought to Soliman, he falls in love with her, but, learning that she and Erastus are in love, honourably gives her to Erastus, and they return to Rhodes. However, unable to subdue his love for her, Soliman has Erastus killed and returns to attack Rhodes in an attempt to win Perseda. At the last, Perseda, dressed as a man, dies fighting to defend the city, and Soliman also dies. Davenant retains much of the story: his heroine, Ianthe, also defends Rhodes dressed as a soldier, while Solyman is less lustful and more civilized in Western fashion. Love set against Honour is important, but also a French concern, an emphasis on Reason, that should be superior to such passions as love, anger or jealousy.

*Rhodes I* opens with a picture of the city with the Turkish fleet approaching. Villerius, the Grand Master of Rhodes, complains of the coming war and the demands of his military advisers, who, like the military leaders on both sides in the Civil War, are keener on confrontation,

> Who measure not the compass of a crown
> To fit the head that wears it, but their own;
> Still hind'ring peace, because they stewards are
> Without account, to that wild spender, war.

(All survivors of the war knew the heavy cost of the fighting.) Alphonso, a newly wed Sicilian knight, is present, and refuses to return to his new bride, Ianthe, feeling that Honour requires him to stay and fight. As Cavalier Lovelace had earlier stressed the priority of Honour over Love, so Alphonso insists that Cavalier women are of the same mind:

> Honour is colder virtue set on fire:
> My honour lost, her love would soon decay:
> Here for my tomb or triumph I will stay.

Likewise, in Sicily, Ianthe is eager to go to Rhodes, and sell her jewels, 'the spawn of shells, and warts of rocks', rather as Henrietta Maria sold her jewellery for war munitions. The Chorus is indifferent to money:

> Wealth the least of our care is,
>     For the Poor n'er are undone;

(Except for their limbs and lives, as once he knew)

> *A vous, Monsieur* of *Paris,*
>     To the Back-Swords of London.

In the second entry, Rhodes is under heavy siege, the Christians fighting bravely, Alphonso especially, as 'the cheerful English get renown'. As Solyman laments Turkish losses, Mustapha brings in captured Ianthe; Solyman is immediately smitten with her courage and beauty, and lets her go to Rhodes. In the city, the women also commit themselves to the battle, giving up their fashions for 'the cold, cold bed of Honour', like the London townswomen who helped dig the defences of Turnham Green against the Royalists in 1642:

> Hence with our Needles, and give us your Spades;
> We, that were Ladies, grow course as our Maids.
> Our Coaches have drove us to Balls at the Court;
> We now must drive Barrows to earth up the Port.

In the third entry, Islam's prophets and the momentum of war drive on Solyman – 'Empire must move apace, /When she begins the race' – while he still expresses concern for Ianthe and her honourable beloved Alphonso. In Rhodes, Ianthe praises Solyman's courteous Western manners towards her: 'He seem'd [as though] in civil France; and monarch there'; Alphonso recognizes Solyman's generosity in returning her, when 'she was his own by right of war', but is growing jealous. Switching back to the Turkish camp, we now, in the later, 'Enlarg'd' Restoration version (published with Part II in 1663), encounter Solyman's queen, the redoubtable Roxolana, now also jealous of the effect of Ianthe, who, she fears, 'now has got that heart which I have lost'.

In the next entry, Solyman is still fretting over Ianthe and Alphonso, the ideal, honourable lovers. In Rhodes, that is being overcome, it is suggested that Ianthe go to plead for a treaty, but Alphonso is jealous. She says that it is he who is false, in suspecting her: 'Could Solyman both life and honour give? /And can Alphonso me of both deprive?' This does not help matters, as Alphonso's increasing jealousy overcomes his Reason, inciting wild attacks on the Turks. In turn, Roxolana suspects that Solyman's eagerness to enter Rhodes is to get to Ianthe: 'He follows passion, I pursue my reason. /He loves the traitor, and I hate the treason.' The Chorus, four voices in recitative, contemplate

> This cursed Jealousie, what is't?
> 'Tis Love that has lost itself in a Mist …
> 'Tis rich corrupted wine of Love,
> Which sharpest vinegar does prove.

It concludes, slightly absurdly,

> It never can sleep, and dreams still awake,
> It stuffs up the Marriage bed with thorns!
> It gores itself, it gores itself, with imagin'd horns.

The final assault takes place, with fierce commands for off-stage action: 'Traverse the cannon! Mount the batt'ries higher! ... That battlement is loose, and straight will down! ... Point well the cannons, and play fast.' The Rhodians defence is weakening; Ianthe among the defenders is wounded; Alphonso is urged to withdraw to set up further defences, but now Duty and Reason are set against Honour and Love. The Turks have not yet overcome; Ianthe and Alphonso, also wounded, are reconciled, and Solyman and Roxolana manage a more limited reconciliation, as he resolves to starve the Rhodians into submission.

The Chorus, however, provides a cheery, triumphant conclusion, mocking the Turks, how although

> With a fine merry Gale
>   Fit to fill ev'ry Sayl,
> They did cut the smooth Sea
> That our Skins they might flea –

(flea: flay. Turks were notorious for flaying alive their prisoners, notably the Venetian commander of Cyprus in 1570; his skin, neatly folded in an urn, is preserved in Venice to this day)

> Still as they landed we firkt them with Sallys,
>   We did bring their silk Shashes
>   Through Sands and through Plashes,
> Till amain they did run to their Gallies.

The Chorus goes on to claim that

> Then the hug'ous great *Turk*
> Came to make us more work,
> With enow men to eat
> All he meant to defeat.

This may be a suggestion of non-European cannibalism; or simply a joke, like that in *Henry V* about the Dauphin longing 'to eat the English'. At the end, they point out that Alphonso has kept his Ianthe, and the Turks have been held off, 'While we drink good Wine, and you drink but Coffy.'

This musical drama having been a success, Davenant went further, to please the authorities, as well as a wider audience. Following Cromwell's renewed campaign against the Spanish, and Robert Blake's sinking of sixteen Spanish ships off the Canaries in April 1657, his next production, performed in the restored old Cockpit Theatre in July 1658, of *The Cruelty of the Spaniards in Peru*, was well chosen. His old enemy, Henry Herbert, was to complain that it was put on 'in Oliuers tyme, and soly in his favour, wherein he sett of the justice of Oliuers actinges by comparison with the Spanish and endeauored thereby to make Oliuers cruelty appear mercys, in respect of the Spanish crueltys; but the mercys of the wicked are cruell'.[10]

*Cruelty*, an odd, populist exercise, based partly on *The Teares of the Indians* (translated by John Phillips), and dedicated to Cromwell, consisted of tableaux and mimed actions interspersed with music and songs by way of comment; extra entertainment was provided by interspersed gymnastic performances – the 'Somerset', 'Sea-Horse', 'Spring', 'Self- Spring', the 'Porpoise'; a printed text provided an explanation. After a 'wild symphony', the first backcloth image, conflating darkest Peru with the West Indies, depicted a wood with 'Coco-trees, Pines and Palmitos', with 'Munkies, Apes and Parrots', and, on a flat further back, 'Vallies of Sugar-Canes'.

The Chief Priest appears in feathers, with a sun image on his breast. A song on their society's lack of riches, cities, forts and even clothes suggests that Davenant, like Shakespeare's Gonzago, had read Montaigne, probably in Florio's translation. He declares,

> Whilst yet our world was new,
> When not discover'd by the old;
> E're begger'd slaves we grew,
> For having Silver Hills, and Strands of Gold,
> We danc'd and we sung,
> And lookt ever young,
> And from restraints were free,
> As waves and winds at Sea.

After a dance, when two apes dance on a taut, stretched rope, the next entry depicts the arrival of the Spanish fleet, with the Peruvians amazed and fleeing. One speech might be seen as directed at severe puritans:

'What Race is this, who for our punishment /Pretend that they in haste from Heav'n were sent /As just destroyers of Idolatry?' A song recognizes their doom at the hands of these oppressors, a dance expresses horror. Now follows Peruvian civil war, resulting from a disputed succession consequent upon an Inca taking a second wife: 'But Kings who move / Within a lowly sphear of private love /Are too domestick for a Throne'. The war is presented through martial music and dance. Then the Peruvians are shown routed by a smaller Spanish force; the Peruvians lament, and the Spanish dance their victory (with 'castanietos').

After 'a doleful pavane', images present prisons, with basting of an Incan prince over a fire, and torture of natives and some newly-arrived English mariners ('which may be suppos'd to be lately landed there to discover the Coast'), as a speech declares the Spaniards' reaction to non-Catholic newcomers:

> ... other Christian strangers landing here,
> Strait to their jealous sight, as spies appear,
> And think they so much worse than heathens deem,
>   That they must tortur'd die.
>   The world still waste must lye,
> Or else a prison be to all but them.

The fifth song, following the theme of Spanish cruelty, also seems to echo Montaigne on human depravity by contrast with animals' instinct (as in *Gondibert*):

> When Beasts each other chase and then devour,
>   'Tis Natures Law, necessity,
> Which makes them hunt for food, & not for pow'r:
> Men for Dominion, Art's chief vanity,
>   Contrive to make men die;
> Whose blood through wantonness they spil,
> Not having use of what they kill.

The Peruvians are shown as laden and beaten, and forced to dance. The final episode shows an English and Peruvian army defeating the Spanish. At this point, the commentary has to admit that this is sheer fantasy: 'These imaginary English forces may seem improper, because the English had made no discovery of Peru, in the time of the Spaniard's first invasion there; but yet in poetical representations of this nature, it may pass as a vision discerned by the Priest of the Sun, before the matter was extant, in order to his prophecy.' A speech looks forward to a future when

> Those whom the insulting Spaniards scorn,
>     And slaves esteem,
> The English soon shall free;
>     Whilst we the Spaniards see
> Digging for them.

The priest's attendant now performs a double somersault; the apes and 'a great Baboon perform a wild dance', the Incans and English also dance and the Spanish do them homage, before a final grand dance. The natives are created as noble and innocent, abused by the Catholic Spanish, and the English as heroic liberators. Like his contemporaries, Davenant portrays America as a land of opportunity, here laden with gold and silver, available for exploitation (like Madagascar). In the context of the current Cromwellian conflict with Spain, this jingoistic quasi-pantomime contributed to the campaign for 'Empire' and primacy over Spain.

Having looked to an improbable heroic future, Davenant then turned back to a heroic Protestant English past, equally anti-Hispanic, when Sir Francis Drake had harried the Spanish in Panama in 1572, with the assistance of the native Cimaroon tribesmen. Despite some puritan unease in Parliament directed at his shows, – in February 1659 the Lords ordered an inquiry into such goings-on, and in April the Commons discussed them[11] – he went ahead with *The History of Sir Francis Drake* (registered in January 1659 and performed a few months later in the Cockpit), based on *Sir Francis Drake Reviv'd* (1626), a much more full-blooded, jingoistic theatrical experience, with noises off, a ship with moving sails, scenery and dramatic action, but still divided by entries rather than acts. This, with *Peru*, was later incorporated in *The Playhouse to be Let* (*Dramatic Works*, Vol. IV).

In the first entry, after a saraband, Captain Rouse tells Drake's son how he has captured a Spanish 'carvel', and intends to pursue the Spanish inland. The Chorus is optimistic: 'That which enlightens, and does lead

/The world, and all that our vict'ries breed, /We in those caverns shall behold, /In seeing man's light mistress, gold.' The second entry pictures the rocky country of the Symerons, with former Moorish slaves made to work in the mines, but now rebellious. The English arrive, as the steersman sings a rousing song:

> Aloof! and aloof! and steady I steer!
>> 'Tis a Boat to our wish,
>> And she slides like a Fish,
> When chearily stem'd, and when you row clear.
>> She now has her trimme!
>> Away let her swim.
> Mackerels are swift in the shine of the Moon;
>> And Herrings in Gales when they wind us,
> But, timeing our Oars, so smoothly we run,
>> That we leave them in shoals behind us.

The Chorus of oarsmen join in:

>> Then cry, One and all!
>> Amain for *Whitehall*!
> The *Diegos* wee'll board to rummidge their Hould;
> And drawing our Steel, they must draw out their Gold.

The steersman looks forward to their successful attack:

> Our Master and's Mate, with Bacon and pease,
>> In Cabins keep aboard,
>> Each as warm as a Lord:
> No Queen, lying in, lies more at her ease.
>> Whilst we lie in wait
>> For Reals of Eight,
> And for some Gold Quoits, which fortune must send.
>> But, alas, how their ears will tingle,
> When finding, though still like *Hectors* we spend,
>> Yet still all our pockets shall jingle ...

The king of the Symerons welcomes Drake with song and dance ('The Lord of the Sea is welcome to Land … his Name more Alarms /The Spaniards then Trumpets or Drums'), and provides one Pedro as a guide, as four Symerons 'dance a Morisco', followed by a chorus of mariners 'within'. The next two entries show a Symeron town and feast, and Drake and Pedro ordering the marching. Pedro climbs a tall tree, with a view of the Pacific; Drake remarks that 'No English keel hath yet that Ocean ploughed', and Pedro replies, 'If prophecy from me may be allow'd, / Renowned Drake, Heav'n does decree /That happy enterprise to thee.' The Chorus confirms this, hinting at more to come: 'This prophecy will rise /To higher enterprise. /The English Lion's walk shall reach as far /As prosp'rous valour dares adventure war.'

A later entry has the Symerons capture a Peruvian bride (Davenant conflates Panama with Peru), who is shown tied to a tree, awaiting Symeron reprisals for Spanish atrocities. Drake is shocked: 'Arm! arm! the honour of my nation turns /To shame, when an afflicted beauty mourns.' In response, he promises that 'No length of studied torments shall suffice /To punish all unmanly cruelties'. The bride's father and groom dance to express their gratitude.

The final entry begins with martial music, showing Panama in the distance with columns of mules laden with 'Wedges of Silver and Ingots of Gold'. Offstage noises indicate clashing of arms, as the English and Symerons defeat the Spanish. The show ends with a general triumphant chorus and grand celebratory dance.

Davenant's three 'operas' were generally popular, but not everyone was impressed. On 5 May, the diarist John Evelyn (no puritan, but orthodoxly minded) wrote that he went 'to see a new opera, after the Italian way, in recitative music and scenes, much inferior to the Italian composure and magnificence; but it was prodigious that in a time of such public consternation such a vanity should be kept up or permitted. I, being engaged with company, could not decently resist the going to see it, though my heart smote me for it.' The times were indeed of political 'consternation' and insecurity; in August 1659, Davenant was briefly in prison again, suspected (probably only on account of his record) of involvement in a Royalist plot, but was released soon after.[12]

In considering Davenant's 'popular-heroic' performances, that enabled his next major enterprise, the revised and expanded second version of *The*

*Siege of Rhodes*, it is appropriate at this point to quote from John Dryden's essay *Of Heroic Plays*, of 1672.

> The first sight we had of them, on the English theatre, was from the late Sir William D'Avenant. It being forbidden him in the rebellious times to act tragedies and comedies, because they contained matter of scandal to those good people, who could more easily dispossess their lawful sovereign than endure a wanton jest, he was forced to turn his thoughts another way, and to introduce the examples of moral virtue, writ in verse, and performed in recitative music. The original of this music, and of the scenes which adorned his work, he had from the Italian operas; but he heightened his characters (as I may probably imagine) from the example of Corneille and some French poets. In this condition did this part of poetry remain at His Majesty's return … We who come after him have received the advantage from that excellent groundwork which he laid.[13]

Now, with the crumbling of the Parliamentarian régime under Richard Cromwell, it was time to look to the future.

# Chapter 11

# Restoration Theatre Restoration (1660–1662)

In response to the gathering crisis, and feelers from royalists in England and on the continent, the Parliamentarian General George Monck and his army marched slowly down from Scotland. John Aubrey later heard that 'he had no more intended the Kings restauration, when he came into England, or first came to London, then his Horse did'. Be that as it may, on 11 February 1660, Monck presented Parliament with ultimatums demanding the recall of Members excluded in 1648 and the dissolution of the Rump Parliament, which effectively marked the end of Parliamentary rule as it stood. He was elected head of a new Council, but declined the offer of supreme power for himself. There was wild rejoicing in the city, as Pepys recorded: 'a great many bonefires, and Bow bells and all the bells in all the churches ... were ringing.'

Clearly, at this juncture it would be a good idea to write something to welcome, and attract the attention of, the new great man. Davenant's new poem, 'To his Excellency the Lord General Monck'[1] came out promptly in March 1660. The opening paragraph celebrates Monck's 'triumphant night' and the city bonfires, while attacking the 'fiery Sects' and 'the Fanatick party'. Praise of Monck's moderation is followed by a surprising main concern of the poem, criticism of the jargonistic language of the dissenters, characterized by 'Scripture-phrase', contrasted with Monck's plain diction (the product of a plain mind):

> You can converse, and in a dialect
> Where no strange dress makes us the truth suspect ...
> They write the style of Spirits, you of Men;
> Yet are their Swords less powerful then your Pen.

The poem concludes with hopes for Monck's future rule, and a significant pun:

> In doubtful Battails we may trust your Sword,
> And in suspected Factions take your word.

On March 17, Davenant obtained a pass to travel to France,[2] presumably to join the royal party at the Château des Colombes, with the Queen and Jermyn. Charles himself sailed from Scheveningen, the harbour for The Hague, in *The Royal Charles*, an 80-gun three-decker, previously named by Parliament as the *Naseby*; the rest of the accompanying flotilla had also been renamed: the *James*, named after Prince James, had been the *Richard* for Richard Cromwell, the *Speaker* (of the House of Commons) became the *Mary*, for Charles's sister; and so on. Charles landed at Dover on 25 May, accompanied by Pepys and Thomas Killigrew, described by Pepys as 'a merry droll, but a gentleman of great esteem with the king', whose sister had borne Charles a daughter, and who was to be Davenant's great rival in the London theatre, and an incontinent dog. Charles was welcomed by Monck, Buckingham, the Mayor (with a Bible for Charles to kiss, which he declared was the thing he best loved in the world) and a good-sized crowd. After his triumphant arrival in London on 29 May, his birthday, to general though not universal rapture, it was time for grovelling welcomes. John Dryden produced a poem, *Astraea Redux*, proclaiming the return of justice and peace:

> At home the hateful names of parties cease,
> And factious souls are wearied into peace ...
> Oh happy age! Oh times like these alone ...
> When the joint growth of arms and arts foreshow
> The world a monarch, and that monarch you.

Davenant followed up in August with a lengthy panegyric (302 lines), 'Poem upon His Sacred Majesties most happy Return to his Dominions'.[3] It was a good chance to remind the King of his availability as a versifying publicist. It was as well to do this, in these early days. As it was, he had been heard complaining of the King's initial lack of forgiveness, as in his refusal to accept Davenant's old friend, the poet Abraham Cowley, even refusing to let him kiss his hand. The King's secretary, Sir Edward Nicholas, heard of 'an imprudent discourse ... from one that pretends to witt, but might very well have more discretion or loyalty, viz. *Sir Wm.*

*Davenant*.[4] Some tactful ingratiation was in order – whatever he may have once written to Benlowes – if he was to get on at all.

Accordingly, the early part of the poem praises the King's merciful forgiveness, inherited from the martyred *'perfect Father'* – who apparently punished his judges by letting them live (not that this king would). Davenant then turns to the 'restoration' of the Church, now to be unified. Priests will therefore no longer 'in *divided shapes* that *Garment* tear' (a reference to Christ's seamless garment, in *John* IX.23). There will no longer be any questioning of the King's standing army. Royal power will combine with Law to restore the privileges of the wealthy, as

> ... onely *Arm'd Pow'r* can *Law* protect,
> And rescue *Wealth* from Crowds, when *Poverty*
> Treads down those Laws on which the *Rich* rely.

Law is only for the benefit of the rich; there is no sympathy expressed for the poor. No contemporary radical – such as a Leveller – could have put it more bluntly. It seems that Davenant saw the situation clearly; it is not clear what he made of it ('but he who hath ears to hear, let him hear'). The expropriation of the many is presented as being for their own good:

> Yet *Law*, where Kings are arm'd, rescues the *Crowd*
> Even from themselves, when *Plenty* makes them proud.

The aristocracy will no longer respond to public feeling, but adhere to the Crown. The public at large fund the King, who, gratifyingly, in turn provides added value through his royal descent and virtues. (At this time, royal expenditure greatly exceeded income.)

Now the poem turns to celebrating the King's virtues: Clemency (again); *'Judgement* deeper than the Sun' and Thought, that can quickly grasp and make cohere 'all objects of the Sun'. Valour follows, with praise of his conduct at the losing battle at Worcester in 1651. Now he praises the shrewdness of ready forgiveness of anti-royalists and defence of the slow payment of recompense for deprived royalists (teaching them patience, a traditional virtue): an allusion to the forthcoming Act of Indemnity and Oblivion, intended as a unifying gesture (though described by Whitehall discontents as an act of indemnity for the King's enemies and oblivion for his friends). People generally will be of one mind with the King, doing only what they ought, in 'great forgiving till no Laws we need'; his agents will be alert to deal with any disaffection, to

> Watch the first Clouds e're storms of Rebels rise.
> Though *Orators* (the Peoples *Witches*) may
> Raise higher Tempests then their skills may lay –

for even Parliament's orators might not be wholly submissive –

> Making a civil and staid *Senate* rude.

Only obedience is acceptable. As for the reformed, unified, determinedly episcopal Church of England (the Act of Uniformity would be passed in May 1662), everyone shall submit, paying tithes to the 'sacred' Anglican priests (who, in a neat blurring of God and Charles, are ambassadors for 'that King' and 'bright Palace'). 'To these we shall with rev'rence Off'rings make,' even though others, from Baptists and Quakers to Catholics, all resented this imposition, as Davenant knew. Custom apparently sanctifies this practice.

The poem now celebrates the King's father, mother, 'heroick Brothers' and sister, before concluding by presenting itself as the instrument for publicizing the King's achievements, instructing Fame, through this, to

> ascend, and strait dispense
> (As far as ever *Thou* wert led by *Verse*,
> Or *Light* ere flew) my *Sov'raign's* full renown.

The poem has done its job as a panegyric, to flatter and support the new authority (while not unaware of future problems), and demonstrate its author's suitability as Royal Public Relations Poet (whatever his real thoughts might be). Despite this, it was not obvious that Davenant was ever to be more than on the outer orbits of the new Court's solar system – he was (rightly) not considered sufficiently 'sound'. He was to make only one more significant poetic engagement to engage with the King, in 1663; meanwhile, he had other, more satisfying ways of making a living.

First of all, there was the theatre situation to be settled, especially as Thomas Killigrew – a notably disreputable friend of Charles's from the European Court days – had got in ahead, getting a warrant from the King on 9 July to form the King's Company of players, while John Rhodes, a bookseller, had a company at the Cockpit (Pepys saw *The Loyal Subject* there on 18 August), Michael Mohun, a veteran actor who had served in the war, had a company at the old Red Bull Theatre in Clerkenwell, and the actor William Beeston was at Salisbury Court.[5]

Davenant got together with Killigrew, and on 19 July, drafted a document for the Attorney General for him to prepare a Bill for Killigrew and himself to set up two playhouses and companies, and, crucially and shrewdly, that 'there shall be no more places of Representations or Companys of Actors', so that 'all others shal be absolutely suppressed' (a duopoly that would please authorities wanting more control). On 21 August 1660, the grant was approved, with the important proviso requiring the two managers 'to peruse all playes that have been formerly written, and to expunge all Prophaneness and Scurrility from the same, before they be represented or Acted'.[6] This moral censorship should have pleased Sir Henry Herbert, now returned to the Office of Revels, except that he saw it as encroaching on his prerogatives. He had had a nice little arrangement going, of £150 a year, with an agreement with Mohun to be paid 40 shillings for every new play approved, and 20 shillings for every old play, plus £4 a week of performance, He now initiated a lawsuit against Killigrew and Davenant, for conspiring to undermine the Office of the Revels; in February 1662 they were acquitted, with costs. (While this was going on, on 26 November 1660, Davenant applied to be Master of the Revels in Ireland, but was disappointed when John Ogilby – whose *Aesop* he had praised in 1651 – got the position in May 1661.)[7] Interestingly, the Royal patent also demanded,

For as much as many plays formerly acted do contain several profane, obscene and scurrilous passages, and the women's parts therein have been acted by men in the habit of women, at which some have taken offence, for the preventing of these abuses for the future, we do hereby strictly command and enjoin that from henceforth ... that all the women's parts to be acted ... for the time to come may be performed by women, so long as their recreations, which by reason of the abuses foresaid were scandalous and offensive, may by such reformation be esteemed, not only harmless delight, but useful and instructive representations of human life.

Nothing could be more moral and sensible. The reality might be somewhat different.

While their theatres and companies were being sorted out, Killigrew and Davenant combined, from 8 to 16 October 1660, to put on plays at the Cockpit (Pepys saw productions of plays by John Fletcher, and, on 11 October, *Othello*, when 'a very pretty lady that sot by me cried to see Desdimona smothered'). Then, in early November, they made their division. Killigrew kept actors from Mohun's company, and the excellent young Edward Kynaston (brilliant at female parts) from Rhodes's company, and prepared to perform as The King's Company at the converted Gibbons's Tennis Court in Vere Street, in rather cramped conditions with no scenery and using leftover props. Davenant agreed with Henry Harris, a good actor and 'painter' (useful in scenery designing and painting), Thomas Betterton, who was to prove the star actor in Restoration theatre, and eight others from Rhodes's company, to perform as The Duke's Company, with the Duke of York as patron. His intention was to convert Lisle's Tennis Court, at Salisbury Court, off Fleet Street (shrewdly, he had entered into a contract to lease the building two months before, for the purpose of converting it into a playhouse).

Killigrew, with less work to do, was able to kick off promptly, first at the Red Bull and then, on 8 November, at his new theatre, with *Henry IV, Part One*. On 19 November, the first performance of a play at the new Court took place, when his company performed Ben Jonson's *Epicoene, or the Silent Woman*, starring Kynaston (when Pepys saw him, on 7 January 1661, he declared that he 'was clearly the prettiest woman in the whole house'). Davenant, the Poet Laureate, wrote the Prologue, insisting on the almost symbiotic relationship of Crown and Stage:

> Greatest of Monarchs, welcome to this place
> Which *Majesty* so oft was wont to grace
> Before our Exile, to divert the Court,
> This truth we can to our advantage say,
> They that would have no King, would have no *Play*:

The *Laurel* and the *Crown* together went,
Had the same *Foes*, and the same *Banishment*.[8]

The company had a busy time: on the same day they performed Davenant's *The Unfortunate Lovers* at Vere Street, and, the next day, Fletcher's and Massinger's *The Beggars Bush* (however could the actors do it?). The pace was relentless: Pepys – already a theatre addict (his diary an invaluable source of information on Restoration theatre) – recorded five different productions by the King's Company from then until 31 December, and six more in the following January. On 8 December, Killigrew put on *Othello* again. In the prologue, written by actor/playwright Thomas Jordan, the speaker admitted the problems of men acting women characters:

> For to speak truth, men act, that are between
> Forty and fifty, wenches of fifteen:
> With bones so large and nerve so compliant,
> When yous call Desdemona, *enter* giant.

Now, however, there was to be a novelty, in accordance with the royal command:

> I come, unknown to any of the rest;
> To tell the news: I saw the lady drest –
> The woman plays today; mistake me not,
> No man in gown or page in petticoat.[9]

This was the first professional English actress on stage; regrettably, her identity is not known.

Kynaston and his fellows continued with their cross-dressing careers for a few years more. There is a story of the King attending a performance of *Hamlet*, when there was a delay: on being told that Queen Gertrude was not yet shaved, he replied, "Ods fish, I beg her majesty's pardon. We'll wait till her barber has done with her."[10]

Davenant, of course, playing the long game and planning extensive improvements, was initially not doing so well. It was not until 12 December that he was at last granted exclusive rights to a number of plays: much of Shakespeare, including *Romeo and Juliet, Twelfth Night, Measure for Measure*, *Much Ado*, *Hamlet*, *King Lear*, *Macbeth*, *Henry VIII* and *The Tempest*, as well as *The Duchess of Malfi*, Denham's *The Sophy*, several Fletcher plays and even his own plays. He had only a relatively small company of principal players to work with, and a theatre to construct, but he had to get started and get some income.

It was not until 29 January 1661, that Pepys was able to see a Davenant production, of Fletcher's *The Maid in the Mill*, at the Salisbury Court Theatre, where 'after great patience and little expectacions from so poor beginnings [he] saw three acts ... to [his] great content'. An uncertain start. Nevertheless, he was there twice more that month, four times in March and three times in April. It is worth remarking that many of the productions there were of plays by the Jacobean dramatist, John Fletcher, whose comedies and tragi-comedies were amongst the most popular with Restoration audiences (and therefore influential upon other writers). Clearly, they were almost guaranteed box-office material, with assured happy endings, genteel upper-class stories of love and broader lower-class comedy, requiring relatively little adaptation, with special effects and costume displays. Several provided opportunities for women actresses to show off their legs in male costumes, always appreciated by audiences. (When Davenant put on *Cambyses* in 1666, his bookkeeper John Downes noted that 'the first time [Jane Long] appear'd in Man's Habit, prov'd as Beneficial to the Company as several succeeding new plays'. The practice could also prove profitable to the actresses in a private capacity. One, Elizabeth Boutell, told spectators, "Tis worth money that such legs appear, /These are not to be seen so cheap elsewhere.')[11] Audiences, numbering about 350–400, were socially mixed but with a predominant presence of Court and upper classes, though middle classes, such as Pepys, and some of the lower orders were also present (as well as orange-sellers and whores). Performances usually started at about 3.30, with preliminary suites of music and 'act tunes' between the acts.

On St George's Day, the Coronation took place, with great magnificence and pageantry, followed by heavy rain, thunder, lightning and a heroic quantity of popular drinking. Pepys 'wondered to see how the ladies did tipple', fell asleep, and wrote how, when he woke, 'I found myself wet with my spewing. Thus did the day end, with joy everywhere.'

At last, on 28 June 1661, Davenant was able to open his new Duke's Playhouse. His designer, probably John Webb, planned a wooden framework to fit inside the walls of the former tennis court, to support the raised stage – 34 feet deep and 30 feet wide – proscenium arch, painted backcloths, wings and machines to move scenery flats and lower gods in thrones, all familiar to Davenant from Caroline masques. In front was a thrust stage of 9 feet by 20 feet, where actors – and actresses – would be close to the gentlemen 'wits' in the pit, where the loutish rakes sat. Shadwell, in *The Virtuoso* (1676), describes how they 'come drunk and screaming into a playhouse and stand upon the benches, and toss their full periwigs and empty heads, and cry, 'Damme, Jack, this is a damned play, prithee, let's to a whore, Jack.' Wycherley's Mrs Pinchwife observed in 1678 that 'none but naughty women sat there, whom [the men] toused and moused'. The performers had to deliver their lines, not in attentive quiet, but through a barrage of backchat, badinage and occasional brawls. The women of all classes contributed to the general distracting clatter of chatter, flirting with the men, while the orange-sellers offered their wares.

The recessed stage with its scenery provided a pictorial, illusionistic effect, the forward stage, close-range, inter-active engagement, a double experience that was to dominate English theatre for many years. The auditorium was lit by chandeliers and wax candles (more expensive but brighter than tallow candles). To the sides and back were boxes for the quality, where seats might cost four shillings, a middle gallery, where Pepys (and, on occasion, his wife) would sit, and a top gallery.

Behind were a music room and scenery store, and behind that and over the theatre itself was the Davenant household residence, which must have become very crowded in time, with his stepsons, Lady Davenant's increasing offspring – nine in all – together with some young actresses boarded there for their own protection. It is to be hoped that dramatic temperaments were restrained. Outbuildings were used for storage, and there was good access for coaches in Portugal Street.

The Company itself was organized financially [12] by formal agreement into fifteen shares, with ten going to Davenant, including for his 'paines and expences to that purpose for many yeeres', for house rent and maintenance, for provision of costumes and properties, and 'to mainteine all the Women that are to perform or represent Womens partes' (though he did not employ women actresses until the theatre opened). The women came from a variety of backgrounds: a few were from 'good' families come down in the world, victims of the Civil War; some were gentlemen's bastards, some daughters of tradesmen from the servant classes. They worked hard enough, with rehearsals in the morning, performances in the late afternoon – and evenings to make the most of. They included Hester Davenport (later seduced by the Earl of Oxford), Mary Saunderson (who married Thomas Betterton) and Jane Long (former mistress of the Duke of Richmond and then of Endymion Porter's son, George). The Earl of Rochester wrote of her, when imagining the King saying,

> When on Portsmouth's lap I lay my head    [Mlle de Kéroualle]
> And Knight does sing her bawdy song,
> I envy not George Porter's bed,
> Nor the delights of Madam Long.

The remaining shares went to the actors. There were also other theatre staff, including men to take the money, the barber, wardrobe keeper, and general helpers.[13]

When Davenant set out for America in 1650, he took with him as secretary, Thomas Cross, who after the capture in the Channel became secretary to the Governor of Barbados, and then a sort of treasurer for Davenant's pre-Restoration theatre activities. Now Davenant's stepson by Davenant's second marriage, he took over this position for the new company. His complaining deputation before the Court of Chancery in 1684 gives a good idea of what organizing the theatre involved: 'the sole trouble of paying the whole charge of the House weekly that is to say the Salaries of all hireling Players both men and Woemen, Musick Master, Dancing Master, Scene-men, Barbers, Wardrobe keepers, Dorekeepers and Soldiers, besides Bills of all kinds, as for Scenes, Habits, Properties, Candles, Oile and other things, and in making and paying, if called for, all the Dividends of the Sharers.'[14] The expenses involved in converting the old tennis court building into a superior theatre were obviously considerable – the ballad about 'Daphne' and his costs spoke of £6,000, which gives a possible figure; by March 1661 he was having to recoup some of them by selling off shares; but he also gave half a share in trust to Olivia Porter, Endymion's widow; half shares also went to George Porter, and to his friend Abraham Cowley.

Nevertheless, on Friday, 28 June, he was able to put on his previous success, *The Siege of Rhodes*, Part I, and on Tuesday, 2 July, Pepys 'took coach and went to Sir Wm. Davenant's opera … the fourth day that it hath begun … [to see] the second part of *The Siege of Rhodes*'. The success of the play was immediate. Two days after seeing it, Pepys went to Vere Street to see Killigrew's production of *Claricilla* – 'the first time I ever saw it, well acted,' he commented, 'But strange to see this house, that used to be so thronged, now empty since the Opera begun; and so it will continue for a while, I believe.'

*Rhodes II* (*Dramatic Works*, Vol. III) differed significantly from the original Part I, in having expanded parts for both Roxolana and Ianthe, partly to take advantage of at last having women capable of doing the characters justice, and also to respond to Restoration audiences' developing tastes, especially for attractive women performers. Furthermore, it was played as a 'just drama' (in Dryden's phrase), in rhyming pentameters, with – again in response to changing taste – regrettably, no jolly chorus, and the only reference to music being to 'symphonies', indicating off-stage battles, with drums, trumpets and cymbals. Ianthe was played by Mary Saunderson and Roxolana by Hester Davenport, Solyman by Thomas Betterton and Alphonso by Henry Harris; the (necessarily) small part of Haly the eunuch was given to John Downes, who was overcome with stage-fright and hissed off the stage, as he explains: 'The King, Duke of York and all the Nobility in the House, as the first time the King was in a Publick Theatre, the sight of that August presence spoil'd me for an Actor.' After this, and to the benefit of posterity, Davenant transferred him to bookkeeper and prompter, recording all the parts, attending all rehearsals and performances, and noting the success of the various plays, as in his *Roscius Anglicanus* (1708). The production itself had its share of opening-night problems, when a board overhead broke, showering dust onto the ladies' bosoms and the gentlemen's wigs, 'which made good sport,' according to Pepys. After that it went well.

Especially for this occasion, Davenant provided a pretendedly modest Prologue to soften up his illustrious audience:

> Hope little from our Poets wither'd Wit;
> From Infant-Players, scarce grown Puppets yet.
> Hope from our Women less, whose bashful fear,
> Wondred to see me dare to enter here:
> Each took her leave, and wisht my danger past;

> And though I come back safe and undisgrac'd,
> Yet when they spie the WITS here, then I doubt
> No *Amazon* can make 'em venture out.
> Though I advis'd 'em not to fear you much;
> For I presume not half of you are such ...

(No one took that seriously). He goes on to regret the lack of money, as the theatrical profession always does, and the consequent limitations of space (though so much greater than at Rutland House):

> Oh Money! Money! if the WITS would dress,
> With Ornaments, the present face of Peace;
> And to our Poet half that Treasure spare,
> Which Faction gets from Fools to nourish War;
> Then his contracted Scenes should wider be,
> And move by greater Engines, till you see
> (Whilst you Securely sit) fierce Armies meet
> And raging Seas disperse a fighting Fleet ...

Soon after this, the speaker retires, he says, 'like an old Rat ... to Parmizan', and the performance begins.

Now, in *Rhodes II*, Solyman has renewed his siege, and Alphonso and the Marshal of Rhodes lament the lack of European help. The siege is causing starvation, and Alphonso and others want a breakout attack: death or glory in the name of Honour, but Governor Villerius reminds them of the plight of the women, and urges some compromise. The desperate populace is rebelling, and demands that Ianthe be sent to plead with Solyman. The pressure of People Power requires a flexible response (as some of the audience would remember):

> Those who withstand
> The tide of flood, which is the people's will,
> Fall back when they would onward row:
> We strength and way preserve by lying still.

A little compromise with 'the people's will' (always a dubious concept) may help preserve stability. It is agreed that Ianthe should go, trusting in Solyman's honour and despite Alphonso's trouble with his jealousy. In the Turkish camp, Solyman in turn complains of pressure from the military: 'I shall find my peace /Destroy'd at home, unless I seek for them /Destructive war abroad.' He does not seem especially magnificent, his peace destroyed not only by his captains but by Roxolana, who is shown in a dominant position in the Turkish court, insisting that 'we monarch's wives', as strong women, are not merely for ornament or entertainment: 'They shall find I'm no European Queen, /Who in a throne does sit but to be seen.' He is even unsettled by Roxolana's nagging, as second wife, for her son: 'I at night /In vain seek sleep with a tempestuous wife,' which produces a comical picture of a henpecked Sultan.

At last Ianthe arrives at the Turkish camp. A dramatic scene is set up in Roxolana's richly decorated pavilion, suggestive of exotic oriental splendour, with Ianthe shown sleeping on a couch, watched by Haly and Roxolana, poised with a Turkish handkerchief in one hand and a dagger in the other: Virtue threatened by Passion. Ianthe wakes, and assures Roxolana that she has no personal plans for Solyman; Roxolana relents her vengeful intentions, and the women are reconciled. After Ianthe's exit, Roxolana and Solyman argue about his lack of attention to his wife, before he sends her away:

> Beauty, retire! Thou dost my pity move!
> Believe my pity, and then trust my love.

These lines would have been in recitative; however they were performed, for some reason they caught Pepys's imagination, so that he set them to music himself. His portrait by John Hayls in 1666 shows him holding the manuscript of his version, of which he was clearly proud. Solyman now soliloquizes about his unhappy situation, how 'with new and powerful arts /Of study'd war I break the hearts /Of half the world, and she breaks mine'.

The last act shows the Turks' successful siege, with the Grand Master's palace on fire (spectacular lighting effects from off stage), fierce fighting (shouting and two battle 'symphonies' fortissimo), Villerius accepting defeat and Solyman showing compassion to the Rhodians. Solyman and Roxolana are reconciled; Alphonso and Ianthe, both wounded and captured separately, are spared by their conquerors and released as exemplary honourable lovers. *Exeunt omnes.*

The Epilogue then pleads for the Poet to receive

> the priv'lege of old servants got:
> Who are conniv'd at, and have leave to Doat ...

and reminds the audience of previous successes, when 'he serv'd your Fathers many years', though recognizing tastes may have changed. Like old mistresses who console themselves

> With thoughts of former Lovers they have had:
> Even so poor Madam-*Muse* this night must bear,
> With equal pulse, the fits of hope and fear;
> And never will against your Passion strive.

Davenant need not have worried; the play was a great success, a Restoration 'smash hit', running for twelve days continuously – remarkable for those days – 'with great Applause', as Downes recorded, and several times afterwards. Far from being old-fashioned, *Rhodes II* was innovative, marking the beginning of the Restoration taste for heroic-romantic drama, characterized by highfaluting speeches on Love and Honour. It was particularly remarkable in providing favourable characterizations of strong, active women, while also touching on the sensitive subject of relationships between rulers and the governed.

On 15 November, Pepys saw it again, when he thought it 'very well done', but by February 1662 he was regretting the absence of the actress Hester Davenport, who had the misfortune to catch the fancy of Aubrey de Vere, Earl of Oxford, who tricked her with a fake marriage ceremony, actually performed by his servants. The morning after, the Earl dismissed her abruptly; in spite of her complaints, even to the King, he could not be made to marry her. She had to settle for becoming his mistress and receiving a pension of 1,000 crowns. By 27 December, the Pepyses thought her replacement, Mary Norton, 'rather better in all respects, for person, voice and judgment'; on 1 January 1663, she was seen in the theatre again, this time watching from 'the chief box', dressed in a velvet gown provided by the Earl. (It is some comfort to know that, later, the Earl was cuckolded, and his daughter married the son of actress Nell Gwyn.)

For all that by-play, *Rhodes II* had many repeats and revivals over the years. One versifying theatre-goer, dismissing Killigrew's theatre, wrote about coming

> to the other Theatre now,
> Where the Knight with his Scenes doth keep much adoe,
> For the Siege of Rhodes all say
> It is an everlasting Play.

In 1665 Pepys still thought it 'the best poem that ever was wrote'. There was even a Royal Command performance in Whitehall: extra money, and triumph indeed.

Davenant followed *Rhodes* with one of his earlier successes, *The Witts*, which itself ran for eight performances, described by Pepys as 'A most excellent play – and admirable scenes [i.e. scenery]'. Betterton played the Elder Pallatine, and Henry Harris the Younger, with the comic actor, Cave Underhill, as Sir Morglay Thwack and Hester Davenport as Lady Ample. Once again, the King, the Duke of York and attendant courtiers were present (perhaps this was when Davenport caught the eye of the Earl of Oxford). Then, in August 1661, he put on *Hamlet*, of which Downes reported, 'No succeeding Tragedy for several Years got more Reputation or Money to the Company than this.' Hamlet was played by Betterton, Horatio by Harris, Gertrude by Davenport and Ophelia by Mary Saunderson, with Cave Underhill as the Gravedigger. Pepys wrote that 'Batterton did the Prince's part beyond imagination', and it was generally thought that this was the actor's finest performance. It seems possible that his interpretation derived ultimately from Shakespeare, as Downes wrote that 'Sir *William* (having seen *Mr. Taylor* of the *Blackfryars* Company Act it, who being instructed by the Author *Mr. Shakespeare*) taught Mr. *Betterton* in every Particle of it; which by his exact Performance of it, gain'd him Esteem and Reputation, Superlative to all other Plays" In fact, Shakespeare had died three years before Joseph Taylor joined the King's Men, but Taylor probably followed the original Burbage interpretation as advised by Shakespeare.

The text that we have is that printed in 1676, itself probably based on the Second Folio of 1637. The language of the play is made easier and more up to date, to be more readily understood – a different audience had to be catered for. In this, Davenant was of his time: Dryden, in the preface to his own adaptation of *Troilus and Cressida* (1679), wrote:

> It must be allowed to the present age, that the tongue in general is so much refined since Shakespeare's time that many of his words, and more of his phrases, are scarce intelligible. And of those we understand, some are ungrammatical, others coarse; and his whole style is so pestered with figurative expressions, that it is as affected as it is obscure.

'Pestered with figurative expressions': often thought of as poetry. As it was, early Shakespeare editions frequently show revisions and simplifications of diction, grammar and style. Mythological and classical references tend to be omitted or smoothed out. Here, the printed edition warns the reader that the text is abbreviated; the acting text is about 500 lines shorter, and, no doubt in view of the relatively small company, various minor characters disappear. The Fortinbras sub-plot is greatly reduced, as is the character of Polonius, himself simplified into a foolish comic. Claudius also is simplified, his sententious rhetoric and worried introspection gone, as he is more clearly a villain.

Hamlet himself is significantly diminished: much of the self-analysis and self-reproach is omitted from his soliloquies; he is less cynical and theatrical, with no advice to the Player about speaking his lines, and with less wit. In general, the play is made less complex, as suggestions of general corruption and incest are toned down, and Hamlet is made less philosophical and more the clear-minded hero of revenge and honour. Davenant would have exploited the facilities of his theatre, with changing scenery – castle battlements, different chambers in the palace, a trapdoor grave in the churchyard. Contemporary costume would have been worn: Hamlet would have been dressed as a Restoration courtier, even if in black, with a broad-brimmed hat, periwig, lace-trimmed shirt, surcoat, full breeches and shoes with ribbon bows. The play had its obvious contemporary relevance, in suggesting the unsettling effect of regicide, and the need for clear government. The production was a great success, as Downes noted, and frequently repeated: Pepys saw it again on 27 November and 5 December.

*Hamlet* was followed on 1 September by *Twelfth Night*, again attended by the King, with Betterton and Harris as Sir Toby Belch and Sir Andrew Aguecheek, with Underhill as Feste; Downes reported that it had 'mighty success by its well Performance'. How it was adapted is not known, as the text was not printed. The success and reputation of Davenant's company is indicated by the fact that, for his October revival of his own *Love and Honour*, the King, the Duke of York and the Earl of Oxford loaned their coronation clothes; the Earl saw Davenport playing Evandra. On 16 December, Davenant put on *The Cutter of Coleman Street*, by Abraham Cowley, updated from 1650 to provide 'reflection much upon the late times', according to Pepys, and 'not a little injurious to the Cavalier Indigent Officers', noted Downes, who reported that it was 'Acted so perfectly well and Exact, it was perform'd a whole week with a full Audience'. 1661 had been a good year for Davenant and his theatre.

The pace was kept up in the new year. In February 1662, he put on his first significant adaptation of Shakespeare, *The Law Against Lovers*, a version of *Measure for Measure* (*Dramatic Works*, Vol. V). Apart from the shift of setting from Vienna to Turin, the most striking changes to the main action were the removal of the brothel gang of Mrs Overdone, Froth and Pompey Bum with the clown constable, Elbow (presumably in accordance with the royal warrant of 1660), and their replacement by the Beatrice–Benedick story from *Much Ado*, so reducing much sexual innuendo (Lucio is sadly diminished), and providing romantic badinage and wit as a substitute. The absence of the comic lowlife removes the balance it provided against the tense argumentation of the main action, while losing the sense of a city where 'corruption [can] boil and bubble / Till it o'er-run the stew', and thinning the society depicted to close-knit members of the upper class. Sexuality in the language is diluted. When asked what she would do to save Claudio, in *Measure* Isabella replies, 'Th'impression of keen whips I'd wear as rubies, /And strip myself to death as to a bed /That longing have been sick for, ere I'd yield /My body up to shame.' In *Law*, her uneasy sexuality is absent:

> Th'impression of sharp whips I gladly would
> As rubies wear, and strip myself
> Even for a grave, as for a bed, ere I
> Would yield my honour up to shame.

The physical 'longing' and 'body' are replaced by the euphemistic social abstraction, 'honour'.

The characters may be discussed in three groups. The first is that of Angelo and his verbal assault upon the rigidly principled Isabella. The most important difference is that Angelo saw Isabella in the nunnery before the action opens, when, as he tells her, 'A double enterprise perplext my mind, /By *Claudio*'s danger to provoke you forth /From that blest shade, and then to try your worth.' Whereas in *Measure* he was innocent and suddenly overwhelmed by the occasion, now he is a calculating examiner, testing her suitability as a wife, so Davenant omits his guilty soliloquies.

In turn, Isabella's concern is with honour and its value. She asks him, 'How little honour then you had obtain'd, /If where but little was, you that had stain'd?' He would have made a poor bargain. In reproving Juliet for sleeping with Claudio, she speaks for women's honour in general:

> When you your honour did to Claudio give,
> Coz'ning your self, you did our sex deceive;
> Honour is publick treasure, and 'tis fit
> Law should in publick forms dispose of it.

Juliet has cheapened the price women may demand; she tells her, 'Sister, you gave much more than was your own.' Her scheme is about the saving of appearances: 'When we good intend by doing ill /We bring necessity t'excuse our ill, /And that our faults, when hidden by our shame /Pass free from blame, if they scape from shame.' She goes so far as to suggest that Juliet trick Angelo by going to bed with him, so that 'Claudio's life you save and lose no fame'. At the end she is married off, not to the older Duke but to his heir, Angelo.

Contrasting with this unlovely pair are the naïve romantic lovers, Claudio and Juliet, who do not meet until the end. The chief loss is the weakening of his speech on the fear of death:

> We lie in silent darkness, and we rot;
> Where long our motion is not stopt; for though
> In graves none walk upright, proudly to face
> The stars, yet there we move again, when our

Corruption makes those worms in whom we crawl.
Perhaps the spirit, which is future life,
Dwells salamander-like, unharm'd in fire:
Or else with wand'ring winds is blown about
The world …

The third group is composed of Beatrice, Benedick (now Angelo's brother), Lucio and Balthazar, with Viola for the singing and dancing ('a saraband, awhile with castanietos' – later, Beatrice and Benedick also dance), who provide witty banter. Together they constitute a cluster of insouciant young libertines – as such, attractive to courtier audiences – not sexually dissolute but irreverent of established custom and authority, especially marriage. Active in their opposition to Angelo and 'the precise', Benedick arranges for a counterfeit warrant to release Claudio, manages to corrupt the judge, Escalus, and leads a group of disbanded officers to attack the prison, and is wounded when that siege is defeated.

Eventually the Duke comes into the open to sort things out, though he is a less dominating character than in *Measure*. At the end, Angelo is put through a process of humiliation when he is brought to remorse by a sequence of visits in his prison cell, in rhyming couplets, by practically the entire cast; finally, the Duke, Beatrice and Benedick oversee his repentance and submission.

*The Law Against Lovers* has many of the qualities of Fletcherian tragi-comedy, with witty, comic episodes, romance and many intrigues, whether to release Claudio or bring Beatrice and Benedick together, less complex and demanding than its original, with a clearer resolution: 'The story of this day, /When 'tis in future ages told, will seem /A moral drawn from a poetic dream.' In itself, it could be seen as a skilful, neat piece of work, combining entertainment and moral satisfaction for its intended audience: under a benevolent, intervening ruler – the Duke, or Charles – the state can be settled and the succession assured. Pepys thought it 'a good play', and enjoyed Viola as 'the little Girle (who I never saw before) dancing and singing'; a year later, he saw her again in *The Slighted Maid*, 'in boy's apparel, she having very fine legs'.

On 1 March, he and his wife were at the first performance of Davenant's adaptation of *Romeo and Juliet*. Harris and Saunderson were in the title rôles, with Betterton starring as Mercutio. Among the changes, a new character was introduced, the wife of Paris, played by Mrs Holden. She made an unforgettable impression, as Downes reports: when she 'enter'd in a *Hurry*, Crying, O my dear Count! She Inadvertently left out O, in the pronuntiation of the word *Count* ! giving it a Vehement Accent, put the House into such a Laughter, that *London* Bridge at low Water was silence to it'. This first-night disaster may have accounted for Pepys's extremely negative response to the production: 'the play of itself the worst that ever I heard in my life, and the worst acted that ever I saw these people do … they were all of them out more or less.' It is perhaps not surprising that Davenant's version was never printed. Despite this setback, the year continued busily, including Webster's *The Duchess of Malfi*, which, wrote Downes, 'fill'd the House 8 Days Successively, it proving one of the best of Stock Tragedies'. In October, Davenant, loyal to the memory of Endymion Porter, put on *The Villain*, by Endymion's more approved son, Thomas, which went well enough for ten days (with a command performance at Court on 1 January 1667), and then in December, as part of the Christmas Revels at the Middle Temple, Samuel Tuke's translation from the Spanish, *The Adventures of Five Hours*. This was attended by his old friend Edward Hyde, now Lord Clarendon, the Lord Chancellor, for whom Davenant wrote a prologue – 'My Lord, you in your early youth did sit, /As patron and as Censor too of Wit.'[15] When put on in the theatre, it proved to be one of the great successes of Restoration theatre and was much admired by Pepys, running for thirteen days. Downes reports Davenant's new scenery for both productions – perhaps as a response to Killigrew's proposed new theatre. On Christmas Eve, Thomas Betterton and Mary Saunderson found time to get married, which made a good end to the year.[16]

# Chapter 12

# Cavalier with Shakespeare (1663–1664)

On 13 January 1663, Davenant at last received the royal patent for his theatre, which provided the occasion for, or, in effect, required, his grateful 'Poem to the Kings most Sacred Majesty'.[1] One wonders whether he really expected Charles himself to divert sufficient leisure time and energy from satisfying Lady Castlemaine's relentless sexual and financial demands to slog through 526 lines of versified adulation, however grovelling (though in the course of it he praised the King's ability to 'Indure a tedious narrative'). The object was to keep his name in the King's mind, and to assure him of their mutual benefit.

From the beginning, his financial difficulties are emphasized, as 'Poets with the Poor now reckoned are': he was never to be recompensed for his Civil War expenses ('thirteen thousand pounds and more', according to his widow; he had asked for repayment for the war munitions he had bought, but this was refused, as was a request for compensation for the loss of a ship),[2] let alone receive his Laureate pension. His successor as Poet Laureate, John Dryden, was to touch lightly on Charles's parsimony to his poets, in his *Threnodia Augustalis*:

> Tho' little was their Hire, and light their Gain,
> Yet somewhat to their share he threw;
> Fed from his Hand, they sung and flew,
> Like Birds of Paradise, that liv'd on morning dew.[3]

Now the writer, in the autumn of his years – all of 57 – with his Bayes no longer green, still hopes for a new sun king.

Davenant returns to his favourite marine imagery, comparing himself to Columbus's sailors, blown by tempests to a new 'great World', as he 'by Storms' is brought to the King. His regrets are less at lack of money as at concern at his loss of 'dexterity of Thought' (his definition of Wit, in the *Preface*). He fears to have lost the poetic heat that maintained the Bayes, 'Spent early in your God-like Father's praise'. He worries about the burdens placed on the young monarch's shoulders. Davenant, sent to colonize Virginia and Maryland, had read Captain John Smith's *History of Virginia* (1624) and knew how forcefully ejected natives could retaliate: 'From Woods they march victorious back agen /To Cities, the Wall'd-Parks of Hearded-Men.' Charles must instead conquer Minds, to gain the love of the conquered (the implication, that Charles is an invader and conqueror, is unfortunate). As throughout his career, he then warns of 'Factions'.

This leads to an extended attack on dissenters obstinately calling for liberty of preaching and refusing to bow to 'Gods on earth'. Charles, 'God-like', uses Law to bring 'an harmonious Word /Out of the various discords of your State':

> That Feaver, Zeal (the People's desp'rate fit)
> You cool, and without bleeding, master it.

This blandly ignores the numerous mutilated bodies of the hanged, drawn and quartered paraded through the city. In a further, rather dubious divine analogy, he declares that 'The truth of Resurrection is by *You* /Confirm'd to all', in that Charles has revived the Church of England, which had 'lost, by *Martyrdom*, the *Head*'. Dissenters' hostility to church ornaments is contrasted, as in his poem for Monck, with their '*Ethnick* Ornaments of Speech' and 'curious Tropes and Figures'. 'All these *You* have forgiv'n': a reference to the Act of Uniformity of 1662, which in practice drove nearly 2,000 clergy (out of about 9,000) out of their livings, and re-imposed fines for non-attendance at the Church of England. Now, after twenty years of 'rapines', Charles has apparently brought the country to wealth (in only three years). He is now the 'Soveraign of the Sea' (remembering his father's great ship), whose expanding fleets will spread 'the vitall heat of Trade', somehow collecting 'all the *Freights* which ev'ry Country yeilds', and – of particular interest to Davenant– frightening off pirates.

With all this, the King can respond to the Arts for recreation, leading Davenant, in full submission cringe mode, to welcome the Acts of 1661 and 1662 intended to control and restrict preaching, printing and speech.

The Muse is now, by her conversion, taught
Gladly to lose that freedom which she sought ...
    Men knew not what they *took* or Monarchs *gave*,
When they did *liberty of Subjects* crave:
Even Poets would, like other Subjects, be
*Licentious Writers* had they *libertie*;
And study all the madness of *freewill*,
Which is, *old English Freedom* to do ill.

Once, he had told the Commons that he had merely suffered from that 'old infirmity of that Nation which hath ever been bred with liberty of speaking'; that was then, this is now. As it is, 'we' (Davenant, Killigrew and their authors) 'the ancient *Drama* have refin'd', with less difficult plots and 'unblemish'd love' stories, such as Mr Podsnap's Young Person could have watched. Charles has brought this 'publick Mirrour' to a perfection of 'Art and Virtue', as it is in his own image.

Now the ageing wearer of a 'wither'd Laurel' fears seeming unworthy of his pinnace flying the 'Poet's Flag' to praise the King. Though poor, he is rich in having such a 'plentious Theme', but it is not obvious, of course, who could take over from him: 'The young will not agree who is too young, /Nor th'old determine who has liv'd too long.' The God-like subject is too great for any artist: 'All *Painters* strait would lay their Pencils by, /Were they enjoyn'd to paint the *Deity*.' Nevertheless, 'since your name should be perpetual made, /*You* must vouchsafe t'accept a *Poet*'s aid.'

In other words: thank you for the theatre; don't forget me – even I could be of use. Perhaps he thought that it was something that had to be done, no matter what he may have thought – elsewhere, different sentiments would be hinted at; meanwhile, to quote Alice's March Hare, 'It was the *best* butter.'

Early in the new year, he and Killigrew combined to oust their remaining theatrical rival, George Jolly, from the old Red Bull; then, on 7 May, Killigrew opened his large new Theatre Royal in Drury Lane, designed to match the Duke's Theatre with scenery flats, trapdoors and other devices. Davenant was not yet ready for his own planned new and improved playhouse, and carried on where he was. In August, in the quiet time, when Court and the Courts were absent, as he had written in his poem,

'The Long Vacation in London', in 1635, he put on a moneymaker pot-boiler entertainment for the ordinary 'citizens' left behind, *The Playhouse to be Let* (*Dramatic Works*, Vol. IV). A 'back-stage' comedy, with five different acts, it opens with the theatre's Housekeeper and a Player lamenting the dead season, disconsolately shelling peas and hoping for some response to their advertisement for temporary tenants. First comes a Frenchman, managing a touring company – a foreign accent is always good for a laugh – who offers them a farce: 'De vise nation bi for tings heroique, /And de fantastique, vor de farce.' The Player is not keen: 'I believe all *French* farces are /Prohibited Commodities, and will not pass current in *England*.' (There was an Act forbidding certain French imports.) He doubts that his ordinary public will like it, since 'all our travell'd Customers are gone /To take the Air with their own Wives, beyond /*Hide-Park* a great way; a homely country mode /Of their fore-fathers', leaving behind 'their poor mistresses /And us behind 'em without Customers'. The remainder simply want to be 'merry at such obvious things /As not constrain 'em to the pains of thinking'. As it is, this theatre is too narrow:

> We'll let this Theatre and build another, where,
> At a cheaper rate, we may have room for Scenes.
> *Brainford*'s [Brentford's] the place!
> Perhaps 'tis now somewhat too far 'i'th'Suburbs;
> But the mode is for Builders to work slight and fast;
> And they proceed so with new houses
> That old *London* will quickly overtake us.

Next comes a Musician offering a novelty: 'Heroique story /In *Stilo Recitativo*'. He explains that

> Recitative Musick is not compos'd
> Of matter so familiar, as may serve
> For every low occasion of discourse.
> In Tragedy, the language of the Stage
> Is rais'd above the common dialect;
> Our passions rising with the height of Verse;
> And Vocal Musick adds new wings to all
> The flights of poetry.

The Musician, told that 'There is another play-house to let, in *Vere Street*' – Killigrew's old theatre –wants to tune his instruments in the actresses' changing room, and is told, 'You may; for they are all gon, Sir, to rob Orchards, /And get the green-sickness in the Country.' The Housekeeper goes on to provide a wonderful picture of popular entertainments, while complaining that

> All the dry old fools of *Bartholomew*-fair
> Are come to hire our house. The German fool,
> Yon Borridge of Hamb'rough, and numberless
> Jack-puddings; the new motion-man of Norwich,
> Op'ra-puppets; the old gentleman
> That professes the galliard on a rope;
> Another rare Turk that flies without wings,
> Rich jugglers with embroider'd budgets, hoop-men,
> And so many tom-tumblers that you'd think
> Lincoln's-Inn field a forest of wild apes.

When she reports the arrival of 'Two very hot Fencers without doublets', who want to hire the theatre for 'a School, where they'd teach the Art of Duel', the Player replies – perhaps 'ripostes' is the right word – 'Tell 'em the *Red Bull* stands empty for Fencers. /There are no Tenents in it but old Spiders: /Go and bid the men of wrath allay their heat /With Prizes there.' (It is good to see Davenant's favourite spiders again.) One man even wants to hire the company's turban, sceptre and throne used by Solyman in *The Siege of Rhodes*. Finally, a Poet offers 'Romances travesti', in which

> You shall present the actions of the Heroes
> (Which are the chiefest Theams of Tragedy)
> In Verse Burlesque.
>
> Player:   Burlesque and travesty? These are hard words,
> And may be French, but not Law-French.

The poet tells him (as Davenant mocks his own theatrical career) that

> Your old great images of
> Love and Honour are esteem'd by some
> Antiquaries now.

The Poet insists that

> the travestie,
> I mean Burlesque, or, more t'explain my self,
> Would say, the mock-heroique must be it
> Which draws the pleasant hither i'th'Vacation,
> Men of no malice, who will pay for laughter.

(The *OED*'s earliest citation for 'mock-heroic' is 1711.) In the end, the Poet gets the nod, and is allowed to select from the company's stock of costumes.

The Second Act of *The Playhouse*, then, is the promised French farce, a free translation of Molière's *Sganarelle, ou le Cocu Imaginaire*, done well enough, with funny French accents and ending with a song sung by Winifred Gosnell, recently maidservant to Pepys's wife, 'Ah, Love is a delicate ting',[4] to accompany a 'Dance a la Ronde'. The next act, the 'heroique story in *Stilo Recitativo*', is Davenant's own *The History of Sir Francis Drake*, and the fourth is *The Cruelty of the Spaniards in Peru*, neither now political gestures in themselves, but simple popular entertainment. The final act, the burlesque promised by the Poet, presents Julius Caesar, Mark Anthony, Lepidus (who says nothing), Ptolomy, Cleopatra and Cornelia, Pompey's widow.

The piece begins with what purports to be an Egyptian (that is, gypsy) dance, before two of Ptolomy's eunuchs discuss the arrival of Anthony and Caesar:

First:    *Rome* now of *Egypt* will quickly beguile us, ...
          *Tyber* is come to play her pranks in *Nilus*.
Second:   If *Tyber* brings her plund'ring base *Burgonians*,
          Farewell on *Nilus*' banks our leeks and onions.
First:    A cruel wight, whose name is Mark *Anthony*,
          So hard of heart that it is held all boney,
          Is here arriv'd for love of our black *Gypsy*,

On *Cleopatra* he has cast a Sheep's eye,
And *Caesar* too, with many a stout *Terrpawling*,
                                        [tarpaulin, sailor]
Landed with him and comes a caterwauling.

Although we are told that Cleopatra 'will simper, at the sight of *Caesar*! /
And oh, how trusty *Tony* means to tease her', the expected love-and-sex
stories are not followed up. Caesar and Antony accuse Ptolomy, who says
that Pompey

Had plunder'd *Nilus'* banks till there was scarce one
Turkey or pig left for the tythes of parson;. ...
And came not here for rescue, but to rob us;
Yet we at last bob'd him who meant to bob us.

Caesar threatens him, but Cleopatra fires up in his defence before
Anthony calms her. He then wants to kill Ptolomy's eunuchs instead,
before they are all reconciled. Now enters Cornelia, comic vengeful
widow, as described by Caesar:

Sly scowling look, though men of Mars ne'er mind it,
Hat black and broad, long cypress down behind it,
Gown short and loose, and her hair under pinner,
                                        [cap with long flaps]
As if locks on cheeks were token of a sinner,
As though, out of zeal, dame laid the French mode by.
Mass, now I think on't, 'tis Pompey's rich widow.
Anthony:  Of mumping minx would we were fairly rid, lo!

Cornelia bickers with Cleopatra, and complains that they are not doing
their duty, but merely having a good time: 'Men, women, and child, you
chief should be killing, /But stead of bombasting you are a billing.' They
succeed in reconciling her:

Anthony:  Widow, be friends! make no more such a hot coil;
          We'll find out rich husband to make you the pot boil.

Caesar points out that there is no point in complaining:

> Yet fortune has done but what does become her;
> In winter w'are hay and grass in the summer.
> Cornelia:  In troth it is true! w'are of that sort all!
> Then farewell, sweet Pompey! since thou wast but mortal.

They all agree to have a dance and a drink; Caesar is out of money, and wants to borrow from Anthony, who has spent all his on women. They then all dance, and Caesar concludes with,

> Let's all to the ale-house go, where tapsters know me;
> Fat Hostess there will trust; lead, King *Ptolomy*!
> Fiddlers will thither come, and never grumble;
> In Play-house they are proud, in ale-house humble.
> Gossips shall tattle there, while tongues will wag on,
> And to my Gypsy's health I'll drink a flagon.

*Exeunt omnes*, except the Playhouse people, who lament that in fact they have made no money; but hope that the audience will come to the theatre, next time. It seems very uninspired stuff and doggerel, though with entertaining glimpses of ordinary life. In not dealing with any of the famous events of Roman history, it seems strangely inconsequential (though in a few years, the Antony and Cleopatra story, aimed partly at Charles, would be performed frequently – Dryden's *All for Love* came out in 1677). Nevertheless, its situations might be thought to have some point, written and performed in the early years of the Restoration: senior figures come from abroad, intending to punish the killers of their leader, but soon turn to amusements and women, and the leader's widow is assuaged. The parallels can easily be sketched in. Perhaps the implicit suggestion is, it's over, let it go: move on, and enjoy yourselves while you can: 'In winter w'are hay, and grass i'the summer.'

The main event of autumn and winter of 1663 was Davenant's production of *Henry VIII*, one of Shakespeare's later, less interesting works, written in collaboration with Fletcher. Always notable for its spectacle and processions, its action is concerned with the Katherine of Aragon and Anne Boleyn conflict. Downes was very enthusiastic:

This play, by Order of Sir *William Davenant*, was all new Cloath'd in proper Habits: the King's was new, all the Lords, the Cardinals, the Bishops, the Doctors, Proctors, Lawyers, Tip-staves, new Scenes; the part of the King was so right and justly done by Mr *Betterton*, he being instructed in it by Sir *William*, who had it from Old Mr *Lowen*, that had his instruction from Mr *Shakespeare* himself, that I dare and will aver, none can or will come near him in this Age, in the performance of that part.

Harris played Wolsey, and was 'little Inferior to that, he doing it with just State, Port and Mein, that I dare affirm, that none hitherto had Equall'd him'. (A portrait of him as Wolsey, by John Greenhill, is the earliest known picture of an English actor in a Shakespearean rôle.)

'Every part was exactly perform'd,' affirmed Downes, 'by the great Care of Sir *William*.' The production ran for fifteen days, and on 1 January 1664, Pepys got to see it, but was not impressed: 'so simple a thing, made up of a great many patches, that, besides the shows and processions in it, there is nothing in the world good or well done.' For all that, the piece became the byword and standard for spectacle. Years later, in the Duke of Buckingham's theatrical mockery of Davenant and Dryden, *The Rehearsal*, the supposed author, Mr Bayes, tells his guests, 'Now, Gentlemen, I will be bold to say, I'll shew you the greatest scene that ever England saw: I mean not for words, for those I do not value; but for state, shew, and magnificence. In fine, I'll justifie it to be as grand to the eye every whit, I gad, as that great Scene in *Harry* the Eight, and grander too, I gad.'

On 7 March 1664, he put on his own earlier play, *The Unfortunate Lovers*. When that was printed in 1643, he included the Prologue and Epilogue, and these appeared again in the 1673 edition, based on this performance. In the Prologue he again accuses the audience of being excessively critical, compared with those of the past: 'Since ten times more of Wit then was allow'd /Your silly Ancestors in twenty year, /You think in two short hours to swallow here.' In the Epilogue, he complains, 'to cry Plays down /Is half the business Termers have in Town; /And still the reputation of their Wit grows strong, /As they can first condemn, though right or wrong.' Pepys saw it four times; on the first night, he was 'not much pleased with it; though [he knew] not where to lay the fault –

unless it was that the house was very empty, by reason of a new play at the other house'.

Nevertheless, 1664 proved a busy year, as Davenant competed with Killigrew's company, including, notably, George Etherege's *The Comical Revenge, or, Love in a Tub*, a lively piece that foreshadowed the characteristic Restoration comedy of manners: Downes reported that it 'got the Company more Reputation and Profit than any preceding comedy'. Later that year, he put on Lord Orrery's rhymed tragedy, *Henry V*. It was probably about this time that he revised his poem to Roger Boyle, then Lord Broghill, now Lord Orrery.[5] It is extraordinarily long, as Davenant considers the necessary changes from one social order to another. Once again, Davenant compares himself to Columbus, discovering a great new world, Orrery, hitherto unappreciated by others. In lines that look back to 'Madagascar', he observes that as Columbus

> knew not, when he first saw Land,
> The place of Silver, Oare, or Golden Sand;
> Nor knew to dive near Rocks where Mermaids dwell
> And lock their Pearles in Cabinets of shell;
> So there are several treasures of your minde,
> Which none but such wise Travellers can find
> As long within your Mindes vast Country stay ...

Just as Columbus had to trade with wild men in America, here there are other men 'of a graver wildness ... solemnly and so austerely mad': puritans, opposed to the theatre. Such men are best defeated by 'Civility, by Nature yours', and 'well establisht Judgement, such as yours, [which] / By perfect strength as certainly secures /The aimes of Pow'r'. The people can be brought to accept authority by such means, especially through entertainments and the arts: 'The Muses Regents were in *Greece* and *Rome*: /In all the civil world they were at home.' He still insists that 'the most important Things (which are /Empire and Arts) require Heav'ns special care'. In this spirit, Orrery is to write patriotic plays, and Davenant to put them on. Civility, Judgement and Wit are the qualities needed in the new government; as he moves towards his conclusion, he hopes for rewards for revealing to the ignorant and uncomprehending the 'rich Reserves' of Orrery-America. As Columbus laid claim to America, so Davenant, as discoverer of the virtues of his subject, so 'by that Title [discoverer] I lay claime to you' – whichever title Boyle now might have.

September saw Davenant's *The Rivals* (*Dramatic Works*, Vol. V), an adaptation of Shakespeare and Fletcher's *The Two Noble Kinsmen*, another patchy, late effort, adapted to Restoration tastes and practice in tragi-comedy, including symmetrical pairing of characters, including the comic lower classes. In *Kinsmen*, two loving young noblemen, defeated in battle, both fall in love with their captor's daughter, Emilia, who – like many readers – can hardly distinguish between them. After their passionate rivalry they duel for her: Arcite, the devotee of Mars, wins, but falls off his horse, with fatal effect. The friends are reconciled, and Palamon, the devotee of Venus, gets Emilia. In *The Rivals*, the theme is the Cavalier favourite of Love versus Honour. Here, after their non-fatal fight, Philander (the Palamon character, played by Betterton) is awarded the chaste Heraclia (played by Mrs Betterton) whilst Harris's Theocles has to settle for the Provost's daughter, Celania (based on *Kinsmen's* Jailor's daughter), who has been driven mad by her unrequited love for him, but whom he can now save. When asked if he can now love her, he replies, absurdly,

> Ay, there's the question which I knew she'd move.
> Know I can love, and since that love does want
> Growth in Heraclia's bosom, I'll transplant
> It into yours.

It's as easy as that. Philander can conclude by declaring,

> My quarrel here with Theocles shall end,
> I lose a rival and preserve a friend.

The familiar situation of the love rivalry of close friends (quasi-brothers) obviously appealed to Davenant, while their relationship seems far more intense and important than their raptures over their hardly known, passive objective.

Within the action of the play, Davenant develops *Kinsmen's* comic scenes of a country schoolmaster's rustic performers of a play (itself similar to *Love's Labours Lost's* entertainment), with an amusing extended routine of Morris dancing, complete with hobby horse, wooden spoons, tabor-playing and horns. (Downes mentions 'a very fine Interlude ... with very Diverting Dances'.) Particularly notable is the great expansion of Celania's part, to exploit the skills of the performer, who is provided with seven songs in her madness, some distinctly reminiscent of Ophelia's. Her final pathetic song begins,

> My lodging it is on the Cold ground,
> 	and very hard is my fare,
> But that which troubles me most, is
> 	the unkindness of my dear.[7]

This was sung by Moll (Mary) Davis, who could sing, dance and play the guitar (Lely later painted her with one). Although parodied by her rival, Nell Gwyn, it was found very affecting, especially by the King, who, as Downes recorded, 'Rais'd her from her Bed on the Cold Ground, to a Bed Royal.' On 11 January 1668, Pepys heard that the King had taken her as a mistress, with an expensive ring, a pension of £1,000 and a house in Suffolk Street. She was to become a serious rival to Nell Gwyn, both on the stage and in Charles's bed. The play itself ran for nine days, and did well.

# Chapter 13

# Rough Magic (1664–1667)

In autumn 1663 or early 1664 came a major Shakespearean adaptation, *Macbeth* (*Dramatic Works*, Vol. V). Downes's description of the 1673 version, put on in the company's new Dorset Garden Theatre, is helpful in suggesting something of this production. He describes the performance as 'drest in all it's Finery, as new Cloaths, new Scenes, Machines, as flyings for the Witches; with all the Singing and Dancing in it … being in the nature of an Opera, it Recompenc'd double the Expence'. Some of the equipment for that production may have strained the powers of the original Duke's Theatre; as it was, it was very successful theatrically and financially, remarkable for its special effects, variety, singing and dancing.

For all the frequent singing and dancing, as by Heccat and the flying (probably male) witches, and special effects, the modified drama is most important, with the language, characterization and theme clarified and thinned, in accordance with contemporary taste and, no doubt, Davenant's sense of his audience's capacity. For example, where, in Act I, Scene ii, Shakespeare's Sergeant is sardonic and brutal –

> Which ne'er shook hands, nor bade farewell to him
> Till he unseam'd him from the nave to th'chops,
> And fix'd his head upon our battlements

he is replaced by Seyton – or Seaton – (who takes over many other parts) with, simply, 'Then, having conquer'd him with single force, /He fix'd his head …' Where Ross had reported on the battle in a dramatic present tense, now Seyton narrates, less effectively:

> From Fyfe great King, where the Norweyan Banner
> Darken'd the Aire and fann'd our people cold …
> Till brave Macbeth oppos'd his bloody rage

> And check'd his haughty spirits; after which
> His army fled. Thus shallow streams may flow
> Forward with violence a while; but when
> They are oppos'd, as fast run back again ...

Changes sometimes produce bathetic effects (as with the streams): when the Sergeant had reported how 'Fortune, on his damned quarrel smiling /Showed like a rebel's whore', Seyton now observes that 'Fortune with her smiles oblig'd a while' – which was nice of her. With Macbeth no longer 'Bellona's bridegroom', and 'Golgotha' omitted, such references are omitted; 'murder' no longer has 'Tarquin's ravishing strides', and when Macbeth had wondered whether

> Will all great Neptune's ocean wash this blood
> Clean from this hand? No; this my hand will rather
> The multitudinous seas incarnadine,
> Making the green one red,

now, less sonorously, he asks, simply,

> Can the Sea afford
> Water enough to wash away the stains?
> No, they wou'd sooner add a Tincture to
> The Sea, and turn the Green into a Red.

Many vivid and complex are sacrificed for easy comprehension: where Macbeth asked night to 'Scarf up the tender eye of pitiful day', he now requests, 'Close up the eye of quick sighted day'. A metaphysical condition for the witches – 'Fair is foul and foul is fair' becomes more to do with the weather: 'To us fair weather's foule, and foule is fair.'

Decorum required various changes: Banquo is killed off stage, his death reported by his son Flean, as are young Macduff and Lady Macduff, and Macbeth; at the end, Macduff brings on, not Macbeth's head (which originally paralleled that of Macdonwald) but his sword. Comedy was not supposed to mix with tragedy, so the indecent Porter scene is cut. The constraints of a limited company enforced some changes, notably in the case of the actor who played Seyton/Seaton, who took over as the wounded sergeant, the Old Man, Ross, Lennox, a Lord, a messenger, as Macbeth's confidant, and for the Doctor, before his final desertion.

The major changes are the simplification of the Macbeths and the parallel promotion of the Macduffs, as their foil and opposites. Macbeth is less complex and harrowed, more ambitious and single-minded, driven by his ambitious wife, who blames him for taking her advice:

> You were a man
> And by the charter of your sex you shou'd
> Have govern'd me. There was more crime in you
> When you obey'd my councils, then I contracted
> By my giving it.

As General's wife, she graciously inquires of the junior officer's wife, Lady Macduff, 'You've been disconsolate. Pray tell me, /Are you in perfect health?' Lady Macduff has been worrying about her husband, but is told she should be pleased with his military successes: 'the bright glories which /He gain'd in Battel might dispel those Clouds.' Davenant was never impressed by war; now Lady Macduff replies, emphatically but rather tactlessly,

> The World mistakes those glories gain'd in war,
> Thinking their Lustre true; alas, they are
> But Comets, Vapours! By some men exhal'd
> From others bloud, and kindl'd in the Region
> Of popular applause, in which they live
> A while; then vanish; and the very breath
> Which first inflam'd them, blows them out agen.

(So much for his flattery of Ormond's slaughters in Ireland.) She is told to go and rest, while Lady Macbeth has a letter to read.

Before the murder, Lady Macbeth says 'There wou'd be Musick in a Ravens voice /Which shou'd but Crook the entrance of the King,' and urges the spirits to 'Empty my Nature of humanity ... That no relapses into Mercy may /Shake my designe'. Stylistic decorum requires that 'dark [not thick] night' to hide her in, not 'dunnest smoke' but a smoak as black as Hell', and Heaven not peep through a 'blanket' but 'the Curtains of the dark'. Theory required symmetry, so, as Banquo's ghost appeared to Macbeth, Duncan's ghost haunts her: 'Why do you follow me? I did not do it.' Her sleep-walking scene, originally intended to arouse sympathy, is only reported. Uxorious Macbeth is psychologically diminished by her illness and death, to a brutal warrior, and says of her death, 'she should have dy'd hereafter, I brought /Her here to see my victims, and not to dye'. Most of his agonizing and despair is reduced or thinned: the reflection on 'the wine of life' is gone; as for 'nothing serious in mortality' life has now 'nothing in it worth a good man's care', his friendless life in the 'sere and yellow leaf' is gone; 'out out short Candle'. Even his final, obstinate heroism is downplayed: no 'And damn'd be he that first cries, Hold, enough'. Instead, hammering home this play's overriding theme, his last words are, 'Farewell vain World, and what's most vain in it, Ambition,' which is as moralistic, obvious and banal as could be.

By contrast, the Macduffs are built up; Lady Macduff even warns her husband against ambition: 'May you be never by Ambition led ... Usurpers lives have but a short event.' When Macduff says, 'My Country's dangers call for my defence,' he is told, 'I am afraid you have some other end / Than meerly Scotland's freedom to defend ... That purpose will appear when rightly scann'd /But usurpation att the second hand.' He replies that his 'aime is not to governe but protect' (an allusion to Cromwell as Lord Protector), but she turns him away from that course. Perhaps surprisingly, the play's final speech is not given to the new monarch, Malcolm, but to loyal Macduff.

The contemporary political appeal was obvious, in showing the disastrous consequences of regicide and attempted revolution, the destructive effect of ambition on potential usurpers, and the benefit of loyalty, especially for the loyal. Pepys saw it four times, the first time on 5 November 1664; in January 1667, he described it as 'a most excellent play in all respects, but especially in divertisement, though it be a deep tragedy; which is a strange perfection in a tragedy, it being most proper here and suitable'; in April 1667 it was 'one of the best plays for a stage, and variety of dancing and music, that ever I saw'. Few people nowadays think so well of Davenant's version.

Not long after this, in April 1665, Davenant put on Lord Orrery's spectacular rhymed tragedy, *Mustapha, The Son of Solyman the Magnificent*, presumably written to profit from *Rhodes II*, with the Bettertons returning as Solyman and Roxolana. Downes recorded: 'All the Parts being new Cloath'd with new Scenes, Sir *William*'s great care of having it perfect and exactly perform'd, it produc'd to himself and Company vast Profit.' At some time, he also produced *King Lear*, probably starring Betterton; it may not have done well, as Downes merely recorded that it was 'Acted exactly as Mr. *Shakespear* Wrote it.' Pepys makes no mention of it.

From 5 June that year until November, the theatres were closed, as a consequence of the terrible Great Plague, that slaughtered between 66,000 and 100,000 people. Killigrew occupied this unwonted interval with improvements to his theatre; it is not known what Davenant did to support his company and family (he may have followed the Court to Oxford). Nevertheless, Davenant was able to stage *Mustapha* again in October and the following January. In March 1667, he put on *The Humorous Lovers*, by his former Civil War commander, the Duke of Newcastle, which Pepys dismissed as 'the most ridiculous thing that ever was wrote', and then his own *The Witts* again, with a very profitable command performance at Court, as well as *Rhodes II*. In August, he produced John Dryden's *Sir Martin Mar-All* (based on Molière's *L'Etourdi*), with the celebrated comedian John Nokes in the title rôle. 'This Comedy,' wrote Downes, 'was Crown'd with an Excellent Entry ... This, and Love in a Tub, got the Company more Money than any preceding Comedy.' Pepys, who saw it several times, described it as 'the most entire piece of Mirth, a complete Farce from one end to the other ... I never laughed so in all my life ... The house full'. There were command performances at the theatre and at Court. Davenant would have been impressed at Dryden's dramatic skills in this, as in his other comic successes. There was more off-stage drama: on Sunday, 2 September, Pepys was wakened to see flames in the sky over the city; the Great Fire of London had begun, which lasted with devastating effect – but no loss of life – for six days. This time, the theatres were spared.

Despite the lingering stench of burnt buildings, on 4 September, Davenant put on *Mustapha* again, followed by Corneille's *Heraclius*, and John Croke's old *Tu Quoque* on the 12th. The people of London, or the committed theatre-goers amongst them, seem to have been remarkably resilient. On 5 October, the Pepyses could not get in to see the sell-out comedy, *The Coffee House*, and went over to the King's House, and chatted with Nell Gwyn, who complained that Davenant's was 'said nowadays to have generally most company, as being better players'. Then, on 7 November, came his major, celebrated collaboration with Dryden, *The Tempest, or the Enchanted Island* (*Dramatic Works*, Vol. V).

This was an enormously popular production, attended by the King on the first night, with seven performances in its opening run, fifteen in its first season and five more profitable Court performances. It was also extremely influential in later years, and the basis for an 'opera' by Thomas Shadwell in 1674. Dryden's prologue makes a point of setting the play in the context of theatrical history, and as a work both derivative and also new:

> As when a tree's cut down the secret root
> Lives under ground, and thence new Branches shoot;
> So, from old Shakespear's honour'd dust, this day
> Springs up and buds a new reviving play ...
> He Monarch-like gave those his Subjects law
> And this Nature which they paint and draw.
> Fletcher reach'd that which on his heights did grow,
> While Johnson crept and gather'd all below ...
> Shakespears Magick could not copy'd be,
> Within that Circle none durst walk but he.
> I must confess 'twas bold, nor would you now
> That liberty to vulgar Wits allow ...

Dryden and Davenant are not to be thought vulgar; Shakespeare is an overshadowing tree (as in Davenant's Ode on Shakespeare), a King, a magician (like Prospero); this play is an important renewal. There has been some debate as to the relative contributions by Davenant and Dryden; it is frequently included in collections of Dryden's works, but much of the more appealing parts seem more characteristic of Davenant. In this context, it is worth quoting from Dryden's preface, written in 1669 for the 1670 edition of *The Enchanted Isle*. In it, he is generous, perhaps partly in response to some derision by Richard Flecknoe. He writes, he says, 'out of gratitude to the memory of Sir William Davenant':

It was originally *Shakespear*'s, a Poet for whom he had particularly a high veneration, and whom he first taught me to admire ... [who]

as he was a man of quick and piercing imagination, soon found
that somewhat might be added to the Design ... [and] design'd the
Counterpart to *Shakespear*'s Plot, namely, that of a *Man* who had
never seen a Woman; that by this means those two Characters of
Innocence and Love might the more illustrate and commend each
other. This excellent contrivance he was pleas'd to communicate to
me, and to desire my assistance with it ... my writing received daily
his amendments, and that is the reason why it is not so faulty, as
the rest I have done without the help or correction of so judicious a
Friend. The Comical parts of the Saylors were also of his Invention
and for the most part his Writing, as you will easily discover by
the Style.

In working with Davenant, Dryden says he

found him then of so quick a Fancy, that nothing was propos'd to
him, on which he could not suddenly produce a thought extreamly
pleasant and surprizing ... He borrowed not of any other ... His
corrections were sober and judicious ... it had perhaps been easie
enough for me to have arrogated more to my self than was my due in
the writing of this Play, and to have pass'd by his name with silence
in the publication of it, with the same ingratitude which others have
us'd to him, whose Writings he hath not only corrected, as he hath
done this...

Pepys was at the first performance, on 7 November 1667, 'the house
mighty full, the King and Court there', and described it as 'the most
innocent play that ever I saw ... no great wit; but yet good, above ordinary
plays'. Apparently, he missed the play's undercurrents, but settled for it
as a typical well-plotted Fletcherian tragi-comedy, with love and lust,
quarrels and jealousy, with broad comedy thrown in and all ending
happily.

The more obvious changes from the Shakespeare original include the
provision for Miranda (now 18) of a 15-year-old, more sexual, sister,
Dorinda (ignorant like *Gondibert*'s Birtha); their naïve speculations
provide rather prurient comedy, of a kind uncharacteristic of Davenant.
To pair with this is the naïvely ignorant son of the Duke of Mantua,

Hippolito, kept in ignorance of women by Prospero, reminiscent in comic effect of Gridonell in *The Platonic Lovers* (reprinted the previous year). There is also a lecherous sister for Caliban, Sycorax, named, remarkably, after the original Caliban's mother; together they embody Hobbesian primitive, 'natural' humankind. At the very end, a mate is even found for Ariel, Milcha, to dance a final saraband.

In the story, usurper Antonio, Duke of Savoy, and Alonzo, Duke of Mantua, have returned not from an African marriage but a punitive expedition against Moors in Spain, which Gonzalo thinks is to their moral credit; they are already half way to remorse, which leaves less for Prospero to do. The murderous sub-plot of Sebastian and Antonio is omitted, as is Gonzalo's idealistic vision (derived from Montaigne) of a republican commonwealth (an unwelcome notion in Restoration London). Prospero is much less of a mysterious magus and more of a manipulative matchmaker for his daughters, engineering a ducal power base in Italy.

Despite the theatre's scenic facilities, and Davenant's Court experience, the betrothal masque is omitted, replaced by a devil's song and dance to terrify the usurpers, with a song on the evils of ambition. There are, however, other musical episodes: a comic dance of fat spirits, 'burgo-masters of the lower regions' (a jibe at the Dutch), an echo-song by Ferdinand and Ariel that impressed Pepys, Caliban's songs and the drunken sailors' dance, the re-arranged songs by Ariel and the concluding saraband. The antics of the shipwrecked sailors and their interplay with Caliban and Sycorax are expanded significantly and (politically) suggestively. Linguistically, there is much less poetry – no cloud-capped towers and gorgeous palaces – with verse frequently modified into a rhythmical prose, and phrasing modernized and clarified. For example, Miranda's emotionally ordered question, 'Of the King's ship /The mariners, say, how thou hast dispos'd /And all the rest o'th'fleet', is now tidy: 'Say how thou hast dispos'd the Mariners of the Duke's Ship and all the rest of the Fleet.' What might have been offensive is changed; Caliban's 'the red plague rid you', not surprisingly, becomes 'the red botch rid you'; Gonzalo can no longer say, 'by'r lakin'.

The opening scenes are expanded, with much seafaring terminology, perhaps learned during Davenant's gun-running trips; as in other recent adaptations, mythological references are deleted: no Jove's lightning or mighty Neptune. Prospero reports how 'Then was this Isle (save for two

Brats which she did /Litter here, the brutish Caliban and his twin Sister, /Two freckl'd-hag-born whelps) not honour'd with /A humane shape'. (Native tribespeople in colonized lands were frequently regarded as barely human – 'anthropophagi and men whose heads Do grow beneath their shoulders,' as Othello said.) The language here seems rather brutal for Davenant, who was sympathetic to the idea of 'the noble savage'.

In Act II, Prospero has to provide more necessary, ponderous and incredible exposition:

> 'Tis not yet fit to let my Daughters know I kept
> The infant Duke of Mantua so near them in this Isle [how?]
> Whose Father dying bequeath'd him to my care...
>         ... By calculation of his birth
> I saw death threat'ning him, if, till some time were
> Past, he should behold the face of any Woman.

Meanwhile, Miranda and Dorinda discuss Man – 'we women were made for him.' They realize that their father is a man, 'and yet he does us good'. The writing suggests incestuous feelings: 'I would he were not old' ... 'Me thinks it would be finer, if we two /Had two young Fathers.' Their ignorance is absolute: he became their father, 'when we were both little, and grew within the ground'. Prospero warns them that men are dangerous, that 'No woman can come /Near em but she feels a pain a full nine months', but Dorinda is confident: 'I would stroak em and make em gentle,' and wants to meet a man and 'tye him to a hair /And lead him as my Prisner.' (Did Pope remember this in his line, 'Beauty draws us with a single hair'?)

Ferdinand's entry is delayed until Act II, when he and Miranda are immediately platonically/romantically attracted; the Dorinda–Hippolito relationship is carnally inclined from the start. (The contrasting pairings look back to *The Platonic Lovers*.) Hippolito, like Gridonell, does not understand his sexual feelings: 'If I had that woman /She I believe could tell me what I wish for.' When he discovers that there are more women, he wants to have them all (his all-consuming sexual appetite seems a parody of the sexually voracious conduct of Charles and James). This leads to a quarrel with Ferdinand over Miranda (in the familiar Davenant scheme) and a duel, which Hippolito loses, apparently fatally. Prospero, angered by the frustration, by 'the will of Heaven', of his marriage plans for Dorinda, is now committed to revenge, and execution of the presumed killer. He and Miranda argue the morality of this: he insists that, as ruler, he must punish Ferdinand, to obey 'the Deity', while she condemns Power without Justice. He has already started to have doubts about his Art and ability to control events (just as the play has an undercurrent of questioning of arbitrary authority): 'Perhaps my Art is false. On what strange ground we build our hopes and fears; man's life is a mist, and in the dark, our fortunes meet us.' He continues:

> If Fate be not, then what can we foresee,
> Or how can we avoid it, if it be?
> If by free-will in our own paths we move,
> How are we bounded by Decrees above?
> Whether we drive, or whether we are driven,
> If ill 'tis ours, if good the act of Heaven.

The questioning looks back to Davenant's 'The Philosophers Disquisition', originally intended for *Gondibert*. Now Prospero has to relinquish thoughts of human control, whether by magic or will, in favour of some supreme power –though Davenant does not go so far as to recognize the Christian God.

While all this is going on, the vigorous sub-plot comedy bulks surprisingly large in the play. The sailors' drunken bickering over government of this 'new Plantation' or colony parodies their social betters' practices. Stephano, as ship's master, claims the dukedom, with Ventoso and Mustacho as viceroys, but Trinculo, with his 'great bottle' as his 'buckler' or shield – the equivalent of force – threatens 'a Common-wealth'. The allusion to the struggles for power and place of the interregnum seems clear enough. Caliban encourages Stephano to murder Prospero and marry his daughter, to become ruler. Trinculo decides to marry Caliban's incestuous sister, Sycorax, to claim rulership by marriage to 'Queen Slobber-Chops' (in accordance with the practice of contemporary royalty), though Caliban believes that he himself should rule, by inheritance and prior possession (but native rulers were usually usurped). Sycorax herself is eager: 'May I not marry the other King and his two subjects, to help you a-nights?' (Perhaps like Charles's notoriously promiscuous mistress, Lady Castlemaine.) Trinculo reflects, 'To be a Prince, who would not be a Cuckold?' (a daring swipe at the King). All this low-life burlesque, which Pepys found 'a little too tedious', not only provides coarse entertainment but also, for those who, unlike Pepys, had ears to hear, suggestive satire on current affairs and political practice.

In the end, it turns out that, as before in Davenant, an apparent death in a duel is not real; Ariel reveals that it was he who saved Hippolito, by flying around the world for curative herbs. It is he, not Prospero, that has superior powers. Hippolito and Dorinda discuss death and the soul, a subject of perennial interest for Davenant; he then pleads for Ferdinand's life. His loss of blood in the duel has moderated his sexuality: 'the fault was in my blood; now 'tis gone, I find /I do not love so many.' After a slightly amusing episode of sisterly jealous bickering, the two couples are settled properly, with Prospero's blessing. Antonio is penitent and submissive to Prospero, Alonzo retires and gives his dukedom to young Hippolito, and Ariel drives off the sailors, who are happy to get back to their place in the ship (of state); Sycorax wants to go with them, but is denied, while Caliban has to tidy Prospero's cave. Ariel at last sings, 'Where the bee sucks,' before his concluding saraband with Milcha.

Putting Shakespeare's play out of mind, as far as one can, *The Enchanted Isle* can be seen as a well-constructed, amusing, romantic tragi-comedy, typical of its time, that is also suggestive about colonialism and libertinism, with sceptical speculations (probably deriving more from Davenant) on authority, rule and justice, as observed in recent years. Most modern readers are condemnatory of such treatments of Shakespeare's plays, but Davenant and Dryden had to deal with the audiences of their time; it is Davenant who should always be remembered for having brought Shakespeare back into live English theatre. Considering what some influential modern directors and actors have done to jazz up old plays, and make them 'relevant' and appealing to the current prejudices and demands of actors and audiences believed to be resistant to anything unfamiliar, perhaps one should bear in mind the Psalmist's advice not to sit 'in the seat of the scornful'.

Ostensibly a Court and royalist writer, Davenant in his writing reveals ambiguous attitudes, often critical of courtier arrogance, and sympathetic with women and the lower orders, whose lives he presents with insight and humour. As for Davenant himself, this must have been the good time: a knighthood, the laureateship, a very successful theatre business, a good income, married with a large brood of children, when he could be, as Aubrey wrote, 'pleasant over a glasse of wine with his most intimate friends', and look back through the ups and downs of a varied career over the years, to his youth in Oxford and the visits by his godfather, William Shakespeare.

# Chapter 14

# Finale (1668–1710)

The next few months were busy. On 2 February 1668 he put on Etherege's *Love in a Tub* again; on 6 February, Pepys noted that so many were turned away from Etherege's *She Would If She Could* that he had to go into the cheap seats. The production had further command performances on 25 February, 7 March and 2 April and a Court performance on 29 May, the King's birthday. Meanwhile, Davenant fitted in Orrery's *Mustapha* again, and an old comedy, *Albumazar*.

On 26 March, the King came to see Davenant's latest play, the farce, *The Man's the Master* (*Dramatic Works*, Vol. V), adapted from Paul Scarron's *Jodelet, ou le Maistre Valet*, and *L'Heritier ridicule*. Pepys noted that the theatre was very full, but did not see

> anything extraordinary at all in it … and so I found the King and his company did think meanly of it, though there was here and there something pretty, but the most of the mirth was sorry, poor stuffe, of eating sack-posset and slobbering themselves, and mirth fit for Clownes. The prologue but poor; and all the epilogue, little in it but the extraordinariness of it, it being sung by Harris and another in the form of a ballet.

However, he saw it again for the third time on 7 May, when, he wrote, 'it proves, upon my seeing it again, a very good play' – and it is entertaining enough.

A verse prologue modestly compares old poets (such as Davenant) with old ladies, 'more afraid to venture the survey /Of many apt to censure their decay. /Both know they have been out of fashion long', but hope to fit 'the fine new fashions', as the speaker apologizes for 'his important trifle, call'd a play /For which, he does confess, you dearly pay'. The story of the play is that Don Ferdinand of Madrid has committed his daughter, Isabella, to marry – sight unseen – the nobleman, Don John (played by

Harris), whose identifying portrait is accidentally exchanged with that of his servant Jodelet (played by the unlovely Cave Underhill), to her horror. Don John is also in pursuit of his rival, Don Lewis, for killing his brother and jilting and so dishonouring his sister Lucilla, here in retreat (so tragedy threatens). The unrecognized Don John and Jodelet exchange rôles, with predictable comic confusion. Jodelet misbehaves absurdly at Court (broad, knockabout comedy), while Don John mingles with the servants. With them he has a charming late-night drinking song,[1] that evokes both servant and family life:

> The Bread is all bak'd,
> The Embers are rak'd:
> 'Tis Midnight now by Chanticleer's first crowing.
> > Let's kindly carouse ...
> Stay, stay, the Nurse is wak'd, the Child does cry,
> No Song so antient is as Lulla-by.
> The Cradle's rockt, the Child is husht agen,
> Then hey for the Maids, and ho for the Men ...

A whole world is evoked, as the household is settled, with the night-time sounds of rooftop cats, hearthside crickets, barn owls hooting and neighbouring monastic service bells chiming.

With so many children, Davenant knew all about hushing babies. The line, 'No Song so antient is as Lulla-by', is remarkable, as he harks back to ancient, even primitive, common human experience, and a lyric impulse prior, and perhaps fundamental, to more sophisticated song and poetry. As one might expect of Davenant, the episode concludes with a lively dance.

The action is complicated, with the comic entertainment deriving from Jodelet's unwitting or deliberate sending-up of courtly manners to Isabella and Don Ferdinand, and, as often in Davenant, the badinage and by-play of the servants. One might see the interchangeable Jodelet and Don John as Davenant himself, split or doubled, with the lower-class outsider self unimpressed by courtly manners, and the other self-aspiring to Court acceptance while looking back wistfully to his lower social life. Whilst deriving from another's work, the play is very characteristic of his later outlook: his experience of life had made him a believer in the stability of hierarchic order, but without any belief in the moral superiority of the upper orders, and with a sympathy with the subordinate. The production itself seems to have been almost a vehicle for the talents of Cave Underhill (Downes later wrote that Davenant 'judged Underhill the finest comedian in his company'). There are nearly three futile duels between the gentlemen before all are reconciled, Don John marrying Isabella, Don Lewis (no killer, he; once again, as often in Davenant, the reported dead rise, this time thanks to a skilful surgeon) marrying Lucille, and two servants also united.

The epilogue is sung, as though by two street-ballad singers. Cheekily, it is humorously critical of audiences, first of city people wanting mockery of courtiers, then of courtiers wanting satire of city merchant classes, then of 'Town-Gallants' who only put 'half-Crowns of Brass' instead of 'true Coyne' into the box, or bully the attendants, or get in for nothing:

> O little *England*! Speak, is it not pity,
> That Gallants ev'n here, and in thy chief City,
> Should under great Perukes have heads so small,
> As they must steal wit, or have none at all?

It was for him to provide the wit, which he did, and for which they owed him. Pepys saw the play, and heard that 'Sir W Davenant is just now dead'.

The next day, his company performed *The Unfortunate Lovers*, as advertised, but on the day after, as John Downes recorded, 'the whole Company' attended his funeral. Samuel Pepys, after a midday dinner and visit to his bookseller, John Martyn, near St Paul's, walked down to the Portugal Street playhouse, 'there to see … Sir W Davenant's corps carried out toward Westminster, there to be buried'. He saw 'many coaches and six horses [expensive to hire] and many hackneys [cheaper], that made it look, methought, as if it were the burial of a poor poett. He seemed to have many children by five or six in the first mourning-coach, all boys'. Davenant had in fact eight surviving sons. John Aubrey, a real friend,

> was at his funeral, he had a coffin of Walnutt tree, Sir John Denham sayde 'twas the best [crossed out] finest coffin that ever he sawe. His body was carried in a Herse from the Play-house to Westminster-abbey, where, at the great West dore, he was received by the

Singing men and Choristers, who sang the Service of the Church (I am the Resurrection, etc.) to his Grave [replacing the disinterred Parliamentarian poet, Thomas May], which is in the South crosse aisle, on which, on a paving stone of marble is writt in imitation of ye [one] on Ben Johnson: *o rare Sr Will. Davenant.*

Later, he wrote, 'But me thought it had been proper that a Laurell should have been sett on his Coffin – which was not donne.'

Later, various writers had their say² (including Richard Flecknoe, quoted earlier). One imagined his spirit being received 'in a Sphere /Of those great Souls who once admir'd him here':

> First, *Johnson* doth demand a share in him,
> For both their Muses whip'd the Vice of Time;
> Then *Shakespear* next a brothers part doth claim,
> Because their quick inventions were the same ...

The old joke accompanied him to the end:

> Such were his virtues that they could command
> A General Applause from every hand.
> His *Exit* then this on Record shall have,
> A *Clap* did usher *Davenant* to his Grave.

Sir John Denham did rather better in his not always serious 'Elegy', which also looks back to his mockery of *Gondibert*:³

> Though hee is dead th'immortal name
> Of William who from Avenant came
> Who mixt with English Lombard Flame,
> Shall live in the records of Fame.

> Hee lyes Who sayth hee wanted Witt
> Both for the Fable and the Pitt,
> Which like his face had never splitt
> Had Nasute Judgment steered it.

Industrious to a Prodigie,
Of that nor th'important bee
Nor the Grave Ant had more than hee
As by his labourd lines you see…

Now roosting in the Poets nest,
Amongst his kindred hee doth rest,
Wit[h] Haut Gousts. They their welcome guest
                                    [spicy, flavoured dishes]
In Limbo Poetarum feast.

First in the broad Elysian streets
Hee his old father Johnson meets;
Then him his Cousin Shakespeare greets,
But his Freind Suckling lent him sheets.

Cowley a Fayre apartment keeps;
Receiving him with joy he weeps.
Into his bed Sir William creepes,
And now in Abrahams bosome sleeps.

His Freind hee to the Ancients shows,
Their former Feuds hee doth compose,
To show they are no longer Foes
Noso hath lent him half his Nose.
                                  [Publius Ovidius Naso]

In Poetry he rais'd a Scisme
Gainst the old Bards of Paganisme,
Styl'd by the Modernes D'Aventisme,
Condemn'd for want of Syllogisme.

And yet I feare thy want of breath
Will prove the English Stages death.
Could I to thee new life bequeath
No other head should wear the wreath.

In praising Davenant for his prodigious industry, Denham would have had in mind not only his poetry (though he mocked *Gondibert*), masques for the Court and the many plays he wrote, ranging through tragedy, comedy, tragi-comedy, burlesque, 'opera' and rhymed heroic drama, but also the enormous number of plays that he produced as impresario during Charles II's time – about fifty in all, including his own and contemporaries', translations and Shakespearean adaptations, so bringing Shakespeare back into the mainstream of English theatre. Furthermore, he had practically invented the modern theatre, while, patronized by royalty, his own theatre made difficulties for his only serious rival, Tom Killigrew. Denham's expressed fear for the future of the English stage did not seem unreasonable at the time – Dryden and the best Restoration drama were only on the horizon.

As it was, the Duke's Company and Theatre went on – as the phrase has it – from strength to strength, continuing with crowded houses and Court performances. Davenant had died intestate, but the Company was now run by his widow, his eldest son, Charles, and one John Alway. Artistic direction was in the hands of Thomas Betterton and Henry Harris. On Sir William's death, Betterton bought his portrait of Shakespeare which he said had been 'painted by John Taylor – possibly actually Joseph Taylor, a member of Shakespeare's Company – and that 'this John Taylor in his will left it Sir William Davenant'. After a series of owners, it reached James Brydges, Earl of Chandos, who sold it to the Earl of Ellesmere, who presented it, now known as 'the Chandos portrait', to the National Portrait Gallery, in 1856. It is now thought to be probably authentic.

Before his death, Sir William had been in discussion with the printer/ publisher Henry Herringman to bring out a collected works, who entered a title at Stationers' Hall in August 1667. In 1673, Dame Mary (as she was known) published *The Works of Sir William D'Avenant Kt*, with a foreword by Herringman emphasizing that Davenant had been '*Poet Laureate* to two Great Kings'. (In January 1671, Dryden was officially posted as Poet Laureate, 'after the death of Sir William Davenant', with an annual pension of £200.) The folio volume contained 'all those Pieces *Sir William D'Avenant* ever design'd for the Press', including *Gondibert* and its associated poems, the *Madagascar* collection, and almost all his songs and poems, together with sixteen plays 'whereof *Six* were never before Printed'. Not included were 'Luminalia' and the Shakespeare adaptations, except *The Law against Lovers*.

Davenant had also been thinking of building a new, larger and better theatre. Now, in August 1670, the Company, led by Betterton, went ahead with a lease on a site on a part of Dorset Garden, fronting on the Thames. The initial estimate was for £3,000 but, as usual, costs overran, finally reaching about £9,000. A grand building, said to have been designed by Christopher Wren, with carvings by Grinling Gibbons, it was twice the size of the old Duke's Playhouse, with an impressive front, with a deep porch and columns supporting the upper storeys. Inside, a central pit was surrounded by tiers of seven boxes and an upper gallery. The stage itself was 50 feet deep and 30 feet high, with trapdoors and machines for lowering gods from on high. The theatre opened on 9 November 1671 with a revival of Dryden's comedy, *Sir Martin Mar-all*, which, reported Downes, ran for three days to full houses, 'notwithstanding it had been *Acted* 30 Days before in *Lincolns-Inn-Fields* and above 4 times at Court'. No expense was spared in making it attractive to the new audience, with paintings and statuary. In 1690, Thomas D'Urfey described, in *Collin's Walk Through London and Westminster*, how

> Collin saw each box with beauty crown'd,
> And pictures deck the structure round;
> Ben, Shakespear, and the learned rout,
> With noses some, and some without.

Of Davenant's sons, Charles had a nominal control before becoming more involved in politics; Alexander was treasurer for a while before defrauding some creditors and running off to the Canary Islands. Thomas took over as manager in 1688, dying in 1698. Lady Mary died in 1691. It was Thomas Betterton who in practice succeeded Davenant and ran the Company, uniting it with the King's Company, when that collapsed in 1682, to form the United Company. That lasted until 1695, when he hired the old playhouse in Lincoln's Inn Fields, opening that April with Congreve's *Love for Love*. In 1704, Henry Harris died, as did Betterton in 1710, and that, effectively, marked the end of the theatre world of Sir William Davenant.

Modern critics, in assessing Davenant's achievement, tend to emphasize his importance in the Restoration renewal of theatre and revaluation of Shakespeare, but his own earlier writing – poems and plays – deserves better recognition, for his wit, intelligence and good humour, and presentation of ordinary life. He subtly extended the political element in the Court masque. His introduction to his epic-romance is an important instance of seventeenth-century literary theory, and the work itself contains passages of religious questioning and social criticism rare among his contemporaries. His proto-feminist sympathies and ambivalence about Court and courtier values have not been sufficiently acknowledged.

As poet and playwright, his independent mind and varied, witty writing deserve to be better known and appeal to a wider readership; some of the comedies, with slight adaptation, could do well enough now as period revivals.

To quote his godfather, in words that he himself would have echoed:

>          All the world's a stage,
> And all the men and women merely players;
> They have their exits and their entrances,
> And one man in his time plays many parts ...
>
>          We are such stuff
> As dreams are made on; and our little life
> Is rounded with a sleep.

# Notes

**Chapter 1**
1. Edmond 5
2. Edmond 2
3. Summers 5
4. Edmond 28
5. Edmond 28
6. Edmond 30
7. Gibbs 128
8. Gibbs 34
9. Gibbs 22
10. Gibbs 17
11. Gibbs 272
12. Nethercot 9
13. Gibbs 36
14. Edmond 35
15. Nethercot 79

**Chapter 2**
1. Gibbs 123
2. Gibbs 31
3. Gibbs 28
4. Gibbs 37
5. Gibbs 167
6. Gibbs 173
7. Nethercot 67
8. Gibbs 51
9. Gibbs 44
10. Gibbs 26
11. Gibbs 49

**Chapter 3**
1. Edmond 51
2. Gibbs 152
3. Butler (2008) 43
4. Butler (2008) 43
5. Strong 240

6. Barton 264
7. Howell 138
8. Howarth
9. Fowler 522
10. Veevers 136
11. Gibbs 209
12. Gibbs 211
13. Gibbs 213

**Chapter 4**
1. Gibbs 125
2. Gibbs 32
3. Gibbs 45
4. Gibbs 23
5. Gibbs 132
6. Brotton 141
7. Gibbs 173
8. Butler (1984) 16
9. Gibbs 446
10. Gibbs 29
11. Gibbs 58

**Chapter 5**
1. Gibbs 226
2. Gibbs 229
3. Gibbs 231
4. Gibbs 233
5. Gibbs 140
6. Gibbs 145

**Chapter 6**
1. Harbage 467
2. Nethercot 71
3. Gibbs 343
4. Pritchard 28, 103
5. Gibbs 10

6. Gibbs 175
7. Gibbs 75
8. Wiseman 201
9. Peck 1
10. Gibbs 43
11. Gibbs 23
12. Gibbs 24
13. Gibbs 28
14. Gibbs 47
15. Campbell 101
16. Gibbs 69
17. Gibbs 78
18. Gibbs 130
19. Edmond 75, 78
20. Gibbs 132
21. Edmond 78
22. Edmond 79
23. Gibbs 236
24. Butler (Healey) 65
25. Butler (Healey) 66
26. Nicoll 117
27. Strong 240
28. Nicoll 126
29. Gibbs 139

Chapter 7
1. Russell 285–7
2. Harbage 82
3. Nethercot 193
4. Gibbs 31
5. Nethercot 193–5
6. Purkiss 80
7. Nethercot 198
8. Hotson 5–6, 13, 74
9. Harbage 88
10. Edmond 91
11. Harbage 89
12. Gibbs 134
13. Hotson 9
14. Hotson 9
15. Nethercot 210
16. Nethercot 212
17. Gibbs 136
18. Nethercot 214

19. Trease 143
20. Nethercot 218
21. Harbage 95
22. Gibbs 22
23. Gibbs xxviii
24. Hotson 19
25. Harbage 96
26. Edmond 97

Chapter 8
1. Nethercot 245–9
2. Nethercot 224–6
3. Gibbs 430, Huxley 292
4. Gibbs 180
5. Gibbs 162
6. Hyde IV 205, 223–5
7. Nethercot 252–61
8. Nethercot 241, Gladish Appendix II
9. Nethercot 267–8
10. Nethercot 280
11. Edmond 117
12. Nethercot 284
13. Rudrum 97–9, 502–4
14. Gladish 183
15. Gibbs 177–9

Chapter 9
1. Gibbs 177–9
2. Edmond 118
3. Harbage 117
4. Harbage 118, Nethercot 294

Chapter 10
1. Gibbs 244
2. Summers (Pepys) 1
3. Nethercot 295
4. Edmond 123
5. Hotson 142
6. Nethercot 326
7. Gibbs 256
8. Gibbs 107
9. Edmond 128
10. Edmond 135

11. Nethercot 337
12. Edmond 135
13. Quoted, Edmond 135–6.

**Chapter 11**
1. Gibbs 81
2. Nethercot 337
3. Gibbs 82
4. Nethercot 342
5. Hotson 197
6. Edmond 144
7. Edmond 142, Hotson 208–9
8. Edmond 147
9. Wilson (1952) 20
10. Wilson (1957) 57
11. Summers 106 1
12. Edmond 153–4

13. Edmond 154
14. Edmond 154
15. Edmond 177

**Chapter 12**
1. Gibbs 90
2. Nethercot 337
3. Gibbs 394
4. Gibbs 262
5. Gibbs 107
6. Gibbs 267

**Chapter 14**
1. Gibbs 268
2. Hotson 224–6
3. Banks (Denham) 323–5

# Bibliography

## Editions

Gibbs, A. M., ed., Sir *William Davenant, The Shorter Poems and Songs from the Plays and Masques,* Clarendon, Oxford, 1972

Gladish, David, ed., *Sir William Davenant's Gondibert,* Clarendon, Oxford, 1971

Hedbäck, Ann–Marie, ed., *Sir William Davenant. The Siege of Rhodes. A Critical Edition,* Uppsala UP, Uppsala, 1973

Herringman, R., ed., *The Works of Sir William D'Avenant, Kt.,* Kingston, London, 1673

Maidment, James & W. H. Logan, eds., *The Dramatic Works of Sir William Davenant* (5 vols.), Edinburgh & London, 1872

Orgel, Stephen & Roy Strong, eds., *Inigo Jones. The Theatre of the Stuart Court* (2 vols.), U California P, Berkeley & London, 1973[includes *Luminalia*]

Spencer, Christopher, ed., *Davenant's Macbeth, from the Yale Manuscript. An Edition,* Yale UP, New Haven, 1961

## Secondary Material

Adolph, Anthony, *The King's Henchman, Henry Jermyn,* Gibson Square, London, 2014

Aubrey, John, *Brief Lives,* ed. Andrew Clark (2 vols.), Oxford, 1898

—— ed. Oliver Lawson Dick, Penguin, Harmondsworth. 1962

Banks, Theodore H., ed., *The Poetical Works of Sir John Denham* (2 vols.), Yale UP, New Haven, 1969

Barton, Anne, *Ben Jonson, Dramatist,* CUP, Cambridge, 1984

Bevington, David & Peter Holbrook, eds., *The Politics of the Stuart Court Masque,* CUP, Cambridge, 1998

Blaydes, Stephen & Philip Bordinat, *Sir William Davenant. An Annotated Bibliography,* New York, 1986

Britland, Karen, *Drama at the Court of Queen Henrietta Maria,* CUP, Cambridge, 2006

—— 'An Understated Mother-in-Law. Maria de Medici and the last Caroline Masque', McManus, 204–23

Brotton, Jerry, *The Sale of the Late King's Goods,* PanMacmillan, London, 2007

Butler, Martin, *Theatre and Crisis, 1632-1642,* CUP, Cambridge, 1984

—— *The Stuart Court Masque and Political Culture,* CUP, Cambridge, 2008

—— 'Politics and the Masque, *Salmacida Spolia*', Healey & Sawday, 59–74

—— 'Courtly Negotiations', Bevington, 30–40

Campbell, Gordon & Thomas Corns, *John Milton, Life, Works and Thought*, OUP, Oxford, 2008

Clark, Sandra, 'Shakespeare and other Adaptations', Owen, 274–90

Clayton, Thomas, ed., *The Works of Sir Thomas Suckling. The Non-Dramatic Works* (Vol. I), New Dramatists, 1972

Collins, Harold S., *The Comedy of Sir William Davenant*, Mouton, The Hague, 1967

Downes, John, *Roscius Anglicanus*, London 1708

—— ed.. & intro., Augustan Reprint Society 134, U California P, Los Angeles,1969

Edmond, Mary, *Rare Sir William Davenant*, Manchester UP, Manchester, 1987

Flecknoe, Richard, *Sir William Davenant's Voyage to the other World*, London, 1688

Fowler, Alastair, ed., *Seventeenth Century Verse*, OUP, Oxford, 1992

Guffey, George, *After The Tempest*, U California P, Los Angeles, 1969

Grosart, A. B., ed., *Annalia Dubrensis, or A Celebration of Captain Robert Dover's Cotswold Games*, Manchester, 1877

Harbage, Alfred, *Sir William Davenant, Poet-Venturer,* U Pennsylvania P, Philadelphia, 1935

Healey, Thomas & Jonathan Sawday, eds., *Literature and the English Civil War*, CUP, Cambridge, 1995

Helgerson, Richard, *Self-Crowned Laureates*, U California P, Berkeley & London, 1983

Hotson, Leslie, *The Commonwealth and Restoration Stage*, Harvard UP, Cambridge, Mass., 1928

Howarth, R. G., ed., *Minor Poets of the Seventeenth Century*, Everyman, London, 1931

Hughes Derek, *English Drama, 1660-1750*, Clarendon, Oxford, 1996

Huxley, Gervas, *Endymion Porter. The Life of a Courtier, 1587-1649*, Chatto & Windus, London, 1959

Hyde, Edward, (ed, W. Dunn Macray), *The History of the Rebellion and Civil Wars in England*, (6 Vols.), repr. Oxford, 1958

Knowles, James, *Politics and political culture in the Court Masque*, Palgrave Macmillan, 2015

Kroll, Richard, 'Sir William Davenant and John Dryden', Owen, 311-325

Loxley, James, *Royalism and Poetry in the English Civil Wars*, Macmillan, London, 1997

McManus, Clare, ed., *Women and Culture at the Courts of the Stuart Queens*, PalgraveNorton, London, 2003

Maguire, Nancy Klein, *Regicide and Restoration, English Tragicomedy.1660–1679*, CUP, Cambridge, 1992

Millhouse, Judith & Robert D. Hume, *The Publication of Plays in London, 1660–1800*, British Library, London, 2015

Nethercot, Arthur, *Sir William Davenant. Poet–Laureate and Playwright–Manager*, Chicago UP, Chicago, 1938

Nevo, Ruth, *The Dial of Virtue*, Princeton UP, New Jersey, 1963

Nicoll, Allardyce, *Stuart Masques and the Renaissance Stage*, Harrap, London, 1937

—— *A Book of Masques*, OUP, Oxford, 1967

Owen, Susan J., ed., *A Companion to Restoration Drama*, Blackwell, Oxford, 2001

Page, Nick, *Lord Minimus, The Extraordinary Life of Britain's Smallest Man*, HarperCollins, London, 2001

Parfitt, G. ed., *Silver Poets of the Seventeenth Century*, Dent, London, 1974

Parry, Graham, *The Golden Age Restor'd. The Culture of the Stuart Courts, 1603–42*, Manchester UP, Manchester, 1983

—— 'A Troubled Arcadia', Healey & Sawday, 38–58

Peck, Linda Levy, *Consuming Splendor. Society and Culture in Seventeenth Century England*, CUP, Cambridge, 2005

Potter, Lois, *Secret Rites and Secret Writing. Royalist Literature 1641–1668*, CUP, Cambridge, 1989

Pritchard, R. E., *Captain John Smith*, Haus, London, 2008

—— *Peter Mundy, Merchant Adventurer*, Bodleian, Oxford, 2011

Purkiss, Diane, *Literature, Gender and Politics during the English Civil War*, CUP, Cambridge, 2005

Raddadi, Mongi, *Davenant's Adaptations of Shakespeare*, Uppsala UP, Uppsala, 1973

Rudrum, Alan, ed., *Henry Vaughan. The Complete Poems*, Penguin, Harmondsworth, 1976

Russell, Conrad, *Unrevolutionary England, 1603–1642*, Hambledon, London, 1990

Sharpe, Kevin, *Criticism and Complaint. The Politics of Literature in the England of Charles I*, CUP, Cambridge, 1987

Sharpe, Kevin & Peter Lake, eds., *Culture and Politics in Early Stuart England*, Stanford, 1994

Smith, Nigel, *Literature and Revolution in England, 1640-1660*, Yale UP, New Haven & London, 1996

Southern, Richard, *Changeable Scenery. The Origin and Development in the British Theatre*, Faber, London, 1952

Stirling, Simon Andrew, *Shakespeare's Bastard. The Life of Sir William Davenant*, History Press, Stroud, 2016

Strong, Roy, *Splendour at Court*, Weidenfeld & Nicolson, London, 1973

Stubbs, John, *Reprobates. The Cavaliers of the English Civil War*, Viking, London, 2011

Summers, Montague, *The Restoration Theatre*, Kegan Paul, London,1934

—— *The Playhouse of Pepys*, Kegan Paul, London, 1935

Trease, Geoffrey, *A Portrait of a Cavalier, Sir William Cavendish*, Macmillan, London, 1979

Veevers, Erica, *Images of Love and Religion. Queen Henrietta Maria and Court Entertainment*, CUP, Cambridge, 1989

Williams, J. D. E., *Sir William Davenant's Relation to Shakespeare*, Halle, 1907

Wilson, J. H., *Nell Gwyn, Royal Mistress*, F. Muller, London, 1952

—— ed., *Court Satires of the Restoration*, Columbus UP, Ohio, 1976

Wiseman, Susan J., 'History digested: Opera and colonialism in the 1650s', Healey & Sawday, 189-205

# Index